An English Translation and the Correct Interpretation of Laozi's Tao Te Ching

英譯並正解老子道德經

附 《道德經》艱深句子正解並白話對譯

by

KS Vincent POON（潘君尚）

BSc, CMF, BEd, MSc

Kwok Kin POON（潘國鍵）

BA, DipEd, MA, MPhil, MEd, PhD

The SenSeis

First Edition
July 2020

Published by
The SenSeis 尚尚齋
Toronto
Canada
www.thesenseis.com
publishing@thesenseis.com

ISBN 978-1-989485-15-6

In Loving Memory of Our Beloved

Pui Luen Nora TSANG（曾佩鑾）

Acknowledge one's pure inherent nature and
embrace primitive simplicity - *Tao Te Ching*

隸書 Clerical Script   68x35cm 2000AD
Source: *A Collection of Kwok Kin Poon's Calligraphy*

Table of Contents

There are so many diverse things - *Tao Te Ching*

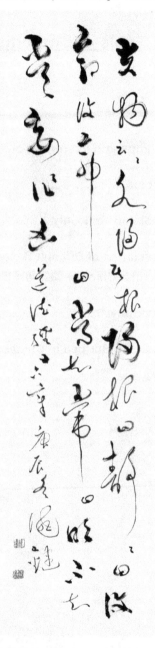

草書 Cursive Script 129x38cm 2000AD
Source: *A Collection of Kwok Kin Poon's Calligraphy*

INTRODUCTION

It is the most beneficial to act with no
personal differentiation and intent - *Tao Te Ching*

篆書 Seal Script   67x31cm 2000AD
Source: *A Collection of Kwok Kin Poon's Calligraphy*

Introduction

(I)

Tao Te Ching (《道德經》, or *Dao De Jing*), presumably written by Laozi (老子, who is also known as Lao Dan 老聃, Li Er 李耳, or Li Dan 李聃) of the 6th century BC, is one of the most famous and influential philosophical works in Chinese history. Being the foundational canon of Taoism (道家), *Tao Te Ching* outlines the characteristics and roles of the fundamental Tao (道) and its Te (德, Manifestation of Tao) in the formation and maintenance of all in the Universe. Written in fewer than 6000 Chinese characters, *Tao Te Ching* also depicts the underlying nature of governance[i] and some natural laws, which, remarkably, include modern scientific concepts such as atomic theory[ii], chemical equilibrium[iii], polarities[iv], as well as the quantum uncertainty principle[v]. Accordingly, despite its age of over 2500 years, *Tao Te Ching* remains a monumental text that must be read by all.

(II)

Unfortunately, *Tao Te Ching* is often misinterpreted by many for more than two thousand years. Their failures can largely be categorized into four types:

1. Misinterpreting through the lenses of Taoist Religion (道教) and Huang–Lao (黄老) concepts. One typical example is erroneously taking Laozi had advised one to completely rid all desires to become a celestial being (神仙), which often leads to misinterpreting "鬼" as "ghosts" and "神" as "gods" or "dieties" in *Tao Te Ching*.[vi] Laozi had only asked one to minimize desires and had never addressed the existence of supernatural entities. Heshang Gong (河上公), one of the most prominent masters of Taoist Religion and

the earliest commentators of *Tao Te Ching*, had often committed this type of error.

2. Misinterpreting through the lenses of Confucianism. Thus, characters such as "仁", "慈", "善", "德" are often misinterpreted by applying Confucian values.[(vii)] Laozi abhorred the establishment of Confucian "moral virtues", and so he could not have cherished them in *Tao Te Ching*. As Confucianism is widespread among Chinese academia, this type of misinterpretation is frequently committed by many scholars, including the renowned Wang Bi (王弼), Kang Youwei (康有為), Zhang Mosheng (張默生), Gao Heng (高亨), and James Legge.

3. Misinterpreting Chinese characters like "若", "似", and "或" as "seemingly", "resemble", and "perhaps".[(viii)] Such misinterpretations often give rise to the incorrect impression that Laozi was advising one to be pretending, scheming, and calculating. Laozi had always cherished acting by one's simple primitive nature and so would never have asked one to be pretending or disingenuous.

4. Committing a combination of misinterpretations outlined in 1, 2, or 3. This type of error usually results in multiple self-contradictions and inconsistencies, which further generate confusions and mystifications in understanding *Tao Te Ching*.

(III)

As such, this book aims to provide readers with a clear, concise, consistent, and correct English translation and interpretation of *Tao Te Ching*[(ix)], which is presented here in a line-by-line format accompanied by ample annotated footnotes. Footnotes include justifications and references for interpreting key Chinese characters as well as brief discussions on various general misinterpretations. Further, to facilitate easy reading, the bare translated text is supplemented in a separate section, while the correct interpretation of difficult and complex sentences in vernacular Chinese (《道德經》艱深句子正解並白話對譯) in another.

It is my sincere hope that the world can finally understand the actual thought of Laozi, the wise sage of Taoism.

KS Vincent Poon
July 2020.

(i) See Section One, Chapters 17 - 19, 29 - 31, 57 - 60, 65 - 67, 72 -75, and 78-80.

(ii) See Section One, Chapter 21.

(iii) See Section One, Chapters 36, 40, and 77.

(iv) See Section One, Chapter 42.

(v) See Section One, Chapters 14 and 21.

(vi) See Section One, Chapter 60, as well as footnotes 6 and 527 in Section Two. Laozi had always asked one to leave behind selfishness and be selfless. By contrast, Taoist religion contends one can follow certain practices to become a long-living celestial being (升仙/長生不老), a concept that is actually selfish and incompatible with Laozi's teachings.

(vii) See Section One, Chapter 8 Line 23, Chapter 49 Line 134, Chapter 54 Line 147, Chapter 59 Line 160, Chapter 63 Line 170, Chapter 67 Line 182, and Chapter 79 Line 213. See also the corresponding footnotes of these lines in Section Two.

(viii) See Section One, Chapter 5 Line 18, Chapter 15 Line 47, Chapter 78 Line 211, Chapter 4 Lines 10 and 11 , Chapter 20 Line 62, Chapter 29 Line 87, and Chapter 61 Line 165. See also the corresponding footnotes of these lines in Section Two.

(ix) The current English interpretation is based on the original Chinese text of 81 chapters provided in *Laozi's Tao Te Ching with Wang Bi's Commentaries* (《老子王弼注》).

Pristine tranquillity - *Tao Te Ching*

楷書 Standard Script 69x31cm 2000AD
Source: *A Collection of Kwok Kin Poon's Calligraphy*

SECTION ONE

Translation and Interpretation

A sturdy tree of one's entire embrace - *Tao Te Ching*

隸書 Clerical Script   123x43cm 2000AD
Source: *A Collection of Kwok Kin Poon's Calligraphy*

An English Translation and the Correct Interpretation of Laozi's Tao Te Ching

by KS Vincent POON (潘君尚) & Kwok Kin POON (潘國鍵)

第一章 Chapter 1

1. 道可道，非常道; 名可名，非常名。無名天地之始，有名萬物之母。

The Tao (道, Tao, Path, or Way) that can be spoken or described is not the "Immutable and Everlasting Tao (常道)"[1]. The Name (名) that can be named or spelt out is not the "immutable and everlasting Name (常名)". That which is "unidentifiable and nameless (無名)" is the Originator (始) of the Universe (天地)[2], whereas that which is "identifiable and with names (有名)" (i.e. 德, Te, or Manifestation of Tao)[3] is the Mother of all things.[4]

2. 故常無，欲以觀其妙; 常有，欲以觀其徼。

Therefore, the "immutable and everlasting Tao (常道)" and the "unidentifiable and nameless (無名)" can hopefully (欲) be used (以) to examine (觀) the unimaginable underlying wonders (妙) of Tao; whereas, the "immutable and everlasting Name (常名)" and the "identifiable and with names (有名)" can hopefully be used to examine (觀) the fundamental path that all things follow (徼) [5] [6]

3. 此兩者，同出而異名，同謂之玄。玄之又玄，眾妙之門。

Both the "unidentifiable and nameless" and the "identifiable and with names" stem from the same source, but we merely labelled them differently. Similarly, both are regarded as great mysteries (玄)[7]. Mysteries upon mysteries, such are the doors and gates to all wonders (眾妙) of Tao and the Universe.

第二章 Chapter 2

4. 天下皆知美之為美, 斯惡已; 皆知善之為善, 斯不善已。

All under Heaven recognize the beauty of the beautiful, and in doing this, they have the idea of what ugliness is; they all recognize the goodness of the good, and in doing this, they have the idea of what not good is.[8]

5. 故有無相生, 難易相成; 長短相較, 高下相傾; 音聲相和, 前後相隨。

Hence, the idea of "existence" and "non-existence" emerge from each other; "difficult" and "easy" give rise to each other; "long" and "short" compare with each other; "high" and "low" contrast each other; "notes" and "tones" harmonize each other; "front" and "back" accompany each other.

6. 是以聖人處無為之事, 行不言之教。萬物作焉而不辭, 生而不有, 為而不恃, 功成而弗居。夫唯弗居, 是以不去。

This is why a wise sage (聖人)[9] deals with (處) all matters by "not acting with any personal differentiation and intent (無為)"[10] and implements (行) enlightenment (教)[11] of others through the wordless (不言)[12]. All things spring up naturally without diction (不辭). Tao begets (生) all without anything (不有) and acts (為) without relying on any other (不恃).[13] Tao accomplishes but never claims any achievement. Alas, it is precisely because (唯)[14] it does not claim any achievement that its achievements shall never depart away (不去)[15] from all things.

第三章 Chapter 3

7. 不尚賢, 使民不爭; 不貴難得之貨, 使民不為盜; 不見可欲, 使民心不亂。

Not honouring (尚) distinguished individuals (賢) keeps the people away from rivalry among themselves; not prizing (貴) goods that are difficult to procure keeps the people away from becoming thieves; not presenting anything that can provoke selfish desires (欲) keeps the people's minds away from unrest.

8. 是以聖人之治, 虛其心, 實其腹, 弱其志, 強其骨。

Therefore, the wise sage governs to empty (虛) the people's minds (to rid their minds of narcissistic and arrogant ideas), to fill (實) their bellies (to rid their thoughts of unnecessary greed), to weaken their wills (to prevent them from carrying out conceited acts), and to strengthen their bones (to maintain their natural healthy bodies).

9. 常使民無知無欲, 使夫智者不敢為也。為無為, 則無不治。

The wise sage constantly seeks to keep the people without acquired knowledge (無知) and without selfish desire (無欲); this will make those who are clever with acquired intelligence (智者) have no place nor condition to apply their skills. If one acts (為) to not act with any personal differentiation and intent (無為), then there is nothing that one cannot govern or manage well.

第四章 Chapter 4

10. 道沖而用之或不盈。淵兮似萬物之宗。

Tao is inherently "void and empty (沖)" and utilizes this to apply (用) itself; since it is infinitely "void and empty", it is everywhere and invariably (或)[16] never exhaust (不盈) itself. Deep and unfathomable (淵) indeed (兮), it (似)[17] is the most revered fundamental root (宗) of all things.

11. 挫其銳, 解其紛; 和其光, 同其塵。湛兮似或存!

Tao dims (挫) all brilliance (銳). Tao disintegrates (解) all chaos (紛). Tao harmonizes (和) all light (光). Tao adapts and merges (同) with the muddy and obscure surroundings (塵). Indeed, Tao is so profound and buried (湛) within that it (似) always (或) exists (存)![18]

12. 吾不知誰之子，象帝之先。

I do not know whose offspring it is; I imagine (象)[19] it existed before Heaven (帝)[20]. [21]

第五章 Chapter 5

13. 天地不仁，以萬物為芻狗; 聖人不仁，以百姓為芻狗。

The Universe does not follow the concept of being benevolent (仁). It treats all things with no mercy as if they are straw-made dogs (芻狗)[22]. The wise sages also do not follow the concept of being benevolent; they treat all people with no mercy as if they are straw-made dogs, no different from all other things.[23]

14. 天地之間，其猶橐籥乎？虛而不屈，動而愈出。

Isn't the dynamic realm of our Universe (天地之間)[24] like that of a bellows (橐籥)? When it is left idle, it keeps its original nature of endless (不屈)[25] emptiness (虛); when operated, the air is expelled, and it becomes more agitated.

15. 多言數窮，不如守中。

Accordingly, speaking too much (多言) invariably results in the loss (窮) of all arguments (數)[26]; hence, it is better to follow and keep one's original idle tranquillity (守中)[27]. [28]

第六章 Chapter 6

16. 谷神不死，是謂玄牝。

The Valley Spirit (谷神) never dies.[29] Thus, it is known as "The Mysterious Motherly Channel of All Things (玄牝)"[30].

17. 玄牝之門，是謂天地根。

The valve (門) of "The Mysterious Motherly Channel" is the root of the Universe.

18. 緜緜若存, 用之不勤。

This valve indeed does (若)[31] exist (存) without end (緜緜) and applies itself without any laborious effort (勤).

第七章 Chapter 7

19. 天長地久。天地所以能長且久者, 以其不自生, 故能長生。

The Universe is long-enduring and lasts for ages. The reason why the Universe can endure and last thus long is because it does not live of, or for, itself (不自生). This is how it can last and endure for so long (長生).

20. 是以聖人後其身而身先, 外其身而身存。

Hence, the wise sages put their own selves last and thus find their own selves in the most foremost place (先); they abandon (外)[32] their own selves and thus find their selves well-preserved.

21. 非以其無私耶？ 故能成其私。

Is this not because of their selflessness (無私)? Due to their selflessness, they are able to bring about their own selves.

第八章 Chapter 8

22. 上善若水。水善利萬物而不爭, 處衆人之所惡, 故幾於道。

The most well-versed in Tao (上善) is (若)[33] water. Water excels in benefiting all things without competing with others and is always willing to occupy any low place that everyone dislikes (惡). Hence, water resembles (幾)[34] Tao.

23. 居善地; 心善淵; 與善仁; 言善信; 正善治; 事善能; 動善時。

The distinguished ones reside (居) themselves at places (地) that are rich in Tao (善)[35]; their minds (心) settle in the abyssal niches (淵)[36] where Tao rests; they befriend (與)[37] those (仁)[38] who are passionate with Tao; their words (言) are with the trustworthiness (信) of Tao; their governances (正)$^{(39)}$ follow the principles of Tao (治)$^{(40)}$; they employ (事)$^{(41)}$ talents (能) that are well-versed in Tao, and they always act (動) following the timing (時) that is dictated by Tao.$^{(42)}$

24. 夫唯不爭, 故無尤。

Alas, it is because the distinguished ones do not compete with others that no one can thus blame (尤) them for anything.

第九章 Chapter 9

25. 持而盈之, 不如其已; 揣而梲之, 不可長保。

Those who hold (持) and also accumulate (盈) are inferior to those who abandon (已)$^{(43)}$. Those who hammer (揣)$^{(44)}$ to become acute and sharpen (梲)$^{(45)}$ themselves cannot be preserved (保) for too long.$^{(46)}$

26. 金玉滿堂, 莫之能守; 富貴而驕, 自遺其咎。

Those who are abundantly wealthy (金玉滿堂) never keep and secure their wealth forever. Those who are conceited because of their wealth are delivering (遺) themselves into misfortunes and tragedies (咎)$^{(47)}$.

27. 功遂身退, 天之道。

Accordingly, when one's work has been accomplished (遂)$^{(48)}$ and one's name has become distinguished, withdrawing into seclusion (身退) is the way of Nature (天)$^{(49)}$.

第十章 Chapter 10

28. 載營魄抱一, 能無離乎？專氣致柔, 能嬰兒乎？滌除玄覽, 能無疵乎？

Resting (載)$^{(50)}$ one's mind (營魄)$^{(51)}$ to embrace the singular (一) Tao, how can the mind and Tao not be (能無)$^{(52)}$ separated (離) in the first place? Holding (專)$^{(53)}$ one's inherent natural forces (氣) to become (致) the most gentle (柔), how can one's gentleness match that of a baby? Cleansing (滌除) one's mind (玄覽)[54] of imperfection, how can there not be any imperfection (疵)[55] in the first place?[56]

29. 愛民治國, 能無知乎？天門開闔, 能無雌乎？明白四達, 能無為乎？

Loving the people and ruling the state, how can one not use acquired intelligence (知)[57]? Monitoring the opening and closing (開闔) of the valve of Motherly Nature (天門)[58], how can one not apply one's motherly way (雌)?[59] Achieving a thorough understanding (明白)[60] that reaches all corners of the Universe (四達)[61], how can one not first study and learn (為)[62] acquired knowledge?[63]

30. 生之, 畜之。生而不有; 為而不恃; 長而不宰。是謂玄德。

Tao begets (生) all things and nurtures (畜)[64] them. It begets them without anything (不有)[65] and acts without relying on any other (不恃)[66]; it oversees (長)[67] all without dominating (宰) over them. Such is known as the "Most Mysterious Manifestation (玄德)[68] of Tao".

第十一章 Chapter 11

31. 三十輻, 共一轂。當其無, 有車之用。

In a wooden wheel, thirty spokes (輻) assemble around the hub (轂)[69]; it is at (當)[70] the empty space (無) of the hub that grants the usefulness (用) of the entire cart.[71]

32. 埏埴以為器。當其無, 有器之用。

When the clay is fashioned (埏埴)[72] into vessels (器), it is at (當) the empty space that grants them their usefulness.

33. 鑿戶牖以為室。當其無, 有室之用。

The door and windows (戶牖) are chiselled out (鑿) from the

walls to form a habitable room (室); it is at the empty space within the doors and windows that grants the room to be useful and habitable.

34. 故有之以為利, 無之以為用。

Hence, a solid entity (有之) merely facilitates (利) the application of the void; ultimately, the void (無之) is where one finds usefulness and utility.

第十二章 Chapter 12

35. 五色令人目盲; 五音令人耳聾;

Feeding one's eyes with all the five colours (五色, i.e., all the different colours) excessively will make one go blind; delivering one's ears with all the five musical notes (五音, i.e., all types of music) immoderately will make one go deaf;

36. 五味令人口爽; 馳騁畋獵, 令人心發狂; 難得之貨, 令人行妨。

Providing one's tongue with all the five flavours (五味, i.e., all the different tastes) exorbitantly will impair (爽)[73] one's sense of taste; riding horses (馳騁) and hunting (畋獵) obsessively will make one lose sanity (狂); rare and treasured valuables will motivate one to act (行) towards harming and taking advantage of others (妨)[74].

37. 是以聖人為腹不為目。故去彼取此。

This is why the wise sages only seek to satisfy the bare necessity of their bellies (腹)[75] and choose not to be enslaved by what can be seen (目).[76] Hence, the wise sages leave behind the former mindset of indulgence and choose to take this latter mindset of frugality.

第十三章 Chapter 13

38. 寵辱若驚，貴大患若身。

Honour (寵) and humiliation (辱) are (若)[77] one's anxieties (驚); great tragedies (大患) are regarded so high (貴)[78] that they have become (若) one's own self (身).

39. 何謂寵辱若驚？ 寵為下。得之若驚，失之若驚。是謂寵辱若驚。

What is "honour and humiliation are one's anxieties"? Honour, which is regarded as superior, ultimately becomes (為) humiliation, which is regarded as lowly (下).[79] Having honour brings about anxiety, losing it also brings about anxiety. Such is "honour and humiliation are one's anxieties".[80]

40. 何謂貴大患若身？ 吾所以有大患者，為吾有身。及吾無身，吾有何患？

What is "great tragedies are regarded so high that they have become one's own self"? The reason why I face great tragedies is because I highly regard my precious self. If I do not regard my own self, how then can tragedies be bestowed upon me?

41. 故貴以身為天下，若可寄天下；愛以身為天下，若可託天下。

Hence, for those who highly regard all under Heaven as themselves (身), all under Heaven can be (若) entrusted (寄) to them; for those who cherish (愛)[81] all under Heaven as themselves, all under Heaven can be confided (託) to them.

第十四章 Chapter 14

42. 視之不見，名曰夷；聽之不聞，名曰希；搏之不得，名曰微。

For an entity that cannot be seen, we name it Yi (夷, The Big)[82]; for an entity that cannot be heard, we name it Xi (希, The Tranquil Silence)[83]; for an entity that we cannot hold or grasp (搏), we name it Wei (微, The Without)[84].

43. 此三者不可致詰，故混而為一。其上不皦，其下不昧。繩繩不可名，復歸於無物。

These three qualities cannot be thoroughly examined nor inquired (致詰)[85], and so they can be together (混) regarded as One[86]. The very top of One is not bright, clear, nor distinct (皦)[87], while the very bottom of One is not dull (昧)[88]. The One is endless (繩繩)[89], cannot be named, and eventually returns to the state of no matter (無物)[90].

44. 是謂無狀之狀，無物之象。是謂惚恍。迎之不見其首，隨之不見其後。

This One is hence called the form of the formless (無狀), phenomenon (象) of the matter-less (無物). It can also be said it is in a state of uncertainty (惚恍) of existence. When one faces it, one cannot see its front; when one chases after it, one cannot see its back.

45. 執古之道，以御今之有。能知古始，是謂道紀。

Grasping the ancient way of Tao can thus empower one to oversee and command (御)[91] any realm (有)[92] of the present day. If one is able to comprehend the origin of the ancient Tao (古始)[93], then one can be said (謂) as having retained the rules and principles mandated by Tao (道紀)[94].

第十五章 Chapter 15

46. 古之善為士者，微妙玄通，深不可識。夫唯不可識，故強為之容。

Those in the past who were adept (善)[95] at following Tao to deal with all matters (士)[96] were deeply profound and extraordinary (微妙)[97] as well as connected themselves with Nature (玄通)[98]. They were so profound (深) that they were beyond our comprehension (識). Alas, for they could not be fully comprehended, I can only barely (強)[99] attempt to provide some description (容) of them here:

47. 豫焉若冬涉川; 猶兮若畏四鄰; 儼兮其若容; 渙兮若冰之將釋; 敦兮其若樸; 曠兮其若谷; 混兮其若濁。

reluctant (豫) indeed (焉), they were (若)[100] stepping on frozen streams; cautious (猶) indeed, they were fearful of their surroundings (四鄰); solemn (儼) indeed, they were respectful of rules and principles (容)[101]; scattering (渙) indeed, they were (將)[102] melting (釋) ices which were evanescent and hard to define; sincere, plain, and honest (敦) indeed, they were living solely by their primitive simplicities (樸); brilliant and vast (曠)[103] indeed, they were open valleys (谷); murky (混) indeed, they were obscure (濁).

48. 孰能濁以靜之徐清? 孰能安以久動之徐生? 保此道者, 不欲盈。夫唯不盈, 故能蔽不新成。

What can induce cloudiness (濁), by applying (以)[104] tranquillity (靜), to consequentially (之)[105] and gradually (徐) be cleared up (清)? What can make stillness (安), by applying perpetual dynamic actions (久動), to consequentially and gradually emerge (生)? (Only Tao, nothing else.) Those who understand (保)[106] this rationale never like (不欲) to be overfilled (盈) in any aspect. Alas, for they are not overfilled in any aspect, they are then able to be inconspicuous (蔽)[107] and take no accomplishment (成) as their own (新)[108].[109]

第十六章 Chapter 16

49. 致虛極, 守靜篤。萬物並作, 吾以觀復。夫物芸芸, 各復歸其根。

Those who follow Tao pursue (致) to nullify (虛) themselves to the utmost degree (極) and safeguard (守) their inherent tranquilities (靜) with absolute diligence (篤)[110].[111] All things dynamically generate and develop (作) together, and I observe them all inevitably return (復) to their eventualities. Alas, there are so many diverse (芸芸) things, yet every one of them always returns to its respective root (i.e., Tao).

50. 歸根曰靜，是謂復命。復命曰常，知常曰明。不知常，妄作凶。
Returning to the root is known as being Tranquil (靜), which is otherwise known as returning (復) to the Natural Destiny (命)[(112)]. Returning to the Natural Destiny is known as adhering to the Immutable (常). Understanding this Immutable is known as Enlightenment (明). If one does not know nor understand this Immutable and acts rashly (妄作) without due consideration, then one shall face ominous outcomes (凶).

51. 知常容。容乃公；公乃王；王乃天；天乃道；道乃久。沒身不殆。
Knowing this Immutable (常) empowers one to forbear (容) all.[(113)] Forbearing all means one is unselfish and selfless (公); being unselfish and selfless means one is the most desirable for all (王)[(114)]; being the most desirable for all means one is following the way of Nature (天)[(115)]; following the way of Nature means one is walking the path of Tao (道). Tao is everywhere, exists all the time, and never ends (久). Accordingly, walking the path of Tao shall enable one to be free from all peril (不殆) in one's entire life (沒身). [(116)]

第十七章 Chapter 17

52. 太上，下知有之；其次，親而譽之；其次，畏之；其次，侮之。
For the finest (太) of superior rulers (上), their subjects (下) only know of their existences (有) but do not realize their governances.[(117)] For the lesser rulers, their subjects are close (親) to them and so commend (譽) them. For the even lesser rulers, their subjects fear (畏) them. For the least of the least rulers, their subjects openly insult and despise (侮) them.[(118)]

53. 信不足？焉有不信焉! 悠兮, 其貴言。

Are the words above not enough (不足) to be credible (信)? How (焉) can they not be credible![119] With this concern (悠)[120] in mind, indeed, rulers should weigh heavily (貴) when they give speeches or decrees (言)[121].

54. 功成事遂, 百姓皆謂我自然。

When the state has accomplished an enormous undertaking, all its people shall hence only say, "We are as we are, of our natural selves (自然)!"

第十八章 Chapter 18

55. 大道廢, 有仁義; 慧智出, 有大偽;

When the great and ultimate Tao is not followed (廢), benevolence (仁) and righteousness (義) appear.[122] When acquired wisdom and intellect come about, great hypocrisy (大偽) appears.[123]

56. 六親不和, 有孝慈; 國家昏亂, 有忠臣。

When there is no harmony (不和) among the six kinships (六親)[124], filial piety (孝) and parental devotion (慈) appear.[125] When the state is in chaos, loyal subordinates (忠臣) appear.[126]

第十九章 Chapter 19

57. 絕聖棄智, 民利百倍; 絕仁棄義, 民復孝慈; 絕巧棄利, 盜賊無有。

If a society abandons living by the examples of the so-called sages (聖)[127] as well as leaving behind acquired wisdom (智), then its people will benefit (利) a hundredfold.[128] If a society abandons living by benevolence and righteousness, then true filial piety will be revived among its people.[129] If a society abandons living by clever schemes (巧) and renounces cherishing personal gains (利), then there will be no thieves or robbers.

58. 此三者以為文不足, 故令有所屬：見素抱樸, 少私寡欲。

As the three narrations above are insufficient to completely illustrate (文) my contentions, so allow (令)[130] me to pen (屬)[131] further: one should acknowledge (見)[132] one's pure inherent nature (素)[133] and embrace primitive simplicity (樸), deride selfishness (私) and minimize (寡) selfish desires (欲).[134]

第二十章 Chapter 20

59. 絕學無憂。唯之與阿, 相去幾何？善之與惡, 相去若何？人之所畏, 不可不畏。

If one insulates (絕) oneself from acquiring knowledge and not follow scholarly disciplines, then one shall be free from worries. The uttering of a polite "Yes! (唯)" and the exclamation of an angry "Ah! (阿)", how different are they? What is defined as "good" and what is defined as "bad", how different are they? Nonetheless, one should fear or respect anything that everyone fears or respects (畏).[135]

60. 荒兮其未央哉！衆人熙熙, 如享太牢, 如春登臺。我獨泊兮其未兆, 如嬰兒之未孩, 儽儽兮若無所歸。

Tao is indeed so vast and spacious (荒)[136] that it has no limit (未央)[137], of course! The masses form jolly crowds, feeling happy, hurried and excited (熙熙)[138]; they all seem to be attending a full banquet dining on meat from sacrificial ceremonies (太牢)[139] or have ascended upon an elevated terrace (臺) on a beautiful spring day. It is just me alone, however, who appears to be tranquil (泊) indeed and yet to surface (未兆)[140]; I seem to be as primitive as a baby who has yet to smile (未孩)[141] and as laid-back (儽儽)[142] indeed as a person who has no direction or goal (所歸).

61. 衆人皆有餘，而我獨若遺。我愚人之心也哉！沌沌兮，俗人昭昭，我獨昏昏；俗人察察，我獨悶悶。

Everyone has lots to spare (餘), while I alone am (若)[143] the one who has lost (遺) everything. Indeed, I am a foolish man with a senseless mind! How ignorant and foolish (沌沌)[144] indeed I am! Other people are brilliant and conspicuous (昭昭)[145], while I alone am obtuse and undiscerning (昏昏)[146]. They all are so intelligent and discerning (察察)[147], while I alone am dim-witted (悶悶)[148].

62. 澹兮其若海，飂兮若無止。衆人皆有以，而我獨頑似鄙。我獨異於人，而貴食母。

Tranquil (澹)[149] indeed, I am (若)[150] the still sea; restless as the high winds (飂)[151] indeed, I am without any restraint (止). Everyone is acting for a reason (以)[152], while I alone appear to be dim-witted (頑) and (似)[153] inferior. I alone am different from all others and value (貴) the nurturing Mother Nature (食母)[154],[155].

第二十一章 Chapter 21

63. 孔德之容，惟道是從。道之為物，惟恍惟惚。惚兮恍兮，其中有象；恍兮惚兮，其中有物；窈兮冥兮，其中有精。

The rules and principles (容)[156] of the great yet vacuous (孔)[157] Manifestation of Tao (德) only follow Tao. When Tao manifests to become objects, it is in a state of uncertainty (惚恍)[158]. A state of uncertainty indeed, within it, there are phenomena (象)[159]. A state of uncertainty indeed, within it, there are matters (物). Unfathomable depth (窈冥)[160] indeed, within it, there are minuscule essences (精)[161] of all things.

64. 其精甚真，其中有信。自古及今，其名不去，以閱衆甫。

These minuscule essences are genuine (真) in existence and can be observed and tested (信)[162]. From the long past to the present, Tao's Name (名, i.e., Manifestation of Tao)[163] has never departed (不去)⁽¹⁶⁴⁾ away and is relied (以)⁽¹⁶⁵⁾ upon to endow (閱)⁽¹⁶⁶⁾ the birth of all things (眾甫)⁽¹⁶⁷⁾.⁽¹⁶⁸⁾

65. 吾何以知眾甫之狀哉？以此。

How do I know the physical forms (狀) of the birth of all things? Solely by the above rationale (以此)⁽¹⁶⁹⁾.

第二十二章 Chapter 22

66. 曲則全, 枉則直; 窪則盈, 敝則新; 少則得, 多則惑。是以聖人抱一為天下式。

It is the ones that are humble and submissive (曲)⁽¹⁷⁰⁾ to Tao that can be fully preserved (全)⁽¹⁷¹⁾;⁽¹⁷²⁾ it is the ones that are crooked (枉)⁽¹⁷³⁾ that can be straightened (直); ⁽¹⁷⁴⁾ it is the ones that are dented (窪)⁽¹⁷⁵⁾ that can be filled (盈); it is the ones that are worn (敝) that can become new (新); it is the ones that are deficient (少) that can attain (得); it is the ones that are rich (多) that can become unsettled (惑).⁽¹⁷⁶⁾ Thus, the wise sages embrace the singular (一)⁽¹⁷⁷⁾ Tao as the principle (式) of all under Heaven.

67. 不自見, 故明; 不自是, 故彰; 不自伐, 故有功; 不自矜, 故長。

Not showing one's brilliance (自見)⁽¹⁷⁸⁾ thus enables one to become enlightened (明); not being self-assertive and arrogant (自是) thus enables one to be celebrated by all others (彰); not being boastful of one's accomplishment (伐)⁽¹⁷⁹⁾ thus enables one's merits (功) to be recognized; not being complacent (自矜) thus enables one to acquire growth and supremacy (長).

68. 夫唯不爭, 故天下莫能與之爭。古之所謂曲則全者, 豈虛言哉！誠全而歸之。

Alas, it is because if a person does not compete with others, then no one under Heaven can compete with that person. People of the past once said only those who are humble and submissive (曲) to Tao can be preserved (全); how can that be just empty words! Indeed (誠), complete preservation belongs (歸) to those who do not compete with others.

第二十三章 Chapter 23

69. 希言自然。故飄風不終朝, 驟雨不終日。孰為此者？天地。天地尚不能久, 而況於人乎!

Words that cannot be heard (希言)[180] are a fundamental nature (自然) of the Manifestation of Tao. Therefore, sounds from violent winds (飄風)[181] do not last for a whole morning (朝), and noises from sudden torrential rains (驟雨) do not last for an entire day. What directs all these? The Universe. Even the Universe cannot make its own act last forever, let alone (況於) mere humans!

70. 故從事於道者: 道者同於道; 德者同於德; 失者同於失。

Hence, from the point of those who follow and serve (從事)[182] under Tao: those with Tao shall act the same way (同) as Tao; those with the Manifestation of Tao shall act the same way as the Manifestation of Tao; those who fail (失) both shall act the same way as failing both.

71. 同於道者, 道亦樂得之; 同於德者, 德亦樂得之; 同於失者, 失亦樂得之。信不足? 焉有不信焉!

Those who act the same way as Tao shall have Tao happily embracing (樂得) them; those who act the same way as the Manifestation of Tao shall have the Manifestation of Tao happily embracing them; those who act the same way as failing both shall have the way that fails both happily embracing them. Are the words above not enough to be credible? How can they not be credible![183]

第二十四章 Chapter 24

72. 企者不立, 跨者不行; 自見者不明, 自是者不彰; 自伐者無功, 自矜者不長。

Those who lift their heels (企)[184] can never stand firm; those who crouch down (跨)[185] can never walk; those who show their brilliance can never be enlightened; those who are self-assertive and arrogant are never celebrated by all others; those who are boastful of their accomplishments (伐)[186] are never recognized for their merits; those who are complacent can never acquire any growth or supremacy (長).[187]

73. 其在道也, 曰餘食贅行。物或惡之, 故有道者不處。

All these impulsive and ostentatious behaviours, from the standpoint of Tao, are known as rotten leftover delicacies (餘食)[188] as well as bodies of ugly tumours (贅行)[189], which are always (或)[190] loathed (惡) by the people (物)[191]. Hence, those who have grasped the way of Tao never put (處)[192] themselves to act in such manners.[193]

第二十五章 Chapter 25

74. 有物混成, 先天地生。寂兮寥兮, 獨立不改。周行而不殆, 可以為天下母。

There is a certain entity that is homogenously turbid yet natural (混成)[194] and born before the birth of the Universe.[195] Formless (寂寥)[196] indeed, it singularly exists, never changes, cycles periodically (周行), and never grows tired (不殆)[197]. Hence, it can manifest (為) itself to become the Mother (母)[198] of all under Heaven.

75. 吾不知其名, 字之曰道, 強為之名曰大。大曰逝, 逝曰遠, 遠曰反。故道大, 天大, 地大, 王亦大。

I do not know its name, so I shall designate (字) it as Tao; if one wants to be more specific, we can only barely (強)[199] call it great. It is great; hence (曰)[200], it flows everywhere in all directions (逝)[201]. It flows everywhere in all directions; hence, it can reach the ultimate limit (遠)[202]. It can reach the ultimate limit; hence, it must return back (反) to the great Tao. Therefore, Tao is great, Nature is great, Earth is great, and the most desirable for all (王)[203] is also great.

76. 域中有四大，而王居其一焉。人法地；地法天；天法道；道法自然。

In our realm (域)[204], there are then four greats, and the most desirable for all takes up (居)[205] one of them. Yet, humankind takes its law (法)[206] from Earth; Earth takes its law from Nature; Nature takes its law from the Tao. Tao takes its law naturally from itself (自然) (i.e., Tao is what it is).[207]

第二十六章 Chapter 26

77. 重為輕根，靜為躁君。是以聖人終日行不離輜重。 雖有榮觀，燕處超然。

Gravity and prudence (重) are the foundational roots of frivolity and imprudence (輕). Tranquil stillness (靜) is the lord (君)[208] of rash actions (躁). Accordingly, the wise sages, night and day (終日), do not leave behind (不離) their heavy supplies (輜重)[209] to walk with frivolity and imprudence. Even though they are honourable and distinguished (榮觀)[210], their minds are still unmoved and at ease (燕處)[211], taking prudence and tranquillity to transcend above the mundane world (超然)[212] [213].

78. 奈何萬乘之主，而以身輕天下？ 輕則失本，躁則失君。

Why then (奈何) would the rulers of great states (萬乘)[214], for their own sakes (身), take all under Heaven lightly with imprudence (輕)? If they take the path of imprudence, they shall then lose their foundations (本) to rule. If they act rashly, they shall lose their thrones (失君)[215].

第二十七章 Chapter 27

79. 善行無轍迹; 善言無瑕讁; 善數不用籌策; 善閉無關楗而不可開; 善結無繩約而不可解。

Those who are well acquainted (善) with Tao carry out their tasks (行) without leaving any trace (轍迹)[216]; those who are well acquainted with Tao speaks without any fault (瑕讁)[217]; those who are well acquainted with Tao calculate without the need of any instrument (籌策)[218]; those who are well acquainted with Tao use no bolts or bars (關楗)[219] to shut a door that can never be thus opened; those who are well acquainted with Tao use no tie with ropes or strings (繩約)[220] to make knots that can never be thus loosened.

80. 是以聖人常善救人, 故無棄人; 常善救物, 故無棄物。是謂襲明。

Therefore, the wise sages are invariably adept at exclusively using Tao to assist (救)[221] all kinds of people, for their very own original natures (故)[222] do not leave anyone behind (棄人); the wise sages are invariably adept at exclusively using Tao to assist in facilitating all kinds of affairs (物)[223], for their very own original natures do not leave any affair unattended (棄物).[224] Such is called "Catching the Enlightenment (襲明)".

81. 故善人者, 不善人之師; 不善人者, 善人之資。

Accordingly, those who are well acquainted with Tao are teachers of those who are not well acquainted with Tao; those who are not well acquainted with Tao are resources and materials (資) for those who are well acquainted with Tao.

82. 不貴其師, 不愛其資, 雖智大迷, 是謂要妙。

If one does not value one's teachers and not treasure (愛) one's resources, then one is still greatly baffled (大迷) in the way of Tao, even if one is extremely intelligent. Such is called "The Most Profound and Wonderful Mystery (要妙) Tao"[225].

第二十八章 Chapter 28

83. 知其雄，守其雌，為天下谿。為天下谿，常德不離，復歸於嬰兒。知其白，守其黑，為天下式。

Understanding one's masculine strength (雄) yet upholding (守) to act with feminine tenderness (雌) enables one to become the lowest point of the valley (谿)[226], which is the most desirable place for all under Heaven. If one becomes the lowest point of the valley for all under Heaven, then the everlasting Manifestation of the immutable Tao (常德) shall never leave (離)[227] one, and so one returns to the state of a newborn baby, original and simple. Accordingly, knowing the clean and clear (白) aspect of the Manifestation of Tao yet upholding its obscure and muddy (黑) aspect is the principle (式) of all under Heaven.[228]

84. 為天下式，常德不忒，復歸於無極。知其榮，守其辱，為天下谷。為天下谷，常德乃足，復歸於樸。

If one applies the principle of all under Heaven, then one shall never stray (忒)[229] from the everlasting Manifestation of the immutable Tao and so is able to return all back to the "limitless infinity (無極)" (i.e., Tao). Knowing how to achieve high glory yet upholding humiliation is assuming the role of the lowest point of the valley (谷)[230] of all under Heaven. If one assumes the role of the lowest point of the valley of all under Heaven, then one shall reach upon (足)[231] the everlasting Manifestation of the immutable Tao (常德) and so is able to return all back to the original simplicity (樸)[232].

85. 樸散則為器。聖人用之，則為官長。故大制不割。

When this original simplicity disperses (散) and manifests itself in the physical world, it becomes all sorts of worldly entities (器)[233]. When wise sages administrate (用)[234] these entities and (則)[235] become the leader of all officials (官長), they, therefore, administrate via Tao (大制)[236] without any personal discernment (不割).[237]

第二十九章 Chapter 29

86. 將欲取天下而為之, 吾見其不得已。天下神器, 不可為也。為者敗之, 執者失之。

For those who wish to oversee all under Heaven under their rule (為)[238], I do not see they will succeed (已)[239]; all under Heaven collectively is an entity of extraordinary nature (神器)[240] and cannot be ruled. Those who rule it with their own differentiations and intents shall eventually fail (敗), while those who tightly take hold (執) of it with absolute dominance shall eventually lose it.

87. 故物或行或隨; 或歔或吹; 或強或羸; 或挫或隳。

After all (故)[241], there are (或)[242] some people (物)[243] who are emphatic and assertive (行)[244], while some who are mild and submissive (隨)[245]; some who blow through their noses (歔)[246], while some who blow through their mouths (吹)[247]; some who are strong and sturdy (強), while some who are weak and frail (羸)[248]; some who humble (挫)[249] themselves to Tao, while some who (refuse to humble and so) wreck themselves by Tao (隳)[250].[251]

88. 是以聖人去甚, 去奢, 去泰。

This is why the wises sages deal away (去) with indulgence (甚)[252], deal away with conceitedness (奢)[253], and deal away with pride and arrogance (泰)[254].[255]

第三十章 Chapter 30

89. 以道佐人主者, 不以兵強天下。其事好還。師之所處, 荊棘生焉。大軍之後, 必有凶年。

Those who use Tao to assist rulers (人主) never use military might to violently (強)[256] suppress all under Heaven.[257] Such a matter (其事) of violent suppression shall easily (好)[258] produce counter results (還)[259]. Wherever the military is, weeds and thorns (荊棘) shall rise.[260] After a major military operation, there will certainly be bad and ominous years (凶年) to come.

90. 善有果而已, 不敢以取強。果而勿矜; 果而勿伐; 果而勿驕; 果而不得已; 果而勿強。

Accordingly, one should only prefer (善) securing favourable results (果) but not dare to adopt (取) violent suppression. Securing favourable results should not be accompanied by vanity (矜); securing favourable results should not be accompanied by boastfulness (伐); securing favourable results should not be accompanied by arrogance (驕); securing favourable results should be seen by all as something that is absolutely necessary with no other option (不得已); securing favourable results should not be done with violent suppression nor should it be used to justify violent suppression (勿強).

91. 物壯則老, 是謂不道。不道早已!

Indeed, if one is mighty and fierce (壯)[261], one will frail and wither (老)[262], and so it can be said as not following Tao. Whatever that is not following Tao will come to its end (已) very soon (早)![263]

第三十一章 Chapter 31

92. 夫佳兵者, 不祥之器。物或惡之, 故有道者不處。君子居則貴左, 用兵則貴右。兵者不祥之器, 非君子之器, 不得已而用之。恬淡為上。

Alas, even the finest (佳)[264] army is a worldly entity (器) of bad omen (不祥). People (物)[265] always (或)[266] despise it, and so those who have grasped the way of Tao never employ it. The honourable ones (君子), during peaceful times (居)[267], highly regard the left (i.e., good omen), while, during war times (用兵), the right (i.e., bad omen).[268] Hence, the military is considered an entity of bad omen and not a tool for the honourable ones; they only utilize it when there is no other option. One should always hold simplicity and tranquillity (恬淡)[269] in the highest regard (為上).

93. 勝而不美, 而美之者, 是樂殺人。夫樂殺人者, 則不可以得志於天下矣。

A military victory is never wonderful (美). If one does proclaim it to be wonderful, then one is seeing killing others as desirable (樂)[270]. Alas, those who desire to kill others shall not have their aspirations realized (得志)[271] under Heaven.

94. 吉事尚左, 凶事尚右。偏將軍居左, 上將軍居右, 言以喪禮處之。殺人之衆, 以哀悲泣之。戰勝以喪禮處之。

Good and auspicious matters honour (尚)[272] the left, while evil and calamitous matters honour the right. The second in command (偏將軍) of the army is to be positioned (居) on the left; the commanding general-in-chief (上將軍) is to be positioned on the right.[273] This means wars should be treated (處)[274] as rites of mourning (喪禮). For those who have killed many, they should thus weep with great sorrows (悲泣)[275]. Even if they are victorious, they should treat their victories as rites of mourning.

第三十二章 Chapter 32

95. 道常無名樸。雖小, 天下莫能臣也。侯王若能守之, 萬物將自賓。天地相合, 以降甘露。民莫之令而自均。

Tao is immutable (常), has no name (無名), and is primordially original and simple (樸). Although it appears to be puny as well as humble (小)[276], nothing under Heaven can subjugate (臣) it. If rulers (侯王) can uphold Tao in their governances, then all shall naturally submit (賓) to their reigns. As Nature and Earth work together (相合), refreshing dew (甘露) naturally forms. Likewise, the people shall naturally follow (自均)[277] the rulers without any command or decree (令).[278]

96. 始制有名。名亦既有，夫亦將知止。知止可以不殆。

The Originator (始, Tao)[279] manifests and generates (制)[280]
the "identifiable and with names (有名)" (i.e., Te, 德)[281]. Since
the Name (名)[282] is already (亦既) identifiable (有) and thus
limited, one should know where to reach and when to stop (知
止)[283]. Knowing where to reach and when to stop shall allow
one to be free from all peril (不殆).[284]

97. 譬道之在天下，猶川谷之於江海。

One should understand (譬)[285] Tao to all under Heaven is like
that of streams from valleys (川谷) to rivers and seas (江海).

第三十三章 Chapter 33

98. 知人者智，自知者明。勝人者有力，自勝者強。

Knowing and understanding others is only intelligent; knowing and understanding oneself is true enlightenment (明)[286].
Overcoming (勝) others is only being more powerful (有力);
overcoming oneself is true strength (強).[287]

99. 知足者富，強行者有志。不失其所者久，死而不亡者壽。

Those who are satisfied with whatever their circumstances are
always wealthy; those who steadfastly act (強行)[288] by Tao
always have their aspirations realized (有志)[289]. Not losing
one's way (所)[290] in following Tao enables one to last long;
[291] to die but not perish (不亡)[292] enables one to have true
longevity (壽).

第三十四章 Chapter 34

**100. 大道氾兮，其可左右。萬物恃之而生而不辭；功成不名有；衣
養萬物而不為主。**

The great Tao flows and permeates everywhere (氾)[293] indeed (兮); it influences all (左右)[294]. All things rely on (恃) it to
spawn and flourish, yet it does not proclaim (辭) itself to be so.

It claims (名) no credit (有) in its accomplishments. Tao embraces (衣)[295] and nurtures the physical beings of all but never claims to be their master (主).

101. 常無欲可名於小; 萬物歸焉而不為主, 可名為大。以其終不自為大, 故能成其大。

This immutable Tao (常) of no selfish desire (無欲) can be named as puny (小); however, all things follow and adhere (歸) to it, yet it never claims to be their master, so, it can be named as great.   As it never (終不)[296] claims itself to be great, it is thus able to accomplish its greatness.

第三十五章 Chapter 35

102. 執大象, 天下往。往而不害, 安平太。樂與餌, 過客止。

Those who grasp the great phenomenon manifested by Tao (大象)[297] shall have all under Heaven follow (往)[298] them. Such following ensures all under Heaven not to be harmed, and great peace and ease shall arise. Offering people good music and delicacies (餌)[299] can merely attract them as passing guests (過客)[300] only (止)[301].

103. 道之出口, 淡乎其無味。視之不足見; 聽之不足聞; 用之不足既。

When Tao is expressed in or described with words (出口)[302], it is so bland and dull that it is not distinct (無味)[303]. When one sees it, it cannot (不足)[304] be seen. When one listens to it, it cannot be heard. However, when one applies it, it can never be exhausted (既)[305].

第三十六章 Chapter 36

104. 將欲歙之, 必固張之; 將欲弱之, 必固強之; 將欲廢之, 必固興之; 將欲奪之, 必固與之。是謂微明。

If one plans to (將欲)[306] diminish something, one must (固)

first expand (張) it; if one plans to weaken something, one must first strengthen it; if one plans to ruin (廢)[307] something, one must first raise and establish (興)[308] it; if one plans to acquire (奪) something, one must first give (與) it away. This principle is known as the "Enlightenment from Wei (微明)"[309].

105. 柔弱勝剛強。魚不可脫於淵。國之利器不可以示人。

The gentle and weak is better than (勝) the bold and strong. A fish should not leave its abyssal niche (淵)[310]. Instruments that benefit the state (國之利器)[311] should not be displayed to the people.[312]

第三十七章 Chapter 37

106. 道常無為而無不為。侯王若能守之, 萬物將自化。化而欲作, 吾將鎮之以無名之樸。

Tao immutably has no personal differentiation and intent to do anything (無為), yet there is nothing that it cannot do (無不為). If rulers of states (侯王) can uphold Tao in their governances, all things shall (將)[313] naturally live and propagate on their own (自化)[314]. As selfish desires (欲) do arise during natural propagations, I will (將)[315] counter and repress (鎮) them with the original simplicity (樸) of the "unidentifiable and nameless (無名)"[316].

107. 無名之樸, 夫亦將無欲。不欲以靜, 天下將自定。

Applying the original simplicity of the "unidentifiable and nameless (無名)" is just (亦)[317] allowing everything to adhere to (將)[318] having no selfish desire. If all leave behind selfish desires (不欲) to return to their state of inherent tranquillity (靜), then all under Heaven shall (將)[319] naturally settle themselves in serenity (定)[320].

第三十八章 Chapter 38

108. 上德不德, 是以有德; 下德不失德, 是以無德。上德無為而無以為; 下德為之而有以為。

Those with high virtue (上德)[321] do not need any virtue, thus indicating they, in fact, already have virtues. Those with low virtue (下德) fear the loss of their virtues, thus indicating they, in fact, do not inherently have any virtue.[322] Those with high virtue do not need to do anything (無為) to be virtuous, and so there is no (無) reason (以)[323] for them to act (為); those with low virtue need to act (為之) to cultivate their virtues, and so they do have a reason (有以) to act (為).

109. 上仁為之而無以為; 上義為之而有以為。上禮為之而莫之應, 則攘臂而扔之。

Those with high benevolence (上仁) act to cultivate benevolence, but there is actually no reason (以) for them to act.[324] Those with high righteousness (上義) act to cultivate righteousness, and so they do have a reason to act. Those with high propriety act and expect others to follow suit: if others do not respond to them with propriety, they shall bare their arms (攘臂)[325] and coercively drag (扔)[326] the nonconformists to comply.

110. 故失道而後德; 失德而後仁; 失仁而後義; 失義而後禮。

Accordingly, when Tao is lost in a society, virtues (德)[327] appear; when virtues are lost, benevolence appears; when benevolence is lost, righteousness appears; and when righteousness is lost, propriety appears.

111. 夫禮者, 忠信之薄, 而亂之首。前識者, 道之華, 而愚之始。是以大丈夫處其厚, 不居其薄; 處其實, 不居其華。故去彼取此。

Alas, propriety is poor in honesty (忠信) and the main (首) culprit of chaos.[328] Having acquired knowledge and being able to foresee (前識)[329] is actually the most superficial (華) in the realm of Tao and the beginning of stupidity (愚). Thus, those who have great aspirations in following Tao (大丈夫)[330] put (處) themselves where Tao is most rich and sturdy (厚) but not where Tao is poor and thin (薄). They reside themselves at the very solid and genuine core (實) of Tao but not the superficial exterior of it. This is why those who have great aspirations in following Tao leave behind the former of foreseeing and choose the latter of following Tao.

第三十九章 Chapter 39

112. 昔之得一者：天得一以清; 地得一以寧; 神得一以靈; 谷得一以盈; 萬物得一以生; 侯王得一以為天下貞。其致之。
Those that have obtained One[331] since the past are: Nature, which carry One to become pure and clear (清); Earth, which carries One to become settled and established (寧); the spirits, which carry One to obtain their vitalities (靈); the valleys (谷), which carry One to become filled with abundant diversity (盈); all things, which carry One to live and exist (生); the rulers (侯王) of states, who carry One to rule all under Heaven in proper order (貞)[332]. The One (其) fulfils and realizes (致) all their corresponding characteristics (之).

113. 天無以清, 將恐裂; 地無以寧, 將恐發; 神無以靈, 將恐歇; 谷無以盈, 將恐竭; 萬物無以生, 將恐滅; 侯王無以貴高, 將恐蹶。
If Nature does not have One to become pure and clear, it shall (將) perhaps (恐)[333] fracture (裂); if Earth does not have One to become settled and calmed, it shall perhaps shake and quake (發)[334]; if the spirits do not have One to obtain their vitalities, they shall perhaps become exhausted and die (歇); if the valleys do not have One to become filled with abundant diversity, they shall perhaps dry up and become barren (竭); if all things do not have One to live and exist, they shall perhaps become extinct (滅); if the rulers of states do not have One to become noble (貴高)[335], their thrones shall perhaps be overthrown (蹶)[336].

114. 故貴以賤為本, 高以下為基。是以侯王自稱孤、寡、不穀。此非以賤為本邪？非乎？故致數輿無輿。不欲琭琭如玉, 珞珞如石。

Accordingly, one should know that anything noble and distinguished (貴) is based on something lesser and unrefined (賤), while anything superior (高) is rooted (基) in something lowly and primitive (下)[337]. Hence, rulers of states call themselves "The Orphaned (孤)", "The Forsaken (寡)", or "The Incapable (不穀)"[338]. Isn't this a demonstration of the distinguished is based on the lesser and unrefined? Isn't this true? Therefore, the honour of possessing (致)[339] many horses to pull one's carriage (數輿)[340] relies on the inferiority of not possessing any carriage (無輿). The honourable should thus never desire to be as dazzling as jades (琭琭如玉)[341] nor as conspicuous as gemstones on a necklace (珞珞如石)[342].[343]

第四十章 Chapter 40

115. 反者道之動; 弱者道之用。天下萬物生於有, 有生於無。
Restorative countering forces (反)[344] are Tao's actions (動)[345].[346] The weak and the puny (弱) are Tao's apparatus. All under Heaven sprang (生) from the entity that can be conceived and named (有), and the entity that can be conceived and named originates (生) from the one that cannot be conceived nor named (無, i.e., Tao).

第四十一章 Chapter 41

116. 上士聞道, 勤而行之; 中士聞道, 若存若亡; 下士聞道, 大笑之。不笑不足以為道。
Scholars of the highest calibre (上士), when they hear about (聞) Tao, earnestly (勤) act according to it. Scholars of the average calibre (中士), when they hear about Tao, sometimes keep (存) it and sometimes lose (亡) it. Scholars of the lowest calibre (下士), when they hear about Tao, laugh greatly at it; if it were not

laughed at by them, it would not be fit to be Tao.

117. 故建言有之：明道若昧; 進道若退; 夷道若纇; 上德若谷; 大白若辱; 廣德若不足; 建德若偷; 質真若渝; 大方無隅; 大器晚成; 大音希聲; 大象無形; 道隱無名。

Thus, there was a saying from the past (建言)[347]: Tao's clear and bright way (明道) is (若)[348] elusive and obscure (昧); Tao's way to advance forward (進道) is to retreat backwards; Tao's flat and even path (夷道) is rough and uneven (纇纇)[349]; the supreme Manifestation of Tao (上德) is rudimentary and lowly as the bottom of a valley (谷); the cleanest and clearest aspect of the Manifestation of Tao (大白)[350] is obscure and muddy (辱)[351]; the most generous and magnanimous aspect of the Manifestation of Tao (廣德)[352] is still insufficient; the most steadfast and sturdy aspect of the Manifestation of Tao (建德)[353] is weak and frail (偷)[354]; those of primitive and simple (質)[355] pureness (真)[356] are tainted (渝)[357] with many impurities; the most rectangular (大方)[358] shape has no corners (隅)[359]; the most magnificent worldly entity (大器)[360] evolves gradually and requires a long time (晚) to become established (成); [361] the most astounding sound (大音) is not audible (希聲); the great phenomenon manifested by Tao (大象)[362] has no shape nor form (無形); Tao, hence, is unimaginably and wonderfully (隱)[363] "unidentifiable and nameless (無名)"[364].

118. 夫唯道善貸且成。

Alas, hence, it is only (唯)[365] Tao that excels (善) in supplying and furnishing (貸)[366] all as well as accomplishing all things (成).

第四十二章 Chapter 42

119. 道生一; 一生二; 二生三; 三生萬物。萬物負陰而抱陽, 沖氣以為和。

Tao spawned (生) One[367]; One spawned Two[368]; Two spawned Three[369]; Three spawned all things. All things possess the negative (陰, Yin) and embrace the positive (陽, Yang), and the interactions (沖) between these two countering forces (氣) make all things to exist in harmony (和).

120. 人之所惡，唯孤、寡、不穀，而王公以為稱。故物或損之而益，或益之而損。

People surely (唯) dislike "The Orphaned", "The Forsaken", and "The Incapable"; yet, these are the very descriptions that rulers of states call themselves. Accordingly, that which diminishes (損) is actually favoured (益), that which favours is actually diminished.

121. 人之所教，我亦教之。強梁者不得其死，吾將以為教父。

What all other people use to enlighten (教)[370] others, I also use it to enlighten others. "The brutal and the strong (強梁)[371] do not reap a natural and pleasant death (不得其死)[372]", I shall take this admonition as the starting point (父)[373] to enlighten (教) others.[374]

第四十三章 Chapter 43

122. 天下之至柔，馳騁天下之至堅。無有入無閒，吾是以知無為之有益。

The gentlest under Heaven gallops freely (馳騁)[375] within the toughest. Tao is without shape nor form (無有)[376], and so it can penetrate (入) even the toughest object under Heaven that has countless infinitely small spaces (無閒)[377] within it. I, therefore, know that it is the most beneficial to act in the gentlest manner, which is not to act with any personal differentiation and intent (無為)[378].

123. 不言之教，無為之益，天下希及之。

Enlightenment (教)[379] through the wordless and the benefits of not acting with any personal differentiation and intent are rarely (希) recognized and attained (及)[380] by those under Heaven.

第四十四章 Chapter 44

124. 名與身孰親？身與貨孰多？得與亡孰病？是故甚愛必大費, 多藏必厚亡。

Fame (名) or life (身), which one is dearer (親) to you? Life or wealth (貨), which one is more important (多)[381] to you? Attainment (得) of wealth or losing (亡) your life, which one is actually suffering (病)[382]? Accordingly, securing what one prizes shall cost one dearly (大費), while treasuring too many (多藏) shall invariably lead to an enormous loss (厚亡).

125. 知足不辱; 知止不殆; 可以長久。

Knowing to be satisfied with whatever the circumstances shall never bring shame (不辱) to oneself; while knowing where to reach and when to stop (知止)[383] shall never bring peril to oneself. Able to do both shall make one live long (長久)[384].

第四十五章 Chapter 45

126. 大成若缺, 其用不弊; 大盈若沖, 其用不窮。大直若屈, 大巧若拙, 大辯若訥。

The most accomplished (大成) is (若)[385] actually still deficient (缺), but its applications are inexhaustible (不弊)[386]; the most abundant (大盈) is actually hollow and empty (沖)[387], but its applications are limitless.[388] The strictest and the most proper (大直)[389] is actually submissive and yielding (屈)[390] to Tao; [391] the sharpest and the most brilliant (大巧) is actually dim-witted (拙); [392] the most eloquent (大辯) is actually inarticulate (訥)[393].

127. 躁勝寒, 靜勝熱。清靜為天下正。

Rash and fiery actions (躁) may temporarily overcome icy and hostile situations (寒), yet it is tranquillity (靜) that shall ultimately and inexhaustibly overcome boiling fierceness (熱).[394] Pristine tranquillity (清靜) is the true guiding principle (正)[395] of all under Heaven.[396]

第四十六章 Chapter 46

128. 天下有道, 卻走馬以糞; 天下無道, 戎馬生於郊。

When all under Heaven embrace Tao, the people reclaim (卻)[397] their distinguished running horses (走馬) to work and fertilize (糞) the fields. When the world rejects Tao, war horses (戎馬) give birth in the wild (郊).

129. 禍莫大於不知足; 咎莫大於欲得。故知足之足, 常足矣。

There is no calamity (禍) greater than being dissatisfied with one's circumstances and no fault (咎) greater than selfish greed to possess (欲得)[398]. Accordingly, the satisfaction from being satisfied with whatever the circumstances is everlasting (常) satisfaction indeed.

第四十七章 Chapter 47

130. 不出戶知天下, 不闚牖見天道。其出彌遠, 其知彌少。

One can understand all under Heaven without leaving one's home, and one can realize Nature's way (天道) without peeking out (闚) of a single window (牖). If one walks further (彌)[399] away (遠) from one's home, the lesser one knows about the true nature of the world.[400]

131. 是以聖人不行而知, 不見而名, 不為而成。

Accordingly, the wise sages do not travel yet know all under Heaven, do not peek out of a single window yet comprehend (名)[401] Tao, and do not act with any personal differentiation and intent (不為) yet accomplish (成) everything.

第四十八章 Chapter 48

132. 為學日益, 為道日損。損之又損, 以至於無為。無為而無不為。

Pursue (為) learning knowledge day by day increases (益)[402] one to act with personal differentiations and intents. Pursue following Tao day by day diminishes (損)[403] one to act with personal differentiations and intents: diminishing upon diminishing, one shall eventually not (無) act (為) with any personal differentiation and intent. As there is no personal differentiation and intent to do anything, there is nothing that one cannot do (無不為).[404]

133. 取天下常以無事。及其有事, 不足以取天下。

When ruling (取)[405] all under Heaven, one should always (常) never aim to accomplish anything great (事)[406]. When one aims to accomplish something great, one is unqualified (不足) to rule all under Heaven.

第四十九章 Chapter 49

134. 聖人無常心, 以百姓心為心。善者, 吾善之; 不善者, 吾亦善之。德善。

The wise sages do not have a fixed and distinct mindset (常心) of their own; they make the mindset of the people as their own. Anything that the people find good (善者), I also favour it (吾善之) to be good. Anything that the people find not good (不善者), I also favour it (吾亦善之) to be not good.[407] Such is attaining (德)[408] what should be favoured (善) from the people.[409]

135. 信者, 吾信之; 不信者, 吾亦信之。德信。

Anything that the people find trustworthy (信者), I believe it (吾信之) to be trustworthy. Anything that the people find untrustworthy (不信者), I also believe it (吾亦信之) to be untrustworthy.[410] Such is acquiring (德)[411] what should be trusted

(信) from the people.[412]

136. 聖人在天下, 歙歙為天下渾其心。聖人皆孩之。

The wise sages living under Heaven have no prejudice (歙歙)[413] of their own and turn the minds (心) of all under Heaven back to their primitive simplistic natures (渾)[414]. The wise sages make all become newborn babies (孩)[415].

第五十章 Chapter 50

137. 出生入死, 生之徒, 十有三; 死之徒, 十有三; 人之生, 動之死地, 亦十有三。夫何故？以其生生之厚!

From birth to death (出生入死), those who are alive have a body of four limbs and nine orifices (十有三, i.e., the bodily self)[416]; those who are dead have a body of four limbs and nine orifices; while living, those who often (動)[417] risk themselves to go into (之)[418] dire and deadly situations (死地)[419] also have a body of four limbs and nine orifices. Why is this so? It is because the body brings about (以其) too much regard (厚)[420] to one's possessions and bodily life (生生)[421]![422]

138. 蓋聞善攝生者, 陸行不遇兕虎, 入軍不被甲兵。兕無所投其角, 虎無所措其爪, 兵無所容其刃。夫何故？以其無死地。

Alas, I have heard that those who are well acquainted with maintaining (攝)[423] their lives never face any fierce rhinoceros (兕) or tiger when travelling on land and never come into (被)[424] contact with any armed soldier (甲兵) when marching into enemy camps (入軍): the rhinoceros finds no place in them into which to thrust its horn, the tiger finds no place in them in which to fix its claws, and the armed soldier finds no spot in them at which to lay (容)[425] his weapons. Why is that so? For they never put themselves in dire and deadly situations (死地).

第五十一章 Chapter 51

139. 道生之，德畜之；物形之，勢成之。是以萬物莫不尊道而貴德。

Tao begets (生) all things, the Manifestation of Tao nurtures (畜) all things. All things take their shapes and forms (形) according to their natures, and the manners (勢) of all things are then established accordingly. Therefore, all things honour Tao and exalt its Manifestation.

140. 道之尊，德之貴，夫莫之命而常自然。故道生之，德畜之；長之育之，亭之毒之；養之覆之。生而不有，為而不恃，長而不宰。是謂玄德。

Although Tao should be honoured and its Manifestation exalted, all things do not need to be directed (命) by them to invariably (常) follow their own natures. Tao begets (生) all, and its Manifestation nurtures (畜) all; they both rear (長) all, raise (育)[426] all, cultivate (亭)[427] all, develop (毒)[428] all, feed (養) all, and return (覆)[429] all back to Tao. Tao begets all without anything (不有)[430], acts without relying (不恃)[431] on any other, and oversees (長)[432] all without dominating (宰)[433] over them. Such is known as the "Most Mysterious Manifestation of Tao (玄德)".

第五十二章 Chapter 52

141. 天下有始，以為天下母。既得其母，以知其子；既知其子，復守其母。沒身不殆。

All under Heaven comes from the Originator (始, i.e., Tao), which manifests itself to become the Mother of all under Heaven (母, i.e., Te or Manifestation of Tao).[434] As we know the Manifestation of Tao is the mother of all, we can conceive that all matters are the offsprings (子) of the Manifestation of Tao; since we know all matters are the offsprings of the Manifestation of Tao, we should thus dedicate ourselves to pursue (守) the motherly way of the Manifestation of Tao but not its offspring, the materialistic matters. Doing this shall allow one to be free from perils (不殆) in one's entire life (沒身).

142. 塞其兌, 閉其門, 終身不勤; 開其兌, 濟其事, 終身不救。
If one closes off (塞) all senses (兌)[435] and shuts the door (between physical matters and one's mind), then one shall never be exhausted (不勤)[436]. If one advances (開) the senses to achieve (濟)[437] personal accomplishments, then one shall never be assisted (不救)[438] by Tao and eventually become tired and exhausted.

143. 見小曰明, 守柔曰強。用其光, 復歸其明, 無遺身殃。是為習常。
Being able to perceive the Small (小)[439] is known as Enlightenment (明); being able to sustain (守) abiding by the most gentle (柔) is known as true strength (強)[440]. Applying the light (光) of Tao to restore (復歸) one's inherent inner enlightenment (明) shall thus not (無) retain (遺)[441] any harm (殃)[442] for oneself. Such is known as "Comprehending the Immutable (習常)"[443].

第五十三章 Chapter 53

144. 使我介然有知, 行於大道, 唯施是畏。大道甚夷, 而民好徑。
Suppose (使) I understand (知) and am unwaveringly (介然)[444] following (行) the great Tao, I still surely (唯) fear (畏) that I will go astray as I apply (施) myself through this great path of Tao. The great path of Tao is very (甚) smooth and level (夷); yet, people (民) prefer (好) to take alternative narrow paths (徑)[445] that deviate from the way of Tao.

145. 朝甚除, 田甚蕪, 倉甚虛。服文綵, 帶利劍, 厭飲食, 財貨有餘。是謂盜夸, 非道也哉!
They construct (除)[446] too many mansions (朝)[447], which leads to ill-cultivated (蕪) fields and empty granaries (倉). Further, they wear (服) elegant and colourful dresses (文綵)[448],

carry (帶) sharp swords, indulge (厭)(449) themselves with food and drinks, and have excessive (有餘) wealth and possessions (財貨)(450); such people are great robbers (盜夸)(451) and certainly not following the way of Tao!

第五十四章 Chapter 54

146. 善建者不拔; 善抱者不脫。子孫以祭祀不輟。

Those who are adept at instituting (建)(452) never have Tao pulled out (拔) from themselves. Likewise, those who are adept in embracing (抱) Tao never drop (脫) Tao from themselves. Their descendants (子孫) shall thus (以)(453) perpetually (不輟) celebrate (祭祀) their predecessors.

147. 修之於身, 其德乃真; 修之於家, 其德乃餘; 修之於鄉, 其德乃長; 修之於國, 其德乃豐; 修之於天下, 其德乃普。

Cultivating (修) Tao for (於)(454) oneself makes one's manifestation (德)(455) pure and genuine (真)(456) ; cultivating Tao for one's family makes one's manifestation plentiful (餘); cultivating Tao for one's county (鄉) makes one's manifestation flourish (長); cultivating Tao for one's state makes one's manifestation rich (豐); cultivating Tao for all under Heaven makes one's manifestation to be universal (普).(457)

148. 故以身觀身; 以家觀家; 以鄉觀鄉; 以國觀國; 以天下觀天下。吾何以知天下然哉？ 以此。

Accordingly, the cultivation of Tao for the self can be applied to examine (觀)(458) the self, the cultivation of Tao for the family can be applied to examine the family, the cultivation of Tao for the county can be applied to examine the county, the cultivation of Tao for the state can be applied to examine the state, the cultivation of Tao for all under Heaven can be applied to examine all under Heaven. How do I know all under Heaven is like this? Solely because of the above rationale(459).

第五十五章 Chapter 55

149. 含德之厚, 比於赤子。蜂蠆虺蛇不螫, 猛獸不據, 攫鳥不搏。骨弱筋柔而握固。

Those who richly (厚) harbour the Manifestation of Tao (含德)[460] are the same (比)[461] as newborn babies (赤子)[462].[463] Poisonous insects like bees and scorpions (蜂蠆), as well as venomous snakes like serpents (虺蛇), will not sting or bite them; fierce beasts will not seize (據)[464] them; vicious birds of prey (攫鳥)[465] will not strike them.[466] The bones and ligaments of an infant are soft (弱) and tender (柔), yet infants can hold their fists firmly (握固).

150. 未知牝牡之合而全作, 精之至也。終日號而不嗄, 和之至也。知和曰常, 知常曰明。

A newborn baby does not yet know the harmonization (合) between the positive and the negative (牝牡), but it perfectly (全)[467] grows and develops (作)[468]: it epitomizes (至) the greatest essence (精)[469] of Tao.[470] A newborn baby cries (號) all day without its voice becoming hoarse (嗄)[471], for it demonstrates the greatest (至) harmony (和) with Tao. Understanding this natural harmony is known as understanding the Immutable (常)[472]. Understanding this Immutable is known as possessing Enlightenment (明).

151. 益生曰祥, 心使氣曰強。物壯則老, 謂之不道。不道早已。

Those who try to deliberately prolong (益)[473] their own natural lives (生) are known to eventually face ominous omens (祥)[474]. Minds that are headstrong and assertive (使氣)[475] are known as being violent (強)[476]. If one is mighty and fierce (壯)[477], one will frail and wither (老)[478], and so it can be said as not following Tao (不道). Whatever that is not following Tao will come to its end very soon (早已).[479]

第五十六章 Chapter 56

152. 知者不言，言者不知。塞其兌，閉其門；挫其銳，解其分；和其光，同其塵。是謂玄同。

Those who understand (知) Tao do not speak of it; [480] those who speak of Tao do not understand it. One should close off (塞) one's senses (兌)[481], shut one's door connecting the outer world to the inner mind, conceal (挫) one's brilliance (銳), embrace one's simplicity to disintegrate (解) all chaos (分)[482], harmonize (和) one's splendour (光) to make it agreeable, and adapt and merge (同) with one's muddy and obscure surroundings (塵). Such is known as "The Deep and Mysterious Unification with Tao and the Universe (玄同)".

153. 故不可得而親，不可得而疏；不可得而利，不可得而害；不可得而貴，不可得而賤。故為天下貴。

Accordingly, within Tao, one cannot find anything (不可得) to be familiar with (親) nor distant from (疏); one cannot find anything favourable (利) nor harmful (害); one cannot find anything honourable (貴) nor dishonourable (賤). As a result, one becomes the most honourable under Heaven.

第五十七章 Chapter 57

154. 以正治國，以奇用兵，以無事取天下。吾何以知其然哉？以此。

A ruler should rely on (以)[483] the correct way (正, i.e., the way of Tao)[484] to govern and consider (以)[485] employing troops as an evil and ominous (奇)[486] measure. One should take and govern (取)[487] all under Heaven without relying on accomplishing anything great (無事)[488].[489] How do I know this is so? Solely because of the above rationale.[490]

155. 天下多忌諱，而民彌貧；民多利器，國家滋昏；人多伎巧，奇物滋起；法令滋彰，盜賊多有。

When all under Heaven have more prohibitions or censorships

(忌諱), its people tend to be more (彌) poor and stagnant; when the people have more tools to benefit themselves (利器)[491], the state becomes increasing (滋)[492] chaotic (昏)[493]. [494] when the people increasingly have more wits and craftiness (伎巧), more evil ploys and contrivances (奇物) will appear; many laws shall then require to be legislated and enacted (彰), yet more criminals and robbers shall spawn.

156. 故聖人云：我無為，而民自化；我好靜，而民自正；我無事，而民自富；我無欲，而民自樸。

This is why the wise sages once said, "I do not act with any personal differentiation and intent, and so the people shall naturally live and propagate peacefully by themselves (自化)[495]; I favour tranquillity, and so the people shall naturally right (正) themselves in accordance with Tao; I never aim to accomplish anything great (無事)[496], and so the people shall naturally become rich by themselves; I empty myself of any selfish desire (無欲), and so the people shall naturally retain their original simplicity (自樸)."

第五十八章 Chapter 58

157. 其政悶悶，其民淳淳；其政察察，其民缺缺。

When the governing is undiscerning and dim-witted (悶悶)[497], the people shall be simple and honest (淳淳)[498]; when the governing is tactful and discerning (察察)[499], the people shall be slick and cunning (缺缺)[500].

158. 禍兮福之所倚，福兮禍之所伏。孰知其極？ 其無正! 正復為奇，善復為妖。

Tragedies (禍) indeed have good fortunes (福) sitting next to them, while good fortunes indeed have tragedies lurking beneath (伏) them. Who knows which one is the actual ultimate (極)[501] ? Tao itself does not any so-called agreeable (正)[502] sides![503] What is now considered agreeable can return to be recognized as evil and ominous (奇)[504]; what is now considered good (善) can return to be recognized as ominous (妖).

159. 人之迷, 其日固久。是以聖人方而不割, 廉而不劌, 直而不肆, 光而不燿。

The people's confusion (迷) surrounding Tao has subsisted (固) for a long time. Hence, wise sages behave duly (方)[505] according to Tao without any discernment (割)[506], act with integrity (廉)[507] without hurting (劌)[508] any other, behave honestly (直)[509] without creating conflicts (肆)[510], and apply their brilliance (光) without dazzling (燿) anyone.

第五十九章 Chapter 59

160. 治人事天莫若嗇。夫唯嗇, 是謂早服。早服謂之重積德。重積德則無不克。無不克則莫知其極。

In cultivating the self (治人)[511] to serve (事)[512] Nature (天), there is no one more proficient than a farmer (嗇)[513]. Alas, only a farmer can be called to have obeyed (服) Nature from the very beginning (早). Having obeyed Nature from the very beginning can be called as focusing (重) on steadily amassing (積) one's yield (德)[514]. If one focuses on steadily amassing one's yield, then there is no task in which one is not competent (克)[515]. Since there is no task in which one is not competent, one's limit (極)[516] cannot be known.[517]

161. 莫知其極, 可以有國。有國之母, 可以長久。是謂深根固柢, 長生久視之道。

Since one's limit cannot be known, one can then rule (有)[518] the state; ruling the state by applying (之)[519] motherly Nature (母)[520] shall make one's rule to last long (長久).[521] Such is like a tree with deep (深) and firm (固) roots (根柢), which illustrates the principle (道) of longevity and long-lasting vitality (長生久視)[522].

第六十章 Chapter 60

162. 治大國若烹小鮮。以道莅天下，其鬼不神。非其鬼不神，其神不傷人。非其神不傷人，聖人亦不傷人!

In governing a great state, one should be as mindful as cooking (烹) a small fish (小鮮).[(523)] If one applies the principles of Tao in governing (莅)[(524)] all under Heaven, then one's wit (鬼)[(525)] appears not so sound in the mind (神); not that one's wit is not sound in the mind, but one's mind does not harm (傷) anyone. Not that one's mind does not harm anyone, but the wise sages surely (亦)[(526)], by their very natures, never harm anyone![(527)]

163. 夫兩不相傷，故德交歸焉。

Alas, both (兩) parties, the rulers and their people, will then not harm each other (相傷). Thus, all can come together (交)[(528)] to attain (德) the outcome of returning (歸) to the way of Tao.

第六十一章 Chapter 61

164. 大國者下流，天下之交，天下之牝。牝常以靜勝牡，以靜為下。

A great and powerful state (大國) should situate itself at a lowly position like that of the downstream of a river (下流), which is the place of all under Heaven coming together (交)[(529)], and the feminine (牝) way of all under Heaven. Feminine always uses tranquillity to win over masculine (牡) and applies tranquillity to be in a lowly and humbled position (下).

165. 故大國以下小國，則取小國；小國以下大國，則取大國。故或下以取，或下而取。

Hence, if a stronger state (大國) humbles (下) itself towards a weaker state (小國), it shall then earn the acceptance (取)[(530)] of the weaker state. If a weaker state humbles itself towards the stronger state, it shall then earn the acceptance (取) from the stronger state. Hence, there are (或)[(531)] those who humble themselves to acquire the faith of the weaker state, and there are those who humble themselves to gain the trust of the stronger state.[(532)]

166. 大國不過欲兼畜人，小國不過欲入事人。夫兩者各得其所欲。大者宜為下。

The stronger state only wishes to subjugate (兼畜)[(533)] the weaker ones; the weaker state only wishes to adopt (入)[(534)] serving (事)[(535)] the stronger ones. Alas, as such, this ensures both the strong and the weak will get what they desire (所欲). The most important (大者)[(536)] is being humble, regardless of the size of the state.

第六十二章 Chapter 62

167. 道者萬物之奧。善人之寶，不善人之所保。美言可以市，尊行可以加人。

Tao is a safe haven (奧)[(537)] for all things.[(538)] Those who are well acquainted with Tao treasure it, and those who are not well acquainted with it rely on it to safeguard (保)[(539)] themselves. Those who speak nice words (美言) can apply themselves only in the marketplace (市), but those who act (行) according to (尊)[(540)] Tao can gift and benefit (加)[(541)] all people (人).

168. 人之不善，何棄之有？故立天子，置三公，雖有拱璧以先駟馬，不如坐進此道。

For those who are not acquainted (不善) with Tao, why would Tao abandon (棄) them? Thus, establishing the role of a Son of Heaven (天子, i.e., the supreme ruler) and designating (置) the positions of the Three Chief Mentors (三公)[(542)], even though the Son of Heaven possesses (有) the priceless treasure of a grand jade as large as one's embrace (拱璧)[(543)] and the Mentors carry (以)[(544)] the great honour (先)[(545)] of having four-horse carriages (駟馬)[(546)], are no match for a society that naturally (坐)[(547)] progresses to (進)[(548)] reside in Tao.[(549)]

169. 古之所以貴此道者何？ 不曰：以求得, 有罪以免邪？ 故為天下貴。

Why did the wise from the past prize Tao so much? Did they not all say "all wishes (求) shall be granted (得) if one applies Tao; all faults (罪) shall be stripped away (免) if one returns to follow Tao"? Hence, Tao is the most valuable under Heaven.

第六十三章 Chapter 63

170. 為無為; 事無事; 味無味。大小多少, 報怨以德。

Those who follow Tao act (為) to not act with any personal differentiation and intent, conduct (事) all matters without aiming to accomplish anything great, and taste (味) all things without distinguishing any flavour. Great, small, few, many, they do not consider them as such; they merely respond to any enmity (怨) according to their manifestations (德)[550] from following Tao.[551]

171. 圖難於其易, 為大於其細。天下難事, 必作於易; 天下大事, 必作於細。

Wise sages tackle (圖) a difficult issue when it is still easy to manage, and they deal with (為) a great (大) matter when it is still trivial and small; all difficult issues under Heaven always originate (作)[552] from issues that are initially easy to manage, and all great matters (大事) under Heaven always stem (作) from matters that are initially trivial and small.

172. 是以聖人終不為大, 故能成其大。夫輕諾必寡信, 多易必多難。是以聖人猶難之, 故終無難矣。

Therefore, the wise sages ultimately (終)[553] do not do anything great; as such, they can accomplish their greatness. Alas, those who make promises lightly (輕諾) surely lack trustworthiness (寡信), while those who find many things easy shall surely find many difficulties ahead. Hence, even (猶) wise sages find all matters difficult to address. As such, they never do anything great, and so they ultimately never face anything difficult.

第六十四章 Chapter 64

173. 其安易持, 其未兆易謀。其脆易泮, 其微易散。為之於未有, 治之於未亂。合抱之木, 生於毫末; 九層之臺, 起於累土; 千里之 行, 始於足下。

When an issue is still calm and tranquil (安)[554], it is easy to grasp (持)[555] it. When an issue has not risen (兆)[556], it is easy to take measures (謀) against it; when a matter is weak (脆), it is easy to break it apart (泮)[557]; when a matter is still extremely small (微), it is easy to break it up (散)[558]. Actions should be taken before any issue develop, and good governance should occur before any chaos begin. A sturdy tree (木)[559] of one's entire embrace (合抱) that is destined to be chopped down grows from the tiniest sprout (毫末); [560] an overly lavished elevated terrace (臺) [561] of nine levels (九層) rises from (起)[562] the first pile of accumulated (累) soil (土); [563] an exhaustive journey (行)[564] of thousands of miles starts by lifting a single foot (足下)[565]. [566]

174. 為者敗之, 執者失之。是以聖人無為故無敗, 無執故無失。民 之從事, 常於幾成而敗之。慎終如始, 則無敗事。

Those who act with personal differentiations and intents (為) shall eventually fail, and those who hold (執) shall eventually lose hold. This is why the wise sages do not act with any personal differentiation and intent and so never fail; they do not hold and thus never lose hold. People conduct (從)[567] their business (事) and often fail on the eve of success (幾成). If they were as meticulous (慎) in following the way of Tao at the end (終) as they were at the beginning (始), they would not have failed.

175. 是以聖人欲不欲, 不貴難得之貨; 學不學, 復眾人之所過; 以 輔萬物之自然而不敢為。

Accordingly, a wise sage desires no selfish desires and does not treasure rare valuables. A wise sage learns not to learn and restores (復) all people back to their inherent simplicities that they had once lost (過)$^{(568)}$.$^{(569)}$ A wise sage merely (以) $^{(570)}$ acts to facilitate (輔)$^{(571)}$ the natures (自然) of all things and dares not act to serve one's personal intents and purposes.

第六十五章 Chapter 65

176. 古之善為道者, 非以明民, 將以愚之。民之難治, 以其智多。故以智治國, 國之賊; 不以智治國, 國之福。知此兩者亦稽式。
Those in the past who are well-acquainted (善) with Tao act not to make the people more intelligent (明) but rather to make them less intelligent. The people become difficult to govern because (以)$^{(572)}$ they have too much acquired intelligence (智). Those who use acquired intelligence to govern are vandals (賊)$^{(573)}$ to the state, while those who do not are blessings (福) to the state. One should know both cases originate from the same (稽)$^{(574)}$ norm (式) governed by Tao.

177. 常知稽式, 是謂玄德。玄德深矣, 遠矣, 與物反矣, 然後乃至大順。
Being always mindful of this norm is known as the "Most Mysterious Manifestation of Tao (玄德)". This "Most Mysterious Manifestation of Tao" is so deep (深) and far-reaching (遠) indeed that it engages (與)$^{(575)}$ in reverting (反) all worldly matters to their respective inherent simplicities. Eventually (然後), all then (乃) shall reach (至) to the "Great Conformity to Tao (大順)".

第六十六章 Chapter 66

178. 江海所以能為百谷王者, 以其善下之, 故能為百谷王。
The reason why the rivers and seas are able to be the most desirable (王)$^{(576)}$ for waters from all valleys (百谷) is because they are proficient (善) at being positioned below all valleys. This is why they are able to be the most desirable for waters

from all valleys.

179. 是以欲上民，必以言下之；欲先民，必以身後之。

As such, if one wishes to be positioned above (上) the people, then one must put oneself (言)[577] below (下) the people;[578] if one wants to lead (先)[579] the people, then one must put oneself at a position behind (後) all people.

180. 是以聖人處上而民不重，處前而民不害。是以天下樂推而不厭。以其不爭，故天下莫能與之爭。

Therefore, although the wise sages are situated (處) above (上) the people, the people do not find them burdensome (重)[580]; although the wise sages are situated in front leading the people, the people will not find them injurious (害).[581] Hence, all under Heaven are willing to endorse (樂推)[582] them and do not grow weary of and despise (厭) them. Since the wise sages do not compete (爭) with others, no one under Heaven can compete with them.

第六十七章 Chapter 67

181. 天下皆謂我道大，似不肖。夫唯大，故似不肖。若肖，久矣其細也夫！

All under Heaven say although my so-called Tao is great, it (似) appears (肖) not to be so. Alas, it is only because of its unlimited greatness that it appears not to be so. If it appears to be great, it would indeed be small long long time ago![583]

182. 我有三寶，持而保之：一曰慈，二曰儉，三曰不敢為天下先。慈故能勇；儉故能廣；不敢為天下先，故能成器長。

I have three treasures (三寶) that I always uphold (持)[584] and rely on (保)[585]: the first is earnest adoration (慈)[586] of Tao, the second is frugality (儉)[587], and the third is not daring to lead and be the most preeminent (先)[588] among all under Heaven[589].[590] When one adores Tao, one can thus be courageous (勇); when one is frugal, one can thus flourish (廣)[591]; when one dares not to lead and be the most preeminent among all under Heaven, one can thus become (成) a distinguished and talented (器) leader (長) among all.

183. 今舍慈且勇; 舍儉且廣; 舍後且先。死矣！夫慈以戰則勝, 以守則固。天將救之, 以慈衛之。

Today, many abandon (舍) earnest adoration (慈) of Tao yet adopt (且)[592] blind courage (勇), abandon frugality (儉) yet adopt raw prosperity (廣), abandon placing oneself behind (後) all others yet adopt preeminence (先). They shall all perish (死) indeed! Alas, applying earnest adoration (慈) of Tao in battles shall ensure one's victory, while applying it in defending shall make one's garrison firm (固); Nature will (將)[593] then surely come to one's aid (救)[594] and utilize (以)[595] one's earnest adoration of Tao to protect (衛) one's safety.

第六十八章 Chapter 68

184. 善為士者, 不武; 善戰者, 不怒; 善勝敵者, 不與; 善用人者, 為之下。

Those who are skilled (善) at being commanders (士)[596] never show their valour (武); those who are skilled at battles never show their might and anger (怒); those who are skilled at over-whelming (勝) their enemies never need to battle (與)[597] their enemies; those who are skilled at delegating responsibilities (用) to their subordinates (人) always humble themselves below (下) their subordinates.

185. 是謂不爭之德, 是謂用人之力, 是謂配天古之極。

Such is known as the attainment (德)[598] of being not competi-tive[599], the genuine way to unleash the true capabilities (力) of one's subordinates, and being compatible (配) with the pinnacle (極) of the long-established (古) Nature (天).

第六十九章 Chapter 69

186. 用兵有言：吾不敢為主，而為客；不敢進寸，而退尺。

Those who commanded troops once said, "I do not dare to be on the offensive (主); I rather prefer to be on the defensive (客); I dare not advance an inch; I prefer to retire a foot."

187. 是謂行無行；攘無臂；扔無敵；執無兵。

This is known as advancing (行) as if one cannot advance (無行); baring one's arms to fight (攘)[600] as if one does not have any arm to bare; defeating (扔)[601] the enemy as if one is being defeated (無敵)[602] by the enemy; holding one's weapon as if one has no weapon (兵) to hold.[603]

188. 禍莫大於輕敵。輕敵幾喪吾寶。故抗兵相加，哀者勝矣。

There is no greater tragedy (禍) than underestimating or disregarding (輕) one's enemy. Doing so will then (幾)[604] lose all my treasures (寶) that I mentioned previously.[605] Thus, when one raises (抗)[606] an army to counter an enemy (加)[607], the side who is in sorrow (哀) shall prevail.[608]

第七十章 Chapter 70

189. 吾言甚易知，甚易行。天下莫能知，莫能行。

My words are quite easy to understand and quite easy to carry out. Yet, most under the Heaven is unable to understand and carry them out.[609]

190. 言有宗，事有君。夫唯無知，是以不我知。

All narratives (言)[610] should have a foundational basis (宗)[611] supporting them, and all things (事) have a lord (君)[612] behind them. Alas, it is solely because not understanding these that people thus do not comprehend me.[613]

191. 知我者希, 則我者貴。是以聖人被褐懷玉!

Those who understand and acknowledge me are extremely rare (希)[614]; those who model (則)[615] after me are to be treasured (貴). Therefore, the wise sages are the people who wear rags as their outer coverings yet bear jades (懷玉) buried deep within themselves![616]

第七十一章 Chapter 71

192. 知不知, 上; 不知知, 病。

Understanding (知) why many not understand (不知) Tao is superior (上),[617] not understanding (不知) why some understand (知) Tao suffers from exhaustion (病)[618].[619]

193. 夫唯病病, 是以不病。聖人不病, 以其病病, 是以不病。

Alas, because (唯) understanding why suffering (病) is suffering (病) shall then make one not suffer (不病). Wise sages do not suffer because they know why suffering is suffering, and so they never suffer.[620]

第七十二章 Chapter 72

194. 民不畏威, 則大威至。無狎其所居, 無厭其所生。夫唯不厭, 是以不厭。

If the people no longer fear the ruler's might and oppression (威), then the people's great might (大威) shall arrive. A ruler should not arbitrarily alter (狎)[621] the whereabouts of the people's dwellings (居) nor inflict harm (厭)[622] to their livelihoods (生). Alas, it is only if you do not inflict harm on the people, then the people will not inflict harm on you.[623]

195. 是以聖人自知不自見; 自愛不自貴。故去彼取此。

Accordingly, the wise sages understand themselves (自知)[624] yet do not show their brilliance to others (不自見); they care (愛) for themselves but do not elevate (貴) themselves above others.

Thus, the sages leave behind the former path of suppression and choose to follow these latter paths.

第七十三章 Chapter 73

196. 勇於敢則殺; 勇於不敢則活。此兩者, 或利或害。天之所惡, 孰知其故？是以聖人猶難之!

Those who are audacious (勇) in being aggressive (敢)[625] shall face horrendous and unnatural deaths (殺)[626]; those who are audacious in being not aggressive shall live their natural lives. Considering these two scenarios, one is advantageous while the other injurious. Nature has its own dislikes, who knows why? Hence, even wise sages find it so difficult to address![627]

197. 天之道, 不爭而善勝, 不言而善應, 不召而自來, 繟然而善謀。天網恢恢, 疏而不失。

Nature's way is not competitive yet proficient (善) at overcoming (勝), does not speak yet is proficient at responding (應), does not need to be called upon (召) yet shows up (來) by itself, and is at ease (繟)[628] yet excels in scheming (謀). The meshes of the great net (網) deployed by Nature are wide and far apart (恢恢)[629], but nothing is missed (失).

第七十四章 Chapter 74

198. 民不畏死, 奈何以死懼之？若使民常畏死而為奇者, 吾得執而殺之。孰敢？

When the people do not fear death, what is the point of threatening them with death? Suppose the people were always inherently afraid of dying, and if there existed those who were evil and ominous (奇)[630], I could simply seize (執) and execute them. Who then would dare to become like them?

199. 常有司殺者殺。夫代司殺者殺，是謂代大匠斲。夫代大匠斲者，希有不傷其手矣。

Yet, the Immutable (常)[631] already has its way (者) to administrate (司)[632] executions (殺). Alas, anyone who executes in place of the way administrated by the Immutable can be said to be (是謂) an unqualified person chopping up (斲) wood instead of the master carpenter (大匠).[633] Indeed, those who chop up wood in place of the master carpenter rarely (希)[634] not hurt their own hands.

第七十五章 Chapter 75

200. 民之饑，以其上食稅之多；是以饑。

The people starve (饑) because of the heavy (多) reliance on taxes consumed (食稅) by their rulers (上); it is through this that they starve.

201. 民之難治，以其上之有為，是以難治。民之輕死，以其上求生之厚，是以輕死。

The people are difficult to govern because their rulers act with personal differentiations and intents; it is through this that they become difficult to govern. The people take death lightly because their rulers hold their own personal possessions and livelihoods (生)[635] in too high of a regard (厚); it is through this that the people take death lightly.

202. 夫唯無以生為者，是賢於貴生！

Alas, without exception (唯)[636], rulers who do not seek (為)[637] to pursue their personal possessions and livelihoods (生) are certainly (是) far more distinguished (賢) than those who draw heavy taxes and highly regard (貴) their own possessions and livelihoods![638]

第七十六章 Chapter 76

203. 人之生也柔弱，其死也堅強。萬物草木之生也柔脆，其死也枯槁。

When alive, a person's body is soft, gentle, and fragile (柔弱); at death, rigid, stiff, and sturdy (堅強). All things, including plants, are soft and brittle (脆) when they are alive; at death, they are all dried-up and withered (枯槁).

204. 故堅強者死之徒，柔弱者生之徒。

Therefore, rigidity, stiffness, and sturdiness belong to those of the dead, while softness, gentleness, and fragility belong to those that are alive.

205. 是以兵強則不勝，木強則兵。強大處下，柔弱處上。

Hence, those who rely only on raw military might (兵強) will never secure a true victory, a sturdy tree (木強) will be quickly chopped down (兵)[639] to be used as fine lumber. Therefore, being strong and mighty is at (處) the inferior (下), while being gentle and weak is at the superior (上).

第七十七章 Chapter 77

206. 天之道，其猶張弓與？高者抑之，下者舉之；有餘者損之，不足者補之。

Is it not Nature's way like (猶) drawing (張) a bow and arrow? If one draws too high, then one shall depress (抑) it; if one draws too low, then one shall raise it. One diminishes (損) the abundant (有餘) while supplements (補) the insufficient.

207. 天之道，損有餘而補不足。人之道則不然，損不足以奉有餘。

Nature's way diminishes the abundant while supplements the insufficient. Not so (不然) with the way of humans (人之道), which diminishes the insufficient to gift (奉)[640] to the abundant.

208. 孰能有餘以奉天下, 唯有道者! 是以聖人為而不恃, 功成而不處。 其不欲見賢。

Who then can take from the abundant to gift (奉) to all under Heaven? Only Tao, of course (者)[641]! Hence, wise sages act without relying on others (不恃)[642] and accomplish without claiming any credit. They never wish to show that they are distinguished (賢).

第七十八章 Chapter 78

209. 天下莫柔弱於水, 而攻堅強者莫之能勝。 以其無以易之。

There is nothing under Heaven gentler and weaker than water, yet there is nothing better than (勝)[643] it to attack (攻) the mighty and strong (堅強); therefore (以)[644], in this respect (其), nothing can replace (易)[645] it.

210. 弱之勝強, 柔之勝剛, 天下莫不知, 莫能行。

The weak is better than (勝) the strong, and the gentle is better than the bold (剛). Everyone under Heaven knows this, but no one can carry it out in practice.

211. 是以聖人云 : 受國之垢, 是謂社稷主; 受國不祥, 是為天下王。 正言若反。

Thus, the wise sages once said, "A person who can accept (受)[646] all the shame (垢)[647] of a state can be called the master of the state (社稷)[648]; a person who can accept (受) all the misdeeds (不祥)[649] of a state can be called the leader of all under the Heaven." Proper narratives (正言)[650] of Tao are (若)[651] countering ways to restore (反) all back to Tao.[652]

第七十九章 Chapter 79

212. 和大怨, 必有餘怨, 安可以為善 ? 是以聖人執左契, 而不責於人。

Even when a great grievance (大怨) has been reconciled (和),

there still must be some grievance remaining (餘怨). How (安) then can reconciliation be a good (善) solution? Thus, wise sages conduct their businesses only by holding (執) documents that provide evidence of proof (左契)[653] and never demand (責)[654] anything from the people.

213. 有德司契, 無德司徹。天道無親, 常與善人。

Those with the Manifestation of Tao (德)[655] administrate (司)[656] by adhering to documents (契)[657]; those without the Manifestation of Tao administrate (司) by demanding land taxes with the system of Che (徹)[658],[659] Nature's way devotes (親) to no one, yet it always supports (與)[660] those who are well acquainted (善)[661] with Tao.[662]

第八十章 Chapter 80

214. 小國寡民。使有什伯之器而不用; 使民重死而不遠徙。雖有舟輿, 無所乘之; 雖有甲兵, 無所陳之。

An ideal state is small, with very few (寡) people living in it. The ideal governance should result in (使)[663] instruments (器) of more than a hundredfold (什伯)[664] not to be applied (用). It also makes people regard death as a grave matter (重死) and choose not to emigrate (徙) to places far away. Although there are boats and carriages (舟輿), they find no need to ride (乘) on them; although there is an army (甲兵), there is no need to display (陳) it.

215. 使人復結繩而用之。甘其食, 美其服; 安其居, 樂其俗。

The ideal governance makes (使) people return (復) to using string knots (結繩) to count and communicate. The people enjoy (甘) their primitive food and cherish (美) their plain clothes; they are content (安) with their simple dwellings and are happy with their native habits and customs (俗).

216. 鄰國相望, 雞犬之聲相聞。民至老死, 不相往來。

Neighbouring states observe (望) each other, and the cries of fowls and dogs among the neighbouring states can also be heard. Yet, till their deaths (老死), people from different states shall have no contact (往來) with each other.⁽⁶⁶⁵⁾

第八十一章 Chapter 81

217. 信言不美, 美言不信; 善者不辯, 辯者不善; 知者不博, 博者不知。

True and honest words (信言) are never nice, while nice words are never true and honest. Those who are well acquainted (善) with Tao do not argue (辯), while those who argue are not well acquainted with Tao. Those who understand (知) Tao do not understand a wide range (博) of acquired knowledge, while those who understand a wide range of acquired knowledge do not understand Tao.

218. 聖人不積。既以為人己愈有; 既以與人己愈多。

The wise sages never amass (積) anything for themselves. Since they already (既以)⁽⁶⁶⁶⁾ gift (為)⁽⁶⁶⁷⁾ themselves to others, they already possess plenty (愈有)⁽⁶⁶⁸⁾; since they already bestow (與)⁽⁶⁶⁹⁾ themselves upon others, they are already affluent (愈多)^{(670) (671)}.

219. 天之道, 利而不害; 聖人之道, 為而不爭。

The way of Nature benefits (利)⁽⁶⁷²⁾ all without doing any harm; the way of a wise sage gifts (為)⁽⁶⁷³⁾ all without competing with others.⁽⁶⁷⁴⁾

SECTION TWO

Footnotes

Thus, those who have great aspirations
in following Tao - *Tao Te Ching*

草書 Cursive Script   137x34cm 2000AD
Source: *A Collection of Kwok Kin Poon's Calligraphy*

Footnotes

(1) "常" here means "immutable and everlasting (恆/久)". See *Kangxi Dictionary* (《康熙字典》).

    "常", the "immutable and everlasting", can also refer to Tao (道) and its Manifestation (德) later on in the document. One example can be seen in Chapter 28 Lines 83 and 84.

(2) "天地" is literally "天 (Heaven and skies)" and "地 (Earth)". Together, it refers to the entire Universe.

(3) "德" here is not "virtue" as cherished in Confucianism. For further elaborations, see footnote 4.

(4) Tao (道) can be thought of as the "unidentifiable and name-less (無名)" fundamental way that drives and begets all things in the Universe. Tao also manifests itself to become "identifiable and with names (有名)", the custodian and Mother of all things. Wang Bi (王弼) provided an excellent elaboration on these circumstances:

> "凡有皆始於無, 故 '未形'、 '無名' 之時, 則為萬物之始, 及其 '有形'、 '有名' 之時, 則長之育之, 亭之毒之, 為其母也."
> "Everything that exists originated from the unknown void that is indescribable (Tao). Hence, when Tao is 'not yet having any form (未形)' and 'unidentifiable and nameless (無名)', it plays the role of the Originator of all things. Afterwards, when it manifests to 'take form (有形)' and can be 'identifiable and with names (有名)', it rears all, nurses all, perfects all, matures all, and plays the role of Mother of all things."
> (interpreted by KS Vincent Poon)
> Source: 王弼 《老子王弼注》. 台北: 新興書局, 1964, p.003.

Laozi further elaborated on the relationship between "unidentifiable and nameless (無名)" and "identifiable and with names (有名)" in Chapter 40 Line 115:

"天下萬物生於有, 有生於無."

"All things under Heaven sprang from the entity that can be conceived and named, and the entity that can be conceived and named originates from the one that cannot be conceived nor named. "

This "identifiable and with names (有名)", the nurturer and Mother of all things, is referred later on as "Manifestation of Tao (德)" in Chapter 51 Line 139:

"道生之, 德畜之."

"Tao begets all things, the Manifestation of Tao nurtures all things."

Hence, with very few exceptions throughout the document, "德" refers to Tao manifesting itself to become "identifiable and with names (有名)".

The entire *Tao Te Ching* can, therefore, be called *The Book of the Fundamental Way of the Universe and its Manifestation* (道德經).

For further elaborations on "unidentifiable and nameless (無名)", please see Chapter 41 Line 117.

(5) "徼" should be "the fundamental path that all follow (循)", as in *Shuowen Jiezi* (《說文解字》). This is consistent with Wang Bi's (王弼) interpretation of "徼" as "the fundamental path and eventuality of all conceivable things (歸終也)".

"徼", however, cannot be interpreted as "the outer fringe (邊) of Tao". Tao is natural, encompasses all, and homogenous (Chapter 25 Line 74). As such, Tao does not have any inner or outer compartments.

(6) "常無" refers to Line 1's "immutable and everlasting (常道)" and "unidentifiable and nameless (無名)", while "常有" refers to Line 1's" the immutable and everlasting name (常名)" and "iden-

tifiable and with names (有名)".

Line 2 is where Laozi addressed the limitation of his narratives on Tao - if Tao is indescribable, how then can Tao be discussed? Laozi asserted that he could only, at best, use what he called "unidentifiable and nameless (無名)" in the hopes (欲) of examining the indescribable Tao. Similarly, he could, at best, only use what he called "identifiable and with names (有名)" in the hopes of examining the infinitely small and unobservable elements of all identifiable and conceivable entities.

Many, such as Heshang Gong, incorrectly interpreted line 2's "故常無欲以觀其妙" as:

"人常能無欲，則可以觀道之要."

"Therefore, always possessing no desire shall allow one to examine the essential core of Tao."

(interpreted by KS Vincent Poon)

Source: 《老子河上公注》, 卷上, p.1.

Laozi had never asked anyone in *Tao Te Ching* to rid all desire completely:

I.   "Desires do arise during their natural propagations (化 而欲作)" (Chapter 37 Line 106). Desire is obviously a natural product of Tao and accordingly should not be considered as a hindrance in the study of Tao.

II. "If one plans to diminish an entity, one must first expand it...(將欲歙之, 必固張之...)" (Chapter 36 Line 104). Laozi even discussed how one could apply Tao to achieve certain desirable effects.

III. "Deride selfishness and minimize desires (少私寡欲)" (Chapter 19 Line 59). Laozi had never asked anyone to rid all desires completely, he only asked one to minimize selfish desires.

IV. Wise sages (聖人) have at least this one desire: the desire to follow Tao. Hence, Laozi described them as people who wish to place themselves with Tao "居善地" (Chapter 8 Line 23) and desire no selfish desires "欲不 欲" (Chapter 63 Line 175).

Completely ridding all desire may be consistent with some branches of Taoist religion (道教), but that is certainly not consistent with *Tao Te Ching*, the canon of Taoism (道家). This is probably why there are so many incorrect interpretations of "故常無欲以觀其妙; 常有欲以觀其徼" for nearly two thousand years, including that by the renowned Wang Bi (王弼).

The correct interpretation in vernacular Chinese of Line 2 should be:

> "故此, 姑且用這個 '常道' 和 '無名', 希望能夠探索一下道的玄奧深妙; 也姑且用這個 '常名' 和 '有名', 希望能夠觀察一下德的萬物規迹."

(interpreted by Kwok Kin Poon)

(7) "玄" was represented as "元" in the *Complete Library in Four Sections* (四庫全書) version of *Tao Te Ching*. "玄" was considered as a taboo character (避諱) in the *Complete Library in Four Sections*, for Qing Emperor Kangxi's given name was "玄燁".

(8) As such, Tao (道), the fundamental way of the Universe, does not discern with the human concept of "beautiful" or "ugly", "good" or "bad".

(9) "Wise sage (聖人)" in Laozi's *Tao Te Ching* is a person who fully comprehends and earnestly follows Tao, which is very different than that of Confucian's.

(10) "Not acting with any personal differentiation and intent (無為)" does not mean one should not act at all. Laozi merely espoused one should act to follow Tao, the fundamental way of the Universe, instead of following one's personal differentiations and intents. Accordingly, one should act to follow the collective mindset of the people (Chapter 49 Line 134) as well as trust what the people trust and distrust what the people distrust (Chapter 49 Line 135).

To interpret "無為" as "one should not act at all" makes no

sense. Laozi certainly acted to author *Tao Te Ching*, and Tao obviously acts to manifest itself to spawn and nurture all in the Universe.

"無為", hence, should not be comprehended to justify "Limited government (小政府)", "Non-interventionism (不干預)", or "Anarchism (無政府)". In fact, recommendations for rulers of states as well as narrations on how wise sages govern were outlined in numerous chapters throughout *Tao Te Ching*. Therefore, Laozi did not reject the idea of a government or go against the enactment of public policies; he merely contended that an ideal government should exclusively follow Tao.

(11) "教" in "不言之教" should be better interpreted as "enlightenment" rather than "teaching/instruction" seen in other interpretations. This is for three reasons:

First, in Chapter 43 Line 23, the same phrase "不言之教" appeared, and it referred to Nature being a source of enlightenment for all. Nature or Tao does not directly teach or instruct us with words. We can, at best, only be enlightened by it.

Second, Laozi abhorred the idea of one being taught acquired knowledge, as indicated in Chapter 20 Line 59 and Chapter 64 Line 175:

"絕學無憂."

"If one insulates oneself from acquiring knowledge and not follow scholarly disciplines, then one shall be free from worries."

"(聖人)學不學."

"(A wise sage) learns not to learn."

Third, in addition to the meaning of "teach", "教" also carries the meaning of "being enlightened (教化)" or "emulate (效)":

I. "教, 效也" in *Guangya - Shigu III* (《廣雅•釋詁三》).
II. "教, 法也" in *Guangyun* (《廣韻•效韻》).
III. "教, 上所施下所效也" in *Shuowen Jiezi* (《說文解字》).

Source: 中央研究院《搜詞尋字》.

(12) "Wordless" here refers to Nature or Tao, for they do not directly teach or instruct us with words. Hence, the subsequent sentence, "All things spring up naturally without diction (萬物作 焉而不辭)". See also Chapter 23 Line 69.

(13) Most, if not all, interpret "生而不有, 為而不恃" as "begets all things without claiming ownership, accomplishes all tasks without claiming them as its own achievements". This is incorrect for three reasons:

I.   "生而不有, 為而不恃" together can also be found in Chapter 10 Line 30 as well as Chapter 51 Line 140 and, in both cases, is stated as Tao's "Most Mysterious Manifestation (玄德)". How is "begetting all things without claiming ownership, accomplishing all tasks without claiming them as their own achievements" qualify as being the most mysterious and difficult to comprehend?

II.   By contrast, our interpretation of this phrase as "begets all without anything and acts without relying on any other" is much more consistent with "Most Mysterious": all things in our known Universe are spawned from something, while implementation of any individual action must be supported by at least one external factor; an entity, therefore, that can beget something out of nothing (無中生有) while acting without any external aid is, indeed, profoundly mysterious.

III. Some, such as renowned scholar Gao Heng (高亨), contended that "恃" carries the meaning of "grace (恩)" and so "為而不恃" should be interpreted as "gives to all things without claiming grace (施澤萬物而不以為恩)" (高亨 《老子正詁》. 上海: 開明書店, 1949, pp. 8-9.). This is highly questionable since Tao simply does not follow the human concept of "grace" (Chapter 5 Line 13: 天地不仁, 以萬物為芻狗). As such, it is inconceivable that Laozi had to spend time to address whether

Tao claims "grace" or not.

"恃" here means "rely on (依)". See *Kangxi Dictionary* (《康熙字典》). The correct interpretation in vernacular Chinese of "生而不有, 為而不恃" should be:

"全無實質而獨自產生, 毫不依仗而獨自作為."

(interpreted by Kwok Kin Poon)

(14) "唯" here is "because", as in:
   I. "冀之既病, 則亦唯君故" in *The Commentary of Zuo - the Second Year of Duke Xi* (《左傳•僖公二年》).
   II. "予唯不食嗟來之食以至於斯也" in *The Classic of Rites - Tan Gong II* (《禮記•檀弓下》).
   Source: 中央研究院《搜詞尋字》.

(15) "不去" here means "not depart (不離開)", as in *Selections of Refined Literature - Fan Ye - Yi Min Chuan Lun* (《文選•范曄•逸民傳論》): "故蒙恥之賓, 屢黜不去其國." See 《重編國語辭典修訂本》.

(16) "或" here is "invariably/always (常常)" and does not carry its ordinary meaning of "perhaps". According to an annotation of *The Analects - Zi Lu* (《論語•子路》) by Huang Kan (皇侃), "或" can be interpreted as "常 (always)": "不恒其德, 或承之羞. 皇侃疏: 或, 常也, 言羞辱常承之也." See 中央研究院《搜詞尋字》.
   Tao is certainly unlimited and inexhaustible (Chapter 59 Line 161: 莫知其極; Chapter 5 Line 18: 緜緜若存, 用之不勤), and so it is illogical to interpret Laozi had described Tao as "perhaps" inexhaustible.

(17) "似" here is "以", as annotated by Yu Yue (俞樾): "似, 當讀為以, 古以、似通用." See 中央研究院《搜詞尋字》.
   This "以", in turn, means "it (其)", as in *Master Lu's Spring and Autumn Annals - Ben Sheng* (《呂氏春秋•本生》): "非夸以名也, 為其實也." See 中央研究院《搜詞尋字》.
   "似" here cannot carry its ordinary meaning of "like" or

"seemingly". Laozi stated that Tao is the fundamental root and origin of all things (Chapter 1). Accordingly, it is unreasonable to interpret Laozi had described Tao here as "only appears to be like" the origin of all things.

(18) "似" here is "it (其)" (see footnote 17), while "或" here is "always (常常)" (see footnote 16).

"似" here cannot carry its ordinary meaning of "like" or "seemingly", while "或" cannot take its ordinary meaning of "perhaps". Since Tao always exists, it is incorrect to say that Laozi had described Tao as "only seemingly or perhaps" existing.

The correct interpretation in vernacular Chinese of "湛兮似或存" should be:

"(道)極其深厚啊! 它是常常存在的!"

(interpreted by Kwok Kin Poon)

(19) "象" here is "imagine (意想)", as in *Hanfeitzu - Explicating Laozi* (《韓非子•解老篇》): "人希見生象也, 而得死象之骨, 按其圖以想其生也, 故諸人之所以意想者, 皆謂之象也. " See *Kangxi Dictionary* (康熙字典).

(20) "帝" here is "Heaven (天)", as in:

I. "帝青九萬里, 空洞無一物" in Wang Anshi's (王安石) *Gu Yi* (《古意》). See 中央研究院 《搜詞尋字》.

II. "昔在帝堯, 聰明文思, 光宅天下. 疏: 帝者, 天之一名, 所以名帝" in the *Book of Documents - Yao Dian - Preamble* (《書經•堯典序》). See *Kangxi Dictionary* (《康熙字典》).

(21) The correct interpretation in vernacular Chinese of Line 12 should be:

"我不知曉這道是誰所生的, 猜想在天出現前便已存在了吧."

(interpreted by Kwok Kin Poon)

(22) "Straw dogs (芻狗)" were once used in sacrificial ceremo-

nies and were simply discarded when such ceremonies conclud-
ed. See 《重編國語辭典修訂本》.

"芻狗" can also be interpreted separately as "straws (芻)"
and "dogs (狗)". In that case, "straws (芻)" represent non-living
objects, while "dogs (狗)" represent living objects. The Universe
treats both types of objects with no mercy.

(23) Such illustrates a key aspect of Laozi's philosophy: the way
of nature is the ideal way for one to deal with all people. Wise
sages merely mirror the Universe's approach in dealing with all
things, which is to treat everything and everyone without mercy
and discernment.

(24) "天地之間" refers to the realm of Heaven and Earth (i.e., the
Universe) and includes all the dynamic interactions within and
between them. "間" is "realm (閒)", as in *The Classic of Rites
- Record of Music* (《禮記•樂記》): "一動一靜者, 天地之閒也."
See *Kangxi Dictionary* (《康熙字典》).

(25) "不屈" here is "endless (不竭/不盡)", as in *Xunzi - Wang Zhi*
(《荀子•王制》): "使國家足用而財物不屈, 虞師之事也." See 《漢
語大詞典》.

(26) "數" here means "arguments (說)", as in:
   I. "故誦數以貫之, 思索以通之, 為其人以處之, 除其害者以
      持養之. 俞樾平議：誦數猶誦說也…凡稱說必一一數之,
      故即謂之數. 誦數以貫之, 猶云誦說以貫之" in *Xunzi -
      Quan Xue* (《荀子•勸學》).
   II. "孔子對曰：遽數之不能終其物, 悉數之乃留, 更僕未
      可終也" in *The Classic of Rites - Ru Xing* (《禮記•儒
      行》).
      Source: 中央研究院《搜詞尋字》.

(27) "守中" here is "keeping one's original intrinsic idle tranquillity", as annotated by Wang Chunfu (王純甫)："多言數窮, 不如守

中. 中也者, 中也, 虛也, 無也, 不可言且名者也." See 《漢語大詞典》.

"守中" is not "keeping the middle ground". Tao does not follow human points of view, like "good" and "bad", "beautiful" and "ugly" (Chapters 2 and 3). As such, Laozi would have never espoused the idea of taking "the middle ground" between two points of view, for points of view simply do not exist in Tao.

(28) The correct interpretation in vernacular Chinese of Line 15 should be:

"太多說話終會辭窮, 倒不如保持虛靜."

(interpreted by Kwok Kin Poon)

(29) "The Valley Spirit (谷神) " can be regarded as the natural Tao. Some contend it refers to the Spirit of Nurturing, while others see it as the Spirit that is void and mysterious. All interpretations indicate that the Valley Spirit (谷神) is empty and has no shape nor form, and so it can hold, accommodate, and permeate all things.

(30) According to *Kangxi Dictionary* (《康熙字典》), "牝" can be interpreted as "谿谷", which means "the channel at the very bottom between two valleys (兩山間可供流水通過的地帶)", as in *Selections of Refined Literature - Song Yu - Feng Fu* (《文選•宋玉•風賦》): "夫風, 生於地, 起於青蘋之末, 侵淫谿谷, 盛怒於土囊之口." See 《重編國語辭典修訂本》.

(31) "若" here means "is/does/become (乃)", not "seemingly (像)", as in:

I. "若, 又乃也. 《周語》必有忍也, 若能有濟也." See *Kangxi Dictionary* (《康熙字典》).

II. "若, 又假借為乃也." See *Shuowen Jiezi Zhu* (《說文解字注》).

III. "刑德相養, 逆順若成" in *Mawangdui Silk Texts* (《馬王堆漢墓帛書•十六經•姓爭》). See 中央研究院 《搜詞尋字》.

The valve (門) to "The Mysterious Motherly Channel (玄牝)" surely exists, for it is the root of all things (Chapter 5 Line 17), Laozi could not have described it as "seemingly" to exist.

(32) "外" here should be better interpreted as "abandon (棄)", as seen in an annotation by Gao You (高誘): "《呂氏春秋‧有度》有所通, 則貪汙之利外矣. 高誘注：外, 棄也." See 中央研究院《搜詞尋字》.

(33) See footnote 31.

(34) "幾" here means "nearly resemble (近)". See *Kangxi Dictionary* (《康熙字典》).

(35) "善" should be distinguished from its usual meaning of "good", "nice", or "kind". Tao does not discern and so does not label anything as "good", "nice", nor "kind"; only humans do that (see footnote 8). Accordingly, "善" refers to those who are "well-versed in Tao" or "rich in Tao". See also Chapter 15 Line 46 "古之善為士者".

(36) "淵" here is "abyssal niches (深潭/深池)", as in:
 I. "或躍在淵" in the *Book of Changes - Gan* (《易經‧乾》).
 II. "溝流於大水及海者, 命曰川水, 出地而不流者, 命曰淵水" in *Guanzi - Du De* (《管子‧度地》).
 Source: 中央研究院《搜詞尋字》.

(37) "與" here means "befriend (親近)", as in:
 I. "公先與百姓而藏其兵" in *Guanzi - Da Kuang* (《管子‧大匡》). 郭沫若注 "與, 親也".
 II. "時人憚焉, 莫之或與" in *Baopuzi - Outer Chapters - Content with Poverty* (《抱朴子‧外篇‧安貧》).
 Source: See 中央研究院《搜詞尋字》.

(38) "仁" here means "individuals (相人偶)". See *Shuowen Jiezi Zhu* (《說文解字注》).

"仁" here does not take on its usual meaning of "benevolence". Since Tao and the wise sages do not follow the concept of being benevolent (Chapter 5 Line 14: 天地不仁, 聖人不仁), Laozi would have never contradicted himself here to describe the distinguished one as being "benevolent".

(39) "正" here is "governance (政)". See *Kangxi Dictionary* (《康熙字典》).

(40) "治" here means "理", which is "ways and principles (道/義理)". See *Kangxi Dictionary* (《康熙字典》).

(41) "事" here means "appoint (任用)", as in *Mo Yze - Exaltation of the Virtuous I* (《墨子•尚賢上》): "是在王公大人, 為政於國家者, 不能以賢事能為政也." See 中央研究院《搜詞尋字》.

(42) The correct interpretation in vernacular Chinese of Line 23 should be:

> "身住在喜好道的地方; 心宿在深藏道的靜淵; 結交修養道的人們; 說話則本於道的誠信; 治理則遵照道的原則; 任用那依循道的人才; 行動則合乎道的時間."

(interpreted by Kwok Kin Poon)

(43) "已" here is "abandon (棄)". See *Kangxi Dictionary* (《康熙字典》).

Wang Bi (王弼) further elaborated on "持而盈之, 不如其已":

> "持, 謂不失德(得)也.既不失其德又盈之, 勢必傾危.故不如其已者, 謂乃更不如無德無功者也."

"Holding is also known as not losing possession. Not losing possession and still accumulating shall put oneself in a more precarious position. As such, 'inferior to those who abandon' means those who hold and accumulate are worse off than those who do not hold nor accomplish

anything."
(interpreted by KS Vincent Poon)
Source: 王弼《老子王弼注》. 台北: 新興書局, 1964,
p.011.

(44) "揣" here mean "hammer (捶之)". See *Shuowen Jiezi* (《說
文解字》).

(45) "梲" should be "銳", which is "to whet" or "to sharpen". See
footnote 46.

(46) Wang Bi (王弼) provided an excellent elaboration on "揣而
梲之, 不可長保":
"既揣末令尖, 又銳之令利, 勢必摧衂故不可長保也."
"If one hammers the tip of a blade to make it acute and
also whets it to make it sharp, then the blade (becomes
too weak and) shall eventually break and so cannot be
preserved for too long."
(interpreted by KS Vincent Poon)
Source: 王弼《老子王弼注》. 台北: 新興書局, 1964,
p.011.

(47) "咎" here is "tragedy (災)". See *Shuowen Jiezi* (《說文解
字》).

(48) "遂" here means "accomplished (成)". See *Kangxi Dictionary* (《康熙字典》).

(49) "天" here should be interpreted as "Nature (大自然)", as in
the *Book of Changes - The Great Treatise I* (《易經•繫辭上》): "
樂天知命, 故不憂." See 中央研究院《搜詞尋字》.
    This "天" is different than "天" in "天地", where it means "天
(Heaven and skies)" in footnote 2.

(50) "載" here is "(處)", as elaborated by Wang Bi (王弼): "載, 猶

處也." See 王弼《老子王弼注》. 台北: 新興書局, 1964, p.011.
This "處" is "rest (安)", as in:

    I. "昔聖王之處民也, 擇瘠土而處之" in *Discourses of the States - Discourses of Lu II* (《國語•魯語下》).

    II. "何以處我? 鄭玄注 : 處, 猶安也" in *The Classic of Rites - Tan Gong II* (《禮記•檀弓下》).

    Source: 中央研究院《搜詞尋字》.

(51) "營魄" here is "魂魄 (soul and mind)". "營" is "䰠". "載營魄抱一, 能無離乎. 註: 營, 䰠也". See *Kangxi Dictionary* (《康熙字典》). "䰠" is "魂". See *Kangxi Dictionary*.

(52) "能無" here is "is it possible to not? (能不?)", as in:

    I. "法語之言, 能無從乎？改之為貴" in T*he Analects - Zi Han* (《論語•子罕》).

    II. "公子侈, 大子卑, 大夫敖, 政多門, 以介於大國, 能無亡乎" in *The Commentary of Zuo - the Thirtieth Year of Duke Xiang* (《左傳•襄公三十年》).

    Source: 《漢語大字典》.

(53) "專" here is "任", as elaborated by Wang Bi (王弼): "專, 任也." See 王弼《老子王弼注》. 台北: 新興書局, 1964, p.012.
This "任" should be "hold (抱)", as in seen an annotation by Zheng Xuan (鄭玄): "《詩經•大雅•生民》 : 是任是負, 以歸肇祀. 鄭玄箋 : 任, 猶抱也." See 中央研究院《搜詞尋字》.

(54) "玄覽" means "the deepest area of the mind that inspects and understands all things (心居玄冥之處而覽知萬物)", as in *Selections of Refined Literature - Lu Ji - Wen Fu* (《文選•陸機•文賦》): "佇中區以玄覽, 頤情志於典墳." See《重編國語辭典修訂本》.

(55) "疵" here is "imperfection (過失/缺點)", as in the *Book of Changes - The Great Treatise I* (《易經•繫辭上》): "悔吝者, 言乎其小疵也. 陸德明釋文 : 疵, 瑕也." See 《漢語大字典》.

(56) "載營魄抱一", "專氣致柔", and "滌除玄覽" are all things that one should not do. To intentionally embrace Tao (載營魄抱一) means one is already absent of Tao in the first place. Trying to become the most gentle is futile, for one can never match the gentleness of a newborn baby, which is the richest in Tao (See Chapter 55 Line 149). Cleansing the mind (滌除玄覽) requires the existence of imperfections in the first place, for one must know what to cleanse. All these actions are futile and ultimately stray away from Tao. One should, therefore, simply "keep one's original intrinsic idle tranquillity" (Chapter 5 Line 15: 不如守中) and allow Tao to naturally act. Accordingly, Line 30 concludes Tao does all, for there is no need for anyone to purposefully do anything to follow Tao. See also footnote 63.

The correct interpretation in vernacular Chinese of Line 28 should be:

"抱持道來安頓自己的魂魄, 能不兩者(道和魂)先已分離嗎?
抱守真氣致使柔軟, 你可及得上嬰兒嗎? 洗淨心鏡, 能不心
裏先有瑕疵嗎?"

(interpreted by Kwok Kin Poon)

(57) "知" here is "acquired intelligence (智)". See *Kangxi Dictionary* (《康熙字典》).

One should distinguish this "acquired intelligence (智)" from the wisdom of following Tao that Laozi cherished. "Acquired intelligence (智)" refers to a trained or learned wit that is used to manipulate others to serve a purpose. Hence, "acquired intelligence (智)" certainly deviates from the path of Tao. Wang Bi (王弼) nicely elaborated this in his annotations of this phrase:

"術以求成, 運數以求匿者, 智也. 玄覽無疵, 猶絕聖也. 治國
無以智, 猶棄智也. 能無以智乎, 則民不辟而國治之也."
Source: 王弼《老子王弼注》. 台北: 新興書局, 1964,
p.012.

It is also important to recognize that Laozi had never contended a ruler should be ignorant or unintelligent. Laozi merely asserted that rulers should exercise their wisdoms to follow Tao and Nature in their governing; otherwise, they shall face ominous outcomes (Chapter 16 Line 50: 不知常, 妄作凶).

(58) "Valve of Motherly Nature (天門)" refers to the "valve of The Mysterious Motherly Channel (玄牝之門)" seen in Chapter 4 Line 17.

(59) "Motherly/feminine way (雌)" here refers to the puny "motherly" way of the self. One's selfish gentle motherly way contrasts the great gentle feminine and motherly way of the "valve of Motherly Nature (天門)", which is also known as "valve of The Mysterious Motherly Channel (玄牝之門)" in Chapter 4 Line 17. Note "牝" carries the meaning of "feminine/motherly (畜母)". See *Kangxi Dictionary* (《康熙字典》).

(60) "明白" here means "thorough understanding", as in *Zhuangzi - The Way of Heaven* (《莊子•天道》): "夫明白於天地之德者, 此之謂大本大宗, 與天和者也." See 《漢語大詞典》.

(61) "四達" here means "reaching all corners of the Universe (通達四方)", as in *Zhuangzi - Ingrained Ideas* (《莊子•刻意》) : "精神四達并流, 無所不極, 上際於天, 下蟠於地. 成玄英疏: 流, 通也.夫愛養精神者, 故能通達四方." See 《漢語大詞典》.

(62) "為" is better interpreted here as "study and learn (學習/研究)", as in *The Analects - Yang Huo* (《論語•陽貨》) : "人而不為《周南》、《召南》, 其猶正牆面而立也與?" See 中央研究院《搜詞尋字》.

Instead of "act", interpreting it here as "study and learn" is more consistent with Chapter 20 Line 15's "絕學無憂" and Chapter 64 Line 175's "學不學". Achieving a thorough understanding of Tao without acquiring human knowledge is a key concept espoused in *Tao Te Ching*.

(63) Like footnote 56, "愛民治國", "天門開闔" and "明白四達"

are all things that one should not do. Ruling and protecting the people (愛民治國) requires one to use acquired intelligence. Monitoring Motherly Nature (天門開闔) requires one to apply one's preconceived motherly way to discern. Achieving a thorough understanding that reaches all corners of the Universe (明白四達) requires one to study and learn human knowledge. All these actions are futile and ultimately stray away from Tao. One should, therefore, simply "keep one's original intrinsic idle tranquillity" (Chapter 5 Line 15: 不如守中) and allow Tao to naturally act. Accordingly, Line 30 concludes Tao does all, for there is no need for anyone to purposefully do anything to follow Tao.

The correct interpretation in vernacular Chinese of Line 29 should be:

"愛護百姓治理國家, 能不自己運用智能嗎？ 大自然陰柔產道閥門開開關關, 能不自己視它做你的陰柔產道嗎？ 明白道理通達四方, 能不自己先學習知識嗎?"

(interpreted by Kwok Kin Poon)

(64) "畜" here is "nurtures and rears (養育)", as in the *Book of Odes - Odes Of Bei - Ri Yue* (《詩經•邶風•日月》): "父兮母兮, 畜我不卒. 朱熹注：畜, 養." See 中央研究院《搜詞尋字》.

(65) See footnote 13.

(66) Ibid.

(67) "長" here should be better interpreted as "oversee/supervise (主管/執掌)", as seen in the following:

I. "故可使治國者使治國, 可使長官者使長官, 可使治邑者使治邑" in *Mo Yze - Exaltation of the Virtuous II* (《墨子•尚賢中》).

II. "使一郡皆寒, 賢者長一縣, 一縣之界能獨溫乎?" in *Lunheng - Ganxu* (《論衡•感虛》).

III. "許由鞠躬, 辭長九州" in Xi Kang's (嵇康) *Admonitions to the Emperor from the Imperial Mentor* (《太師箴》).

Source: 中央研究院《搜詞尋字》.

(68) See Line 140, as well as footnote 13.

(69) "Hub (轂)" is the hole in the centre of a wooden wheel to which the axle is attached.

(70) "當" here is "at (在)", as in *The Commentary of Zuo - the Ninth Year of Duke Xiang* (《左傳•襄公九年》) ："當今吾不能與晉爭." See 中央研究院《搜詞尋字》.

(71) If the hole of the hub is completely filled with no empty space, then the axle can never be placed. This then renders the wheel useless.

(72) "埏埴" here means "the process of using water and clay to produce pottery vessels (用水和泥來製作陶器)", as in Kuan Huan's (桓寬) *Yan Tie Lun*《鹽鐵論》："鑄金為鉏, 埏埴為器." See 《重編國語辭典修訂本》.

(73) "爽" here means "impair (損壞)", as in *Guangya - Shigu IV* (《廣雅•釋詁四》) ："爽, 傷也." See 中央研究院《搜詞尋字》.

(74) "妨" here means "harm/obstruct (損害/阻礙)", as in *The Commentary of Zuo - the Third Year of Duke Yin* (《左傳•隱公三年》): "且夫賤妨貴, 少陵長, 遠間親, 新間舊, 小加大, 淫破義, 所謂六逆也." See《重編國語辭典修訂本》.

(75) "腹" here refers to "果腹", which means "only filling the stomach (填飽肚子)", as in Liu Zongyuan's (柳宗元) *Zeng Wang Sun Wen* (《憎王孫文》) ："充嘯果腹兮, 驕傲驩欣." See《重編國語辭典修訂本》.
　　See also line 8 for the same "腹".

(76) "為腹不為目" is well explained by Wang Bi (王弼):

"為腹者以物養己, 為目者以物役己, 故聖人不為目也."

"Those who seek to satisfy the basic needs of their bellies make use of things to nourish themselves, while those who seek to satisfy their eyes make use of things to enslave themselves. Thus, wise sages never seek to satisfy their eyes."

(interpreted by KS Vincent Poon)

Source: 王弼《老子王弼注》. 台北: 新興書局, 1964, p.014.

(77) See footnote 31.

(78) "貴" here means "high regard (重視)", as in *Zhengzitong* (《正字通》): "貴, 尚也." See 中央研究院《搜詞尋字》.

(79) Why "Honour ultimately becomes humiliation"? Wang Bi (王弼) wrote:

"寵必有辱, 榮必有患, 驚辱等, 榮患同也."

"Honour must be accompanied by humiliation, while glory must be accompanied by tragedy. Hence, anxiety, humiliation, glory, tragedy, etc. are all one and the same."

(interpreted by KS Vincent Poon)

Source: 王弼《老子王弼注》. 台北: 新興書局, 1964, p.015.

(80) The correct interpretation in vernacular Chinese of Line 39 should be:

"什麼叫做榮寵和羞辱乃都令人惶恐的呢? 因為尊尚的榮寵總必成為卑下的羞辱. 所以, 得了榮寵乃惶恐, 這和失去榮寵是惶恐一樣."

(interpreted by Kwok Kin Poon)

(81) "愛" here is "cherish (愛惜)", as in:

   I. "是以聖人愛精神貴處靜" in *Hanfeitzu - Explaining Laozi* (《韓非子•解老》).

II. "夫鴈順風以愛氣力" in *Huainanzi - Youwu* (《淮南子•脩務》).

Source: 中央研究院《搜詞尋字》.

(82) "夷" here may take the meaning of "big (大)", as in *The Book of Odes - Sacrificial odes of Zhou* (《詩經•周頌》): "降福孔夷." See *Kangxi Dictionary* (《康熙字典》).

(83) "希" here may take the meaning of "tranquil silence (靜寂無聲)". Heshang Gong (河上公) annotated "希" here as "無聲曰希", while Lu Deming (陸德明) annotated it as "靜也". See 中央研究院《搜詞尋字》.

(84) "微" here may take the meaning of "without (無/沒有)", as in:
   I. "微管仲, 吾其被髮左衽矣. 何晏集解：馬曰：微, 無也. 無管仲則君不君、臣不臣, 皆為夷狄" in *The Analects - Xian Wen* (《論語•憲問》).
   II. "微趙君, 幾為丞相所賣" in *Records of the Grand Historian - Biography of Li Si* (《史記•李斯列傳》).

Source: 中央研究院《搜詞尋字》.

(85) "致詰" here means "thoroughly examined or inquired (究問)". "致" here means "thoroughly examined (推極/窮究)", as in *The Classic of Rites - The Great Learning* (《禮記•大學》): "欲誠其意者, 先致其知." See 《重編國語辭典修訂本》.

   "詰" is "問 (inquired)". "此三者, 不可致詰. 註: 詰, 問也." See *Kangxi Dictionary* (《康熙字典》).

(86) The "One" here refers to the "One" found in Chapter 42 Line 119.

(87) "皦" here means "clear and distinct as a gemstone (玉石之白也)". See *Shuowen Jiezi* (《說文解字》).

(88) "昧" here means "dull (不明)". See *Kangxi Dictionary* (《康

熙字典》).

(89) "繩繩" here means "the appearance of being endless (相續不絕的樣子)", as in *The Book of Odes - Odes Of Zhou And The South - Zhong Si* (《詩經•周南•螽斯》): "螽斯羽薨薨兮, 宜爾子孫繩繩兮." See 《重編國語辭典修訂本》.

(90) "A state of no matter (無物)" here refers to "not yet having any form (未形)" discussed in footnote 2. This "One" in Line 43 ultimately is in "A state of no matter (無物)", which is Tao's form before it begets all things that can be named. This "One" is the intermediate between Tao (道) and its Manifestation (德), as narrated in Chapter 42 Line 119: Tao spawned One; One spawned Two; Two spawned Three; Three spawned all things (道生一, 一生二, 二生三, 三生萬物).

(91) "御" here means "oversee/govern (治理/統治)":
I. "御, 治也." See *Yupian* (《玉篇•彳部》).
II. "御, 理也." See *Guangyun* (《廣韻•御韻》).
Source: 中央研究院 《搜詞尋字》.

(92) "有" here means "territorial realm (州域)", as in:
I. "方命厥后, 奄有九有. 毛傳：九有, 九州也" in *The Book of Odes - Sacrificial Odes Of Shang - Xuan Niao* (《詩經•商頌•玄鳥》).
II. "此其所以代夏王而受九有也" in *Xunzi - Jiebi* (《荀子•解蔽》).
Source: 中央研究院 《搜詞尋字》.

(93) "古始" refers to "the very origin of the ancient past (古代的開始)", as in the *History of the Northern Dynasties - Volume 10 - Northern Zhou Annals - Emperor Gaozu Wu* (《北史•卷十•周本紀•高祖武帝》)："朕運當澆季, 思復古始." See 《重編國語辭典修訂本》.

(94) "道紀" refers to "rules and principles of Tao (道的規律)".
See 《漢語大詞典》.

(95) See footnote 35.

(96) "士" here means "those who are able to deal with their matters (凡能事其事者偏士)". See *Shuowen Jiezi Zhu* (《說文解字注》).

(97) "微妙" here means "deeply profound and extraordinary(幽深而超乎尋常)", as in *Annotations of Mengzi* (《孟子•注疏》) by Zhao Qi (趙岐): "儒家惟有孟子閎遠微妙, 縕奧難見." See 《重編國語辭典修訂本》.

(98) "玄通" should be interpreted as "connect with Nature (與天相通)". "玄" carries the meaning of "nature (天)", while "通" carries the meaning of "arrive to /connect with (達/徹)". See *Kangxi Dictionary* (《康熙字典》).

(99) "強" here means "barely (勉強)", as in *Strategies of the Warring States - Strategies of Zhao IV* (《戰國策•趙策四》): "老臣今者殊不欲食, 乃自強步, 日三四里." See 中央研究院《搜詞尋字》.

(100) "若" here means "is/does (乃)", not its usual meaning of "seemingly" or "as if". See footnote 31. Laozi had always cherished acting by one's simple primitive nature and would have never asked one to be pretending or disingenuous.

(101) "容" here means "rules and principles (模式/樣式)", as in *The Rites of Zhou - Office of Winter* (《周禮•冬官考工記》) : "凡為甲, 必先為容. 鄭玄注 : 服者之形容也, 鄭司農云, 容謂象式." See 中央研究院《搜詞尋字》.

(102) "將" here is "is/does (乃)", as in *The Book of Expletives* (《

經傳釋詞》): "將, 猶乃也." See中央研究院《搜詞尋字》.

(103) "曠" here means "brilliant and vast (光明/遼闊)", as seen in:

    I.   "曠, 明也" in *Shuowen Jiezi* (《說文解字》).

    II. "曠曠, 大也" in *Guangya - Shixun* (《廣雅•釋訓》).

Source: 中央研究院《搜詞尋字》.

(104) "以" here means "apply/utilize (用/使用)", as indicated in *Yupian* (《玉篇》): "以, 用也." See 中央研究院《搜詞尋字》.

(105) "之" here is often misinterpreted. This "之" actually means "then/consequently (則/就)", as supported below:

    I.   "之, 猶則也" in *The Book of Expletives* (《經傳釋詞》).

    II. "鶉之奔奔, 鵲之彊彊. 毛傳：鶉則奔奔, 鵲則彊彊然" in *The Book of Odes - Odes Of Yong - Chun Zhi Ben Ben* (《詩經•鄘風•鶉之奔奔》).

    III. "華則榮矣, 實之不知" in *Discourses of the States - Discourses of Jin VI* (《國語•晉語六》).

    IV. "故民無常處, 見利之聚, 無之去" in *Master Lu's Spring and Autumn Annals - The Second Month of Spring Almanac - Gong Ming* (《呂氏春秋•仲春紀•功名》).

Source: 中央研究院《搜詞尋字》.

(106) "保" here means "understand (知曉)", as in:

    I.   "有勇有義, 非歌孰能保此? 鄭玄注：保, 知也. 孔穎達疏：不是歌聲辨之, 誰能知其有勇有義" in *The Classic of Rites - Yue Ji* (《禮記•樂記》).

    II. "壹心而不豫兮, 羌不可保也. 王逸注：保, 知也. ...顧君心不可保知, 易傾移也" in *Verses of Chu - Nine Pieces - Grieving I Make My Plaint* (《楚辭•九章•惜誦》).

Source: 中央研究院《搜詞尋字》.

(107) "蔽" here means "hidden/inconspicuous (掩)". See *Kangxi Dictionary* (《康熙字典》). Wang Bi (王弼) further annotated it

as "being covered": "蔽, 覆蓋也." See 王弼《老子王弼注》. 台北: 新興書局, 1964, p.018.

(108) "新" here actually means "親". "親, 又通作新", see *Kangxi Dictionary* (《康熙字典》).

"新" is usually misinterpreted here as "new", which in turn yields two following popular misinterpretations of "夫唯不盈, 故能蔽不新成":

I. "Alas, since they are always not satisfied with themselves (夫唯不盈), they can (故能) break from old traditions (蔽不) and form new ways that are consistent with the times and the way of Tao (新成)."

II. "Alas, since they are content with not being satisfied (夫唯不盈), they are able to preserve their own primitive nature (故能蔽) without establishing any new idea (不新成)."

For I., since Tao is always present with its immutable way, those who follow Tao should recognize there is really nothing new or old in the Universe. Tao is what it is, and so there is no old traditions nor new ways. Accordingly, it makes very little sense to say followers of Tao are pursuing to break something old to form something new.

For II., "蔽" in "能蔽" is obviously a verb, and so cannot be a noun that refers to "primitive nature". Further, it is extremely far-fetched to argue that "able to hide (能蔽)" is a metaphor for "able to preserve primitive nature", for no dictionary has indicated that "蔽" can represent "primitive nature" or the likes.

(109) The correct interpretation in vernacular Chinese of Line 48 should be:

"誰能夠用靜就令混濁得以漸漸清澈? 誰能夠用長久震動則使安靜得以漸漸產生?(唯有道!) 知曉這道理的人, 不愛自滿. 因為不自滿, 故此才能夠隱藏自己, 決不會說親自成就了些什麼."

(interpreted by Kwok Kin Poon)

(110) "篤" here means "fidelity/diligence (忠誠/專一)", as in *Guan-zi - Jun Chen II* (《管子•君臣下》): "小民篤於農, 則財厚而備足." See 中央研究院《搜詞尋字》.

(111) Why must one "nullify oneself to the utmost degree (致虛極)"? All one's accomplishments are actually achieved by Tao, not the self (see Chapter 15 Line 48). Accordingly, one should be humble, tranquil, and disregard the concept of "self" to be able to understand Tao, the fundamental way of all things.

(112) "命" here means "Natural Destiny (天命)", as in *The Analects - Yao Yue* (《論語•堯曰》): "不知命, 無以為君子也. 孔安國注 : 命, 謂窮達之分也." See 中央研究院《搜詞尋字》.
　　As such, "復命" means "returning to the Natural Destiny". All things spawn from the tranquil and Tao, and so they are destined to return back to this tranquil Tao (Chapter 14 Line 43: 復歸於無物).

(113) Tao spawns and bears all things in the Universe. Therefore, understanding the everlasting and immutable way of Tao empowers one to forebear all things in the Universe.

(114) "王" here should mean "the one who is most desirable (天下歸往)". See *Kangxi Dictionary* (《康熙字典》).
　　"王" here cannot take its usual meaning of "kings" or "rulers". If so, "王乃天" makes no sense, as not all kings follow the way of Nature.

(115) "天" here should be interpreted as "Nature (大自然)". See footnote 49.

(116) The correct interpretation in vernacular Chinese of Line 51 should be:
　　"知曉常道, 便會容納一切. 容納一切乃就大公無私; 大公無私乃就萬物所歸往; 萬物所歸往乃就遵循於大自然; 遵循於

大自然乃就依循於道; 依循於道乃就恆久. 這便終身不會危
殆了."
(interpreted by Kwok Kin Poon)

(117) The ideal ruler governs selflessly by way of Tao, and so
the subjects live by their own natures, undisturbed. Hence, the
subjects only know the ruler's existence but not the ruler's governance. Wang Bi (王弼) elaborated on this nicely:

"大人在上, 居無為事, 行不言之教, 萬物作焉而不為始, 故下
知有之而已."

"The ruler, overseeing at the top, governs with no personal differentiation and intent and implements enlightening
others through the wordless. All things merely act but do
not recognize their ruler as the foundation of their lives.
Hence, subjects merely know having a ruler at the top,
nothing more."
(interpreted by KS Vincent Poon)
Source: 王弼《老子王弼注》. 台北: 新興書局, 1964,
p.020.

The correct interpretation in vernacular Chinese of "太上, 下
知有之" should be:

"最好的統治者, 是下面的百姓僅知他的存在(而不知他在統
治)."
(interpreted by Kwok Kin Poon)

(118) For further elaborations by Laozi on this line, please see
chapters 74 and 79.

(119) Tao always acts to deliver consequences that are honest
and impartial (Chapter 21 Line 64: 其精甚真, 其中有信). Accordingly, rulers must be careful in their actions and words, as
illustrated in the subsequence phrase in the same line "悠兮, 其
貴言".

The correct interpretation in vernacular Chinese of "信不足?
焉有不信焉" should be:

"不足信麼? 又豈會有不足信的哩!"

(interpreted by Kwok Kin Poon)

(120) "悠" here means "concern (憂)", as in *Shuowen Jiezi* (《說文解字》).

(121) As "言" here refers to speeches by rulers, it should be better interpreted as "decree (號令)", as in *Kangxi Dictionary* (《康熙字典》): "(言)號令也. 《周語》有不祀則修言."

(122) Tao fundamentally does not act according to human moral concepts of "righteousness", "injustice", "benevolence" and "malevolence" (Chapter 5 Line 13: 天地不仁, 以萬物為芻狗). Accordingly, a society that highly regards "benevolence" and "righteousness" shows that its people must have left Tao and are no longer original and simple (樸).

"Benevolence (仁)" and "righteousness (義)" here refers to the Confucian concepts of benevolence and righteousness (仁義). For further elaborations by Laozi on the shortcomings of various Confucian concepts, please see Chapter 38.

(123) Acquired intellect gives rise to human fraud and deception; if a society cherishes too much intellect, then trickery and corruption shall appear. See Chapter 19 Line 57.

(124) The "six kinships (六親)" are one's father, son, elder brother, younger brother, husband, and wife, as annotated by Wang Bu: "六親, 父子兄弟夫婦也." See 王弼《老子王弼注》. 台北: 新興書局, 1964, p.021.

(125) Filial piety is not needed if close relatives are already harmonious among themselves, full of filial piety. Hence, if a society fears losing filial piety, then it is already devoid of filial piety. Laozi often used the argument of "if one fears losing an entity means one is already devoid of that entity" in *Tao Te*

Ching. See Chapter 38 for another notable example.

(126) Loyal subordinates are not needed nor evident when the state is stable and prosperous. Hence, the appearance of loyal subordinates indicates that the state is in chaos.

(127) This "聖" refers to "the sages" instituted by Confucius's thinking, not Laozi's "wise sages (聖人)" who only follow Tao. Hence, "聖" here is translated as "so-call sages".

(128) With no restraint from human-defined morals and knowledge, people can happily live by their own natures.

(129) See Chapter 18 Line 56 and footnote 125.

(130) "令" here means "allow/let (讓)", as in *Strategies of the Warring States - Strategies of Zhao I* (《戰國策•趙策一》): "故貴為列侯者, 不令在相位." See 中央研究院《搜詞尋字》.

(131) "屬" here means "pen (撰寫)", as in:
  I. "懷王使屈原造為憲令, 屈平屬草槁未定" in *Records of the Grand Historian - Biographies of Qu Yuan and Master Jia* (《史記•屈原賈生列傳》).
  II. "以能誦詩書屬文稱於郡中. 顏師古注：屬謂綴輯之也, 言其能為文也" in the *Book of Han - Biography of Jia Yi* (《漢書•賈誼傳》).
  Source: 中央研究院《搜詞尋字》.

(132) "見" means "acknowledge/know(知道)", as in *Huainanzi - Youwu* (《淮南子•脩務》): "今使六子者易事, 而明弗能見者何? 高誘注：見, 猶知也." See 中央研究院《搜詞尋字》.

(133) "素" here means "one's inherent nature (本性)", as in:
  I. "素, 本也" in *Guangya - Shigu III* (《廣雅•釋詁三》).
  II. "是故虛無者道之舍, 平易者道之素. 高誘注：素, 性也"

in *Huainanzi - Chu Zhen* (《淮南子•俶真》) .
Source: 中央研究院《搜詞尋字》.

(134) The correct interpretation in vernacular Chinese of Line 58 should be:

"上面這三個觀點由於論述的言辭未算足夠, 故此讓我再有
所撰: 了解本性而持守真樸, 少點自我而捨棄私慾."

(interpreted by Kwok Kin Poon)

(135) The wise never put themselves in precarious situations. See Chapter 50 Line 138: "以其無死地".

(136) "荒" here means "vast (大)". See *Kangxi Dictionary* (《康熙字典》).

(137) "未央" here means "no limit (未盡)", as in *Verses of Chu - Li Sa* (《楚辭•離騷》): "及年歲之未晏兮, 時亦猶其未央." See 《重編國語辭典修訂本》.

(138) "熙熙" here means "the appearance of jolly crowds; all feeling happy, hurried and excited (人來人往, 熱鬧紛紜的樣子)", as in *Records of the Grand Historian - Biographies of Usurers* (《史記•貨殖傳》): "天下熙熙, 皆為利來; 天下壤壤, 皆為利往." See 《重編國語辭典修訂本》.

(139) "太牢" refers to "the process of preparing beef, lamb, and pork for a grand sacrificial ceremony to pay respect to the Universe (古代祭祀天地, 以牛、羊、豬三牲具備為太牢, 以示尊崇之意)", as in *Records of the Grand Historian - Biographies of Jing Ke* (《史記•荊軻傳》) : "太子日造門下, 供太牢具." See 《重編國語辭典修訂本》.

(140) "未兆" here means "not yet surfaced (未作之時)", as annotated in *Kangxi Dictionary* (《康熙字典》): "《老子•道德經》我則泊兮其未兆. 註: 意未作之時也."

(141) "孩" here is "smile (小兒笑)". See *Kangxi Dictionary* (《康熙字典》).

(142) "儑" here means "laid-back (懶懈) ". See *Kangxi Dictionary* (《康熙字典》).

(143) See footnote 31. Laozi had always cherished acting in one's natural way and would have never asked one to be pretending or disingenuous.

(144) "沌" here means "the appearance of being ignorant and foolish (愚貌)", as in *Kangxi Dictionary* (《康熙字典》): "沌, 愚貌. 《老子•道德經》忳忳兮.或作沌."

(145) "昭昭" here means "brilliant and conspicuous (明白顯著) ", as in Liu Xie's (劉勰) *The Literary Mind and the Carving of Dragons - Zongjing* (《文心雕龍•宗經》)："故子夏歎書, 昭昭若日月之明, 離離如星辰之行, 言昭灼也." See 《重編國語辭典修訂本》.

(146) "昏昏" here means "obtuse and undiscerning (糊塗不辨是非)", as in *Mengzi - Jin Xin II* (《孟子•盡心下》)："今以其昏昏, 使人昭昭." See《重編國語辭典修訂本》.

(147) "察察" here means "discerning (分別辨析) ", as in the *New Book of Tang - Biography of Tutu Chengcui* (《新唐書•吐突承璀傳》)："以黃門直東宮, 為掖廷局博士, 察察有才." See 《重編國語辭典修訂本》.

(148) "悶悶" here means "dim-witted (渾噩)", as indicated in *Ministry of Education Revised Dictionary of Chinese* (《重編國語辭典修訂本》): "悶悶, 渾噩.《老子》第二十章 , 俗人察察, 我獨悶悶."

(149) "澹" here means "tranquil (恬静)", as indicated in *Kangxi*

Dictionary (《康熙字典》): "澹, 恬靜也. 《老子•道德經》澹兮其若海." Such interpretation can also be seen in the *Book of Han - Biography of Sima Xiangru* (《漢書•司馬相如傳》) : "泊乎無為, 澹乎自持." See 《重編國語辭典修訂本》.

(150) See footnote 31. Laozi had always cherished acting in one's natural way and would have never asked one to be pretending or disingenuous

(151) "飂" here means "the appearance of high winds (高風貌)". See *Kangxi Dictionary* (《康熙字典》).

(152) "以" here means "reason (緣故)", as suggested below :
  I. "以, 故也" in *Zhengzitong* (《正字通》).
  II. "何其久也, 必有以也" in *The Book of Odes - Odes Of Bei - Mao Qiu* (《詩經•邶風•旄丘》).
  Source: 中央研究院《搜詞尋字》.

(153) "似" here is "以", which is "and (而)", as annotated by Yu Yue (俞樾): "而我獨頑似鄙. 似, 當讀為以, 古以、似通用...頑以鄙, 猶言頑而鄙也." See 中央研究院《搜詞尋字》.

(154) "食母" here should be interpreted as "the nurturing mother Nature (乳母)". "母" also carries the meaning of "basis/starting point (本)". All are supported by the following:
  I. "食母, 生之本也" in Wang Bi's *Laozi's Tao Te Ching with Wang Bi's Commentaries* (《老子王弼注》).
  II. "涅非緇也, 青藍也, 茲雖遇其母, 而無能復化已. 高誘注：母, 本也" in *Huainanzi - Chu Zhen* (《淮南子•俶真》). See 中央研究院《搜詞尋字》.
  III. "食母, 乳母.《禮記•內則》大夫之子有食母." See *Ministry of Education Revised Dictionary of Chinese* (《重編國語辭典修訂本》).

(155) The correct interpretation in vernacular Chinese of

"眾人皆有以, 而我獨頑似鄙. 我獨異於人, 而貴食母" should be:

"眾人皆有個原因, 而我獨粗鈍兼鄙陋. 我獨不同於人, 而祇

崇尚生我育我的大自然."

(interpreted by Kwok Kin Poon)

(156) "容" here means "rules and principles (法則/規律)", as supported by:

I. "容, 法也" in *Guangya - Shigu I* (《廣雅•釋詁一》).

II. "夫物有常容, 因乘以導之, 因隨物之容" in *Hanfeitzu - Explicating Laozi* (《韓非子•喻老》).

Source: 中央研究院《搜詞尋字》.

(157) "孔" is "vacuous (空)". Wang Bi (王弼) annotated: "孔, 空也, 惟以空為德, 然後乃能動作從道." See 王弼《老子王弼注》. 台北: 新興書局, 1964, p.024.

(158) "惚恍" here is "in a state of cloudy uncertainty (混沌不清)", as in *Selections of Refined Literature - Pan Yue - Xi Zheng Fu* (《文選•潘岳•西征賦》): "古往今來, 邈矣悠哉, 寥廓惚恍, 化一氣而甄三才." See 《重編國語辭典修訂本》.

(159) See Chapter 14 Line 44.

(160) "窈冥" here is "the appearance of unfathomable depth (深遠渺茫貌)", as in *Huainanzi - Lanming* (《淮南子•覽冥》): "得失之度深微窈冥, 難以知論, 不可以辯說也." See 《重編國語辭典修訂本》.

(161) "精" here is "essence (真氣)", as in:

I. "精, 《增韻》: 真氣也" in *The Essential Comprehensive Dictionary of Ancient and Contemporary Rhymes* (《古今韻會舉要•庚韻》).

II. "一氣能變曰精. 尹知章注: 謂專一其氣, 能變鬼神來教" in *Guanzi - Xin Shu* (《管子•心術下》).

III. "吾欲取天地之精, 以佐五穀, 以養民人. 成玄英疏: 欲

取窈冥之理, 天地陰陽精氣, 助成五穀, 以養蒼生也" in *Zhuangzi - Letting Be and Exercising Forbearance* (《莊子•在宥》).
Source: 中央研究院《搜詞尋字》.

(162) According to Wang Bi's (王弼) annotation, "信" here means "can be tested (信驗)": "信, 信驗也." See 王弼《老子王弼注》. 台北: 新興書局, 1964, p.025.

(163) See Chapter 1 Line 1, the Name.

(164) See footnote 15.

(165) "以" is "rely on (憑藉/仗恃)", as in:
   I.   "富國以農, 距敵恃卒" in *Hanfeitzu - Wu Du* (《韓非子•五蠹》).
   II. "欲知天, 以人事" in *Lunheng - Bu Shi* (《論衡•卜筮》).
   Source: 中央研究院《搜詞尋字》.

(166) "閱" here means "endows (賦與)", as in *Kangxi Dictionary* (《康熙字典》): "閱, 又稟也, 賦與. 《老子•道德經》自古及今, 其名不去, 以閱眾甫. 註: 閱, 稟也. 甫, 始也. 言道稟與萬物始生, 從道受氣."

(167) "眾甫" here is "the birth of all things (物之始也)", as annotated by Wang Bi (王弼). See 王弼《老子王弼注》. 台北: 新興書局, 1964, p.025.

(168) The correct interpretation in vernacular Chinese of Line 64 should be:
   "它(德) 的真氣甚是純正不假, 它裏面有的是可驗證的誠信.
   從古至今, 這德從沒離開過, 靠它來賦與萬物的生長."
   (interpreted by Kwok Kin Poon)

(169) "以此" here means "by the above rationale (此上之所云)", as annotate by Wang Bi (王弼). See 王弼《老子王弼注》. 台北: 新興書局, 1964, p.025.

(170) "曲" here is "submissive and humble (屈曲委細)", as indicated in *Kangxi Dictionary* (《康熙字典》): "《易經•繫辭》曲成萬物而不遺. 疏: 曲, 屈曲委細."

(171) "全" here is "preserve/safeguard (保全)", as supported by:
   I.   "全, 保也" in *Zhengzitong* (《正字通》).
   II. "凡用兵之法, 全國為上, 破國次之" in *The Art of War - Planning an Attack* (《孫子•謀攻》).
   Source: 中央研究院《搜詞尋字》.

(172) It is particularly important to note "曲則全" asks one to be submissive to Tao, not to a ruler. This is supported by a related phrase found in *Zhuangzi - Tian Xia* (《莊子•天下》):
   "人皆求福, 己獨曲全."
   劉文典注: "委順至理則常全, 故無所求福, 福已足矣."
   Liu Wendian's annotation:
   "Those who follow and are submissive to the ultimate way of Tao shall always be preserved; hence, there is no need for them to seek more blessings, for their blessings are already sufficient."
   (interpreted by KS Vincent Poon)
   Source: 劉文典, 《莊子補正》. 雲南: 雲南人民出版社, 1980, p.999.
Accordingly, Laozi had never asked anyone to submit or bow to a ruler in order to preserve oneself (委曲求全).

(173) "枉" here means "crooked (衺曲)". See *Shuowen Jiezi* (《說文解字》).

(174) The correct interpretation in vernacular Chinese of "曲則全, 枉則直" should be:

"曲從於道就可以保全性命, 彎曲就可以伸直."
(interpreted by Kwok Kin Poon)

(175) "窪" here means "dented/lower levelled (凹陷/低下)", as in the *New Book of Tang - Biography of Nanman II* (《新唐書•南蠻傳下》) : "扶南, 在日南之南七千里, 地卑窪." See 中央研究院《搜詞尋字》.

(176) Wang Bi (王弼) elaborated on "少則得, 多則惑" succinctly:
"多則遠其真, 故曰惑也; 少則得其本, 故曰得也."
"The rich are far away from their original and genuine natures; hence, it can be said they can become unsettled. Those who are deficient still attain their original foundations; hence, it can be said they can attain. "
(interpreted by KS Vincent Poon)
Source: 王弼《老子王弼注》. 台北: 新興書局, 1964, p.026.

Indeed, the rich are usually unsettled, for most of them incessantly fear losing their excessive yet unnecessary possessions.

(177) "一" here refers to the singular Tao. See Chapter 10 Line 28 for the same "抱一".

(178) "自見" here means "showing one's brilliance (自我炫耀)", as in Cao Pi's (曹丕) *Discourse on Literature* (《典論論文》) : "夫人善於自見, 而文非一體, 鮮能備善, 是以各以所長, 相輕所短." See《重編國語辭典修訂本》.

(179) "伐" here is "accomplishments (功勞)", as seen in:
   I. "且旌君伐. 杜預注：伐, 功也" in *The Commentary of Zuo - the Twenty-eighth Year of Duke Zhuang* (《左傳

•莊公二十八年》).

II. "（懷王）非有功伐, 何以得專主約！顏師古注：積功
曰伐" in the *Book of Han - Annals of Emperor Gaozu I*
(《漢書•高帝紀上》).
Source: 中央研究院《搜詞尋字》.

(180) See Chapter 41 Line 117.

(181) "飄風" here is "violent winds", as in Cao Pi's (曹丕) *Mis-
cellaneous Poems II* (《雜詩》其二): "惜哉時不遇, 適與飄風會."
See 《重編國語辭典修訂本》.

(182) "從事" here means "follow and serve under (追隨/奉事)"
, as in Niu Sengru's (牛僧孺) *Xuan Guai Lu - Zhang Zuo* (《玄
怪錄•張佐》)："衋慕先生高躅, 願從事左右耳." See 《漢語大詞
典》.

(183) Tao is always honest, impartial, and can continuously
be tried and tested (Chapter 21 Line 64: 其精甚真, 其中有信).
Accordingly, one always faces the eventual and impartial consequences for one's actions without mercy (Chapter 5 Line 13: 天
地不仁, 以萬物為芻狗) as governed by Tao. You reap what you
sow. Such is the gist of Chapter 23 Line 71.
　　For "信不足？ 焉有不信焉", also see Chapter 17 Line 53.

(184) "企" here means "lifting one's heel (舉踵)". See *Shuowen
Jiezi* (《說文解字》).

(185) "跨" here means "踞", which is "crouch (蹲)", as supported
by:
　　I. "跨, 踞也. 《晉語》不跨其國. 註: 猶踞也." See *Kangxi
　　　Dictionary* (《康熙字典》).
　　II. "踞, 蹲也." See *Shuowen Jiezi* (《說文解字》).

(186) See footnote 179.

(187) See Chapter 22 Line 67.

(188) "餘食" here means "rotten leftover delicacies", as annotated by Wang Bi (王弼): "餘食, 盛饌之餘也. 本雖美, 更可藏 (藏, 與穢同)也." See 王弼《老子王弼注》. 台北: 新興書局, 1964, p.028.

(189) "行" here is "bodies/shapes (形)", while "贅" here means "ugly tumours (贅瘤)", as annotated by Sima Guang (司馬光): "《老子本義》引司馬光曰：形、行古字通用. 棄餘之食, 適使人厭, 附贅之形, 適使人醜." See 《漢語大詞典》.

(190) See footnote 16.

(191) "物" here can mean "people (人)", as in *The Commentary of Zuo - the Twenty-eighth year of Duke Zhao* (《左傳•昭公二十八年》): "且三代之亡, 共子之廢, 皆是物也⋯⋯夫有尤物, 足以移人, 苟非德義, 則必有禍." See 中央研究院《搜詞尋字》.

(192) "處" here means "put/situate oneself at (居)". See *Kangxi Dictionary* (《康熙字典》).

(193) The correct interpretation in vernacular Chinese of Line 73 should be:

"這在道裏面呢, 叫做殘羹穢臭與贅疣醜形. 這都是人們常厭惡的, 故有道的人必不會處身其中."
(interpreted by Kwok Kin Poon)

(194) "混成" here means "homogenously turbid yet natural (渾然一體, 自然形成)", as in the *Book of Liang - Volume 13 - Biography of Shen Yue* (《梁書•卷一三•列傳•沈約》)："雖混成以無跡, 寔遺訓之可秉." See 《重編國語辭典修訂本》.

(195) On "有物混成, 先天地生", Wang Bi (王弼) further elaborated:

"混然不可得而知, 而萬物由之以成, 故曰混成也. 不知其誰之子, 故先天地生."

"Homogenously turbid and cannot be grasped nor understood, yet, all things spawn from it. Hence, it can be said it is homogenously turbid yet natural. Since one does not know whose offspring it is, therefore, it must have born before the birth of the Universe."

(interpreted by KS Vincent Poon)

Source: 王弼《老子王弼注》. 台北: 新興書局, 1964, p.028.

(196) "寂寥" here means "formless (無形體)", as annotated by Wang Bi (王弼). See 王弼《老子王弼注》. 台北: 新興書局, 1964, p.029.

(197) "殆" here means "tired (疲乏)", as in *Zhuangzi - Nourishing the Lord of Life* (《莊子•養生主》) : "吾生也有涯, 而知也無涯. 以有涯隨無涯, 殆已." See 《重編國語辭典修訂本》.

(198) See Chapter 52 Line 141.

(199) See footnote 99.

(200) "曰" here is an auxiliary particle, as in Yang Shu Ta's (楊樹達) *Ciquan* (《詞詮》): "曰, 語中助詞." See 中央研究院《搜詞尋字》.

An example of such kind of usage can be seen in *The Book of Odes - Odes Of Bin - Dong Shan* (《詩經•豳風•東山》): "我東曰歸, 我心西悲." See 中央研究院《搜詞尋字》.

Hence, in our context, it can be interpreted as "hence".

(201) "逝" here means "flows everywhere in all direction (行也/無所不至)", as annotated by Wang Bi (王弼). See 王弼《老子王弼注》. 台北: 新興書局, 1964, p.029.

(202) "遠" here means "ultimate limit (極)", as seen below:
 I. "遠, 極也." See 王弼《老子王弼注》. 台北: 新興書局, 1964, p.029.
 II. "極, 遠也" in *Guangya - Shigu I* (《廣雅•釋詁一》)
 See 中央研究院《搜詞尋字》.

(203) See footnote 114.

(204) "域" here is "realm of residence (居處)", as in:
 I. "域民不以封疆之界, 固國不以山谿之險, 威天下不以兵革之利. 朱熹注：域, 界限也" in *Mengzi - Gong Sun Chou II* (《孟子•公孫丑下》).
 II. "人域是域, 士君子也. 司馬貞索隱：域, 居也" in *Records of the Grand Historian - Rites* (《史記•禮書》).
 Source: 中央研究院《搜詞尋字》.

(205) "居" here is "takes up (佔/佔據)", as in:
 I. "居, 據也" in *Guangya - Shiyan* (《廣雅•釋言》).
 II. "故為國任地者, 山林居什一, 藪澤居什一, 溪谷流水居什一, 都邑蹊道居什四, 此先王之正律也" in the *Book of Lord Shang - Calculation of Land* (《商君書•算地》).
 Source: 中央研究院《搜詞尋字》.

(206) "法" here means "law (法則)", as annotated by Wang Bi (王弼). See 王弼《老子王弼注》. 台北: 新興書局, 1964, p.030.

(207) The correct interpretation in vernacular Chinese of Line 76 should be:
 "在人居處的地方裏面, 有四個大, 而天下所歸往者佔其中之一. 人取法於地; 地取法於大自然; 大自然取法於道; 道取法於它自己的本然."
 (interpreted by Kwok Kin Poon)

(208) "君" here is "lord (主)", as in *Xunzi - Jiebi* (《荀子•解蔽》): "心者, 形之君也, 而神明之主也." See 中央研究院《搜詞尋字》.

(209) "輜重" here means "supplies that one carries when one travels (外出時攜載的物資)", as in *Records of the Grand Historian - Biography of Su Qin* (《史記•蘇秦列傳》): "蘇秦為從約長, 并相六國. 北報趙王, 乃行過雒陽, 車騎輜重, 諸侯各發使送之甚眾, 疑於王者." See 《漢語大詞典》.

Laozi likened "輜重" to "gravity and prudence (重)" mentioned earlier in the same line, as suggested by Wang Bi's elaboration on "不離輜重":

> "以重為本, 故不離."
> "(The wise sages) take gravity and prudence as their
> foundation; hence, they never leave it behind."
> (interpreted by KS Vincent Poon)
> Source: 王弼《老子王弼注》. 台北: 新興書局, 1964,
> p.031.

(210) "榮觀" here is "honourable/distinguished (榮名/榮譽)", as seen below:

    I. "名者, 脩身慎行, 懼榮觀之不顯, 非所以讓名也" in *Yanshi Jiaxun - Mingshi* (《顏氏家訓•名實》).

    II. "臣抱疾東荒, 志絕榮觀, 不悟聖恩, 猥復加寵" in the *Book of Song - Biography of Wang Jinghong* (《宋書•王敬弘傳》).

    Source: 《漢語大詞典》.

Heshang Gong (河上公) was incorrect in interpreting "榮觀" here as "宮闕", which means "imperial palace (帝王所居住的宮殿)". Wise sages always wish to preserve their primitive natures (Chapter 15 Line 47: 敦兮其若樸) and be inconspicuous (Chapter 70 Line 191: 被褐懷玉), and so they will never choose to reside themselves in magnificent and flamboyant imperial palaces.

(211) "燕處" here means "at ease (閑居)", as in *The Classic of Rites - Different Teaching of the Different Kings* (《禮記•經解》): "其在朝廷, 則道仁聖禮義之序; 燕處, 則聽雅頌之音." See 《漢語大詞典》.

(212) "超然" here means "transcending above the mundane world (超脫世俗)", as in the *Book of Han - Biography of Dong Zhongshu* (《漢書•董仲舒傳》): "人受命於天, 固超然異於群生." See 《重編國語辭典修訂本》.

(213) The correct interpretation in vernacular Chinese of Line 77 should be:

"重是輕的根基, 靜是躁的主宰. 故此聖人外遊時, 笨重的行
裝物資整天不會離身(寧願走慢些). 雖然享有榮譽, 抱的也
祇會是閑居而超脫世俗的恬靜心態."
(interpreted by Kwok Kin Poon)

(214) "萬乘" here refers to "a great state (大國)", as in *Strategies of the Warring States - Strategies of Zhao III* (《戰國策•趙策三》): "秦萬乘之國, 梁亦萬乘之國." See 《重編國語辭典修訂本》.

(215) 失君 here means "losing the throne (失君位)", as annotated by Wang Bi (王弼). See 王弼《老子王弼注》. 台北: 新興書局, 1964, p.031.

(216) "轍迹" here means "trace (痕迹)", as in Liang Renfang's (梁任昉) *Da Liu Ju Shi* (《答劉居士》): "行無轍迹, 理絕心機." See 《漢語大詞典》.

(217) "瑕謫" here means "fault (過失)", as indicated in *Ministry of Education Revised Dictionary of Chinese* (《重編國語辭典修訂本》): "瑕謫, 比喻過失. 蘇軾《追餞正輔表兄至博羅賦詩為別》何時曠蕩洗瑕謫, 與君歸駕相追攀. 也作 '瑕讁'."

(218) "籌策" here refers to "an instrument for calculating arithmetic (古時計數之竹筳)", as annotated by Gao Heng (高亨). See 高亨《老子正詁》. 上海: 開明書店, 1949, p.64.

(219) "關楗" refers to "bolts and bars that keep the door shut (關

門的木閂)", as annotated by Fan Yingyuan (范應元): "楗, 拒門木也...橫曰關, 豎曰楗." See 《漢語大詞典》.

(220) "繩約" here means "ties with ropes (用繩綑綁)", as in the *Book of the Later Han - Biographies of Confucian Scholars II* (《後漢書•儒林列傳下》): "至如張溫、 皇甫嵩之徒...猶鞠躬昏主之下, 狼狠折棼之命, 散成兵, 就繩約, 而無悔心. 李賢注: 繩約, 猶拘制也." See《漢語大詞典》.

(221) "救" here means "assist (助)". In *Guangya - Shigu II* (《廣雅•釋詁二》): "救, 助也." See 中央研究院《搜詞尋字》.

(222) "故" here is "originally in their nature (本來)", as in:
   I. "故, 本然之詞也" in *The Book of Expletives* (《經傳釋詞》).
   II. "凡禮義者, 是生於聖人之偽, 非故生於人之性也. 楊倞注: 故, 猶本也" in *Xunzi - Xing E* (《荀子•性惡》).
   Source: 中央研究院《搜詞尋字》.

(223) "物" here means "affairs/matters (事情)", as in:
   I. "物, 事也" in *Yupian* (《玉篇•牛部》).
   II. "以鄉三物教萬民而賓興之: 一曰六德, 知、 仁、 聖、 義、 忠、 和; 二曰六行, 孝、 友、 睦、 姻、 任、 恤; 三曰六藝, 禮、 樂、 射、 御、 書、 數. 鄭玄注: 物, 猶事也" in *The Rites of Zhou - Offices of Earth* (《周禮•地官》).
   III. "（晉威公）去苛令三十九物, 以告屠黍. 高誘注: 物, 事" in *Master Lu's Spring and Autumn Annals - Xian Shi* (《呂氏春秋•先識》).
   Source: 中央研究院《搜詞尋字》.

Wise sages applying Tao to resolve all affairs is an example of Tao's ability to disintegrate all problems and chaos (Chapter 4 Line 11: 解其紛).

"物" should not take the meaning of "all things", for non-living things like rocks do not require any assistance from wise sages.

(224) The correct interpretation in vernacular Chinese of " 是以 聖人常善救人, 故無棄人; 常善救物, 故無棄物" should be:

"故此聖人常常依循道來幫助人, 本就不會嫌棄任何人; 也常 常依循道來幫忙做事, 本就不會厭棄任何事物."

(interpreted by Kwok Kin Poon)

(225) "要妙" here is "profound and wonderful mystery (精深微 妙)", as in Sima Guang's (司馬光) *He Shang Du Yi* (《河上督 役》): "高論探要妙, 佳句裁清新." See 《漢語大詞典》.

(226) "谿" literally means "a ravine at the bottom of a valley where all water naturally migrate toward (水注川曰谿)", as anno- tated in *Kangxi Dictionary* (《康熙字典》): "《爾雅•釋水》水注 川曰谿. 疏: 杜預曰: 谿, 亦澗也. 李巡曰: 水出於山入於川曰谿. 宋均曰: 有水曰谿, 無水曰谷."

Accordingly, in our context, "谿" is the place where all things naturally migrate toward, which means it is the most desirable place for all.

(227) "離" here means "leave (去)", as indicated in *Guangya - Shigu II* (《廣雅•釋詁二》): " 離, 去也." See 中央研究院《搜詞 尋字》.

(228) Manifestation of Tao encompasses both clear and mud- dy aspects. This is further reinforced in Chapter 41 Line 117: "the cleanest and clearest aspect of the Manifestation of Tao is obscure and muddy (大白若辱)".

(229) "忒" here is "差也 (strayed from)". See *Kangxi Dictionary* (《康熙字典》).

(230) "谷" here is similar to "谿" in Chapter 28 Line 83. The only difference is "谷" is dry without water, while "谿" is moist with water, as indicated in *Kangxi Dictionary* (《康熙字典》): "宋均 曰: 有水曰谿, 無水曰谷."

(231) "足" here means "止". See *Kangxi Dictionary* (《康熙字典》). "止" is "reach upon (至)", as in *The Book of Odes - Sacrificial odes of Lu - Pan Shui* (《詩經•魯頌•泮水》) : "魯侯戾止, 言觀其旂. 毛傳 : 止, 至也." See 中央研究院《搜詞尋字》.

(232) Wang Bi (王弼) further elaborated this "樸" as "original and genuine (真也)". See 王弼《老子王弼注》. 台北: 新興書局, 1964, p.034.

(233) "器" here is "all sorts of entities (百行/殊類)", as Wang Bi (王弼) suggested: "真散則百行出, 殊類生, 若器也." See 王弼《老子王弼注》. 台北: 新興書局, 1964, p.034.

(234) "用" here means "administrate (治理)", as in:
  I. "子產相鄭, 病將死, 謂游吉曰 : 我死後, 子必用鄭, 必以嚴涖人" in *Hanfeitzu - Nei Chu Shuo* (《韓非子•內儲說上》).
  II. "集眾思, 廣忠益, 諸葛孔明所以用蜀也" in *History of Song - Biography of Yu Jie* (《宋史•余玠傳》).
  Source: 中央研究院《搜詞尋字》.

(235) "則" here is "and (而)", as in *The Commentary of Zuo - the Third Year of Duke Zhao* (《左傳•昭公三年》) : "寡人願事君朝夕不倦, 將奉質幣以無失時, 則國家多難, 是以不獲." See 中央研究院《搜詞尋字》.

(236) "大制" here means "administrate via Tao (以大道治理天下)". See 《漢語大詞典》. Also, see footnote 237 for Wang Bi's (王弼) further elaboration on "大制".

(237) "割" here means "to discern (分)". See *Kangxi Dictionary* (《康熙字典》). On "大制不割", Wang Bi (王弼) further elaborated:
  "大制者, 以天下之心為心, 故無割也."
  "Administrating via Tao is to make the mindset of all un-

der Heaven as one's own. As such, one shall not discern nor discriminate when administrating."
(interpreted by KS Vincent Poon)
Source: 王弼《老子王弼注》. 台北: 新興書局, 1964, p.034.

(238) "為" here is "rule (治理)", as seen in *Xiao Erya - Expanding Old Words* (《小爾雅•廣詁》) : "為, 治也." See 中央研究院《搜詞尋字》.

(239) "已" here is "succeed (成)", as indicated in *Guangya - Shigu III* (《廣雅•釋詁三》) : "已, 成也." See 中央研究院《搜詞尋字》.

(240) "神器" refers to "an entity of extraordinary nature" that is formless, intangible, and cannot be commanded. Wang Bi (王弼) annotated it as "神, 無形無方也. 器, 合成也. 無形以合, 故謂之神器也". See 王弼《老子王弼注》. 台北: 新興書局, 1964, p.034.

(241) "故" here means "after all (畢竟)", as seen in *The Commentary of Zuo - the Ninth Year of Duke Xiang* (《左傳•襄公九年》) : "利物足以和義, 貞固足以幹事, 然故不可誣也." See 中央研究院《搜詞尋字》.

(242) "或" here means "is/are/have (有)", as indicated in *Guangya - Shigu I* (《廣雅•釋詁一》) : "或, 有也." See 中央研究院《搜詞尋字》.

(243) See footnote 191.

(244) "行" here means "the appearance of being emphatic and assertive (剛健貌)", as in *The Analects* (《論語》): "子路行行如也." See *Kangxi Dictionary* (《康熙字典》).

(245) "隨" here is "mild and submissive (順應)", as in:

    I. "隨, 順也" in *Guangya - Shigu I* (《廣雅‧釋詁一》).

    II. "禹敷土, 隨山刊木, 奠高山大川" in the *Book of Documents - Yu Gong* (《書經‧禹貢》).

    Source: 中央研究院《搜詞尋字》.

(246) "歔" here is "blowing through one's nose (鼻出氣爲歔)", as indicated in *The Exegesis of Six-category Characters* (《六書故》). See *Kangxi Dictionary* (《康熙字典》).

(247) "吹" here is "嘘", according to *Shuowen Jiezi* (《說文解字》):"吹, 嘘也." This "嘘" means "blowing through one's mouth (口出氣爲嘘)", as indicated in *The Exegesis of Six-category Characters* (《六書故》). See *Kangxi Dictionary* (《康熙字典》).

(248) "羸" here means "weak and frail (瘦弱)", as in *History of the Southern Dynasties - Biography of Zhou Panlong* (《南史‧周盤龍傳》):"形甚羸而臨軍勇果, 諸將莫逮." See《重編國語辭典修訂本》.

(249) "挫" here means "humble (屈折)", as seen in *Zhuangzi - Heaven and Earth* (《莊子‧天地》):"不以物挫志之謂完. 成玄英疏：挫, 屈也. 一毀譽, 混榮辱, 不以世物屈節, 其德完全." See 中央研究院《搜詞尋字》.

(250) "隳" here means "wreck or obliterate (毀)", as indicated in *Kangxi Dictionary* (《康熙字典》):"隳與毀通." If one does not "humble (挫)" to Tao, then one shall wreck oneself by Tao. This directly echoes Chapter 22 Line 66: "Ones that are humble and submissive to Tao can be fully preserved (曲則全)."

(251) The correct interpretation in vernacular Chinese of Line 87 should be:

    "畢竟在人裏面, 有些剛健, 有些溫順; 有些慣以鼻呼氣, 有些

慣以口呼氣; 有些強壯, 有些羸弱; 有些挫服於道而自全, 有
些不服於道而自毀."

(interpreted by Kwok Kin Poon)

(252) "甚" here means "indulgence (溺愛/溺好)", as in *Shuowen Jiezi Zhu* (《說文解字注》) : "(甚)尤安樂也, ...人情所尤安樂者, 必在所溺愛也."

(253) "奢" here means "conceitedness (自誇/誇張)", as indicated in *Selections of Refined Literature - Sima Xiangru - Zi Xu Fu* (《文選•司馬相如•子虛賦》) : "今足下不稱楚王之德厚, 而盛推雲夢以為高, 奢言淫樂而顯侈靡." See 《重編國語辭典修訂本》.

(254) "泰" here means "pride and arrogance (驕縱/傲慢)", as supported by
    I. "泰, 驕也" indicated in *Yupian* (《玉篇》).
    II. "拜下, 禮也; 今拜乎上, 泰也. 何晏集解 : 時臣驕泰, 故於上拜" in *The Analects - Zi Han* (《論語•子罕》).
    III. "是故君子有大道, 必忠信以得之, 驕泰以失之" in *The Classic of Rites - The Great Learning* (《禮記•大學》).
    Source: 中央研究院《搜詞尋字》.

(255) The correct interpretation in vernacular Chinese of Line 88 should be:
    "故此聖人丟掉溺好, 丟掉自誇, 丟掉驕縱."
    (interpreted by Kwok Kin Poon)

(256) "強" here means "violent (暴)", as indicated *Guangyun* (《廣韻•陽韻》) : "強, 暴也." See 中央研究院《搜詞尋字》.

(257) The correct interpretation in vernacular Chinese of "以道佐人主者, 不以兵強天下" should be:
    "用道來輔助君主的人, 不會以武力來鎮壓天下."
    (interpreted by Kwok Kin Poon)

(258) "好" here means "always easily happen (常常容易發生)", as in Erya (《爾雅•釋草》):"竹篇蓄. 郭璞注：似小藜, 赤莖節, 好生道旁. " See 中央研究院《搜詞尋字》.

(259) "還" here means "counter results (償還/回擊)." See 中央研究院《搜詞尋字》and 《漢語字詞典》.

(260) Why "weeds and thorns (荊棘) shall rise"? The presence of military operations promotes looting and hinders farming. As such, fields will become infertile. Such is succinctly elaborated by Wang Bi (王弼):

> "言師凶害之物也. 無有所濟, 必有所傷, 賊害人民, 殘荒田畝, 故曰荊棘生焉."
>
> Source: 王弼《老子王弼注》. 台北: 新興書局, 1964, pp.035-036.

(261) "壯" here is "mighty and fierce (武力暴興)", as annotated by Wang Bi (王弼):

> "壯, 武力暴興, 喻以兵強於天下者也."
>
> Source: 王弼《老子王弼注》. 台北: 新興書局, 1964, p.036.

(262) "老" here is "frail and wither (衰弱/衰落)", as in:

I. "老, 朽也" in *Shiming* (《釋名》).

II. "師直為壯, 曲為老" in *The Commentary of Zuo - the Twenty-eighth Year of Duke Xi* (《左傳•僖公二十八年》).

III. "治之道, 美不老" in *Xunzi - Cheng Xiang* (《荀子•成相》).

Source: 中央研究院《搜詞尋字》.

(263) The correct interpretation in vernacular Chinese of Line 91 should be:

> "人若壯猛則必自衰弱, 這叫不依循道. 不依循道, 早就完蛋啦!"

(interpreted by Kwok Kin Poon)

(264) "佳" here means "the finest (善/好)", as indicated in *Shuowen Jiezi Zhu* (《說文解字注》).

(265) See footnote 191.

(266) See footnote 16.

(267) "居" here is "at peaceful times (安)", as in:
 I. "居, 安也" in *Yupian* (《玉篇》).
 II. "豈世世賢哉, 其勢居然也" in *Records of the Grand Historian - Annals of Qin Shi Huang* (《史記•秦始皇本紀》).
 Source: 中央研究院《搜詞尋字》.

(268) For "left" and "right", see Line 94.

(269) "恬淡" here is "simplicity and tranquillity (清靜淡泊) ", as in:
 I. "夫虛靜恬淡, 寂寞無為者, 天地之平而道德之至也" in *Zhuangzi - The Way of Heaven* (《莊子•天道》).
 II. "今上治天下, 未能恬倓" in *Records of the Grand Historian - Annals of Qin Shi Huang* (《史記•秦始皇本紀》).
 Source: 《漢語大詞典》.

(270) "樂" here is "desirable (欲)", as indicated in *Jiyun* (《集韻》). See 中央研究院《搜詞尋字》.

(271) "得志" here means "have one's aspirations realized (達到自己的志願)", as in:
 I. "白賁无咎, 上得志也" in the *Book of Changes - Bi* (《易經•賁卦》).
 II. "故四民有業, 各以得志為樂, 惟達者為能通之" in *Selections of Refined Literature - Xi Kang - Yu Shan Ju Yuan Jue Jiao Shu* (《文選•嵇康•與山巨源絕交書》).

Source: 《重編國語辭典修訂本》.

(272) "尚" here is "honour (尊崇/崇尚)", as in:
 I. "尚, 貴也" in *Jiyun* (《集韻》).
 II. "尚, 崇也, 又尊也" in *Zihui* (《字彙》).
 III. "君子尚消息盈虛, 天行也" in the *Book of Changes - Bo* (《易經•剝卦》).
Source: 中央研究院《搜詞尋字》.

(273) It can be said then that the commanding general-in-chief who oversees more killings carries more bad omen.

(274) "處" here is "treat and deal with (處置/辦理)", as in *Records of the Three Kingdoms - Book of Shu - Biography of Zhuge Liang* (《三國志•蜀志•諸葛亮傳》) : "將軍量力而處之." See 中央研究院《搜詞尋字》.

(275) "悲泣" here is "weep with great sorrows (悲傷哭泣)", as in the *Book of Han - Treatise on Punishment and Law* (《漢書•刑法志》) : "齊太倉令淳于公有罪當刑, 詔獄逮繫長安...其少女緹縈, 自傷悲泣." See 《漢語大詞典》.

(276) "小" here is "puny and humble (低微)", as in *Mengzi - Wan Zhang II* (《孟子•萬章下》): "不辭小官." See 《漢語大詞典》.

(277) "均" here is "potter's wheel (鈞)", as indicated in :
 I. "漢志曰, 鈞者、均也. 陽施其氣, 陰化其物, 皆得其成就平均也. 按古多叚鈞爲均" in *Shuowen Jiezi Zhu* (《說文解字注》).
 II. "(均)又通作鈞.《書經•泰誓》厥罪惟鈞" in *Kangxi Dictionary* (《康熙字典》).
This "鈞" here refers to the "Great Potter's Wheel (大鈞)", which is "Nature (天也)", as further elaborated in *Kangxi Dictionary*:
 "《前漢•賈誼傳》大鈞播物, 块圠無垠.註: 如淳曰：陶者作

器于鈞上, 此以造物爲大鈞也. 言造化爲人, 亦猶陶之造瓦
耳."

It can be said then that the people can be naturally enlightened and uplifted by Nature (大鈞) from above as if clays naturally rise towards the top as the "potter's wheel (鈞)" spins.
In the *Book of Han - Biography of Dong Zhongshu* (《漢書•董
仲舒傳》), this analogy was used as a metaphor for the people
(the clay below) following their ruler (towards the top):

"夫上之化下, 下之從上, 猶泥之在鈞."

"Alas, the ones above (rulers) enlighten and uplift the
ones below (the people), the ones below follow the ones
above. This is as if clays naturally rise on a potter's
wheel."
(interpreted by KS Vincent Poon)
Source: 《重編國語辭典修訂本》.

As such, "自均" actually means "to naturally follow the ruler".
Most, however, contend "均" is "evenly (平均)" or "equitably (
公平)" and link "民莫之令而自均" with "天地相合, 以降甘露" to
generate the following incorrect interpretation:

"When Nature and Earth work together, the rain naturally
drops from the skies evenly and equitably without any
command from the people."

This interpretation is incorrect because:

I.   The phrase "民莫之令" obviously means "people (民)"
     "need not be commanded (莫之令)", and so "民莫之令"
     has nothing to do with Nature.

II. Tao does not act "evenly" or "equitably", for it does not
     follow the human concept of benevolence (Chapter
     5 Line 13: 天地不仁, 以萬物為芻狗). As such, Tao
     allows natural disasters to occur without relief. Indeed,
     there are plenty of catastrophic floods and droughts
     each year around the world. Why no relief from Tao?
     Even wise sages do not know (Chapter 73 Line 196: 聖
     人猶難之).

III. This chapter focuses on advising rulers. It makes little sense for Laozi here to have stated "Tao acts without any command from the people". Further, by default, people can never command Tao, so Laozi would have been unreasonable and unnecessary to say it here.

(278) The correct interpretation in vernacular Chinese of "民莫之令而自均" should be:

"百姓無需命令, 也自會遵從上面的君主."

(interpreted by Kwok Kin Poon)

(279) See Chapter 1 Line 1.

(280) "制" here is "make/generate (製造)", as in:

I. "制, 造也" in *Zihui* (《字彙•刀部》).

II. "制彼裳衣, 勿士行枚" in *The Book of Odes - Odes Of Bin - Dong Shan* (《詩經•豳風•東山》).

Source: 中央研究院 《搜詞尋字》.

(281) "Identifiable and with names (有名)" here is "Manifestation of Tao (德)". See Chapter 1 Line 1.

(282) See Chapter 1 Line 1.

(283) "知止" here is "to know where to reach and when to stop (知其所應止之處)", as in *The Classic of Rites - The Great Learning* (《禮記•大學》): "知止而后有定, 定而后能靜. 朱熹《章句》, 止者, 所當止之地, 即至善之所在也." See 《重編國語辭典修訂本》.

(284) The correct interpretation in vernacular Chinese of Line 96 should be:

"道生出了德. 德既已有, 便須知道自己所應至和所應停的地方. 知道自己所應至和所應停的地方, 就可以沒危殆了."

(interpreted Kwok Kin Poon)

(285) "譬" here is "understand (通曉)", as in the *Book of the Later Han - Biography of Bao Yong* (《後漢書•鮑永傳》) : "若乃言之者雖誠, 而聞之未譬. 李賢注：譬, 猶曉也." See 中央研究院《搜詞尋字》.

(286) See Chapter 16 Line 50.

(287) This is because overcoming one's selfish desires to follow the natural and selfless Tao is next to impossible.

(288) "強行" is "steadfastly act (勤能行之)", as annotated by Wang Bi (王弼):
"勤能行之, 其志必獲, 故曰強行者有志矣."
Source: 王弼《老子王弼注》. 台北: 新興書局, 1964, p.039.

(289) "有志" is "have one's aspirations realized (其志必獲)".
Ibid.

(290) "所" here is "the way or principle (道/理)", as in *The Classic of Rites - Questions of Duke Ai* (《禮記•哀公問》) : "求得當欲, 不以其所. 鄭玄注：所, 猶道也." See 中央研究院《搜詞尋字》.

(291) Why "not losing the way of Tao enables one to last long"? Wang Bi (王弼) annotated:
"以明自察, 量力而行, 不失其所, 必獲久長矣."
"Applying Tao's enlightenment to introspect oneself makes one act according to one's capacity, and so one shall not lose one's way in following Tao. Hence, one shall be able to last long indeed."
(interpreted by KS Vincent Poon)
Source: 王弼《老子王弼注》. 台北: 新興書局, 1964, p.039.

(292) How can one die but not perish? Wang Bi (王弼) annotat-

ed:

> "身沒而道猶存."
>
> "The body is gone, yet one's way of Tao still exists."
>
> (interpreted by KS Vincent Poon)
>
> Source: 王弼《老子王弼注》. 台北: 新興書局, 1964,
> p.040.

One's body always expires and shall eventually return to the eternal Tao (Chapter 16 Line 49: 各復歸其根), but one's way of Tao lives on forever.

(293) "氾" here is "flows and permeates everywhere (氾濫/無所不適)", as annotated by Wang Bi (王弼): "言道氾濫, 無所不適." See 王弼《老子王弼注》. 台北: 新興書局, 1964, p.040.

(294) "左右" here is "applies itself in all directions and so influences all", as annotated by Wang Bi (王弼): "可左右上下周旋而用, 則無所不至也." See 王弼《老子王弼注》. 台北: 新興書局, 1964, p.040.

(295) "衣" here is "encompasses and embraces (覆蓋)", as in *Guanzi - Du Di* (《管子•度地》) : "大雨, 堤防可衣者衣之." See 中央研究院《搜詞尋字》.

(296) "終" here is "always (常)", as in *Mo Yze - Exaltation of the Virtuous I* (《墨子•尚賢上》): "故官無常貴, 而民無終賤." See 中央研究院《搜詞尋字》.

   Accordingly, "終不" means "always no" or "never".

(297) "大象" refers to the phenomenon manifested by Tao. This same "大象" can also be seen in Chapter 41 Line 117.

(298) "往" here is "follow and yearn for (歸向)", as indicated in *Jiyun* (《集韻》) : "往, 歸嚮也." See 中央研究院《搜詞尋字》.

(299) "餌" here is "delicacies (餅/餻)", as indicated in *Kangxi*

Dictionary (《康熙字典》).

(300) "過客" here is "passing guests (旅客)" as in Hanfeitzu - Wu Du (《韓非子•五蠹》) : "非疏骨肉愛過客也, 多少之心異也." See 《漢語大詞典》.

(301) "止" here is "an auxiliary word used at the end of a sentence as an intonation (語氣助詞)", as in:
I. "止, 語末助詞" in *Ciqua* (《詞詮》).
II. "既曰歸止, 曷又懷止? 高亨注 : 止, 語氣詞" in The Book of Odes - Odes Of Qi - Nan Shan 《詩經•齊風•南山》.
Source: 中央研究院《搜詞尋字》.

(302) "出口" here means "expressed in or described with words(出言)", as in Mei Yaochen's (梅堯臣) *Feng He Zi Hua Chi Guo Yu Ru Lai Yin Xi Xuan* (《奉和子華持國玉汝來飲西軒》) : "諸君竟相先, 出口論莫奪." See 《漢語大詞典》.

(303) "無味" here means "ordinary and not distinct (平淡無奇)" as in Han Yu's (韓愈) *Song Qiong Wen* (《送窮文》) : "凡所以使吾面目可憎、語言無味者, 皆子之志也." See 《漢語大詞典》.

(304) "不足" here is "cannot (不能)", as in *Xunzi - Zheng Lun* (《荀子•正論》) : "淺不足以測深, 愚不足以謀知." See 《漢語大詞典》.

(305) "既" here is "exhausted (盡)", as in:
I. "既, 盡也" in *Guangya - Shigu I* (《廣雅•釋詁一》).
II. "吾與汝既其文, 未既其實, 而固得道與" in *Zhuangzi -The Normal Course for Rulers and Kings* (《莊子•應帝王》).
Source: 中央研究院《搜詞尋字》.

(306) "將欲" here means "plan to (將要/打算)", as seen in Li Ba's

(李白) *Zeng Wanglun* (《贈汪倫》): "李白乘舟將欲行, 忽聞岸上踏歌聲." See 《漢語大詞典》.

(307) "廢" here is "ruin (傾圮/坍塌)", as indicated in *Shuowen Jiezi* (《說文解字》): "廢, 屋頓也."

(308) "興" is "raise and establish (建立)", as in the *Book of Han -Biographies of Yuan Ang and Chao Cuo* (《漢書•爰盎晁錯傳》): "臣聞漢興以來, 胡虜數入邊地." See 中央研究院《搜詞尋字》.

(309) "Wei (微)" refers to the entity that cannot be held nor grasped. It is manifested by Tao and is part of "One". See Chapter 14 Line 42.

Line 104 outlines the counteracting property of Tao (Chapter 40 Line 115: 反者道之動), which counters one's selfish actions and desires.

(310) If a fish leaves its natural habitat, it will be more likely to be preyed on or captured. Hence, one should not stray away from the natural and nurturing Tao, for one shall be exposed to unnecessary harm (Chapter 16 Line 50: 不知常, 妄作凶).

(311) "國之利器" here is "instruments that benefit the state", which include laws, law enforcement, as well as the military, as seen below:

I. "利器, 利國之器也." See 王弼《老子王弼注》. 台北: 新興書局, 1964, p.042.

II. "賞罰者, 國家之利器也, 所以懲惡勸善, 不以喜加賞, 不以怒增刑" in *Annals of Han - Annals of Emperor Yuan I* (《漢紀•元帝紀上》). See 《重編國語辭典修訂本》.

Such instruments should not be heavily relied upon in governing, for the people benefits the most simply by just following Tao.

(312) The correct interpretation in vernacular Chinese of

"國之利器不可以示人" should be:

　　"有利治理國家的工具(例如軍隊、律法等), 切不可以輕易展
　　示百姓."

　　(interpreted by Kwok Kin Poon)

(313) "將" here is "shall/will/must (必)", as in:
　　I. "將, 必然之詞也" in *Jing Zhuan Shi Ci Bu* (《經傳釋詞
　　　補》).
　　II. "難不已, 將自斃" in *The Commentary of Zuo - the First
　　　Year of Duke Min* (《左傳‧閔公元年》).
　　Source: 中央研究院《搜詞尋字》.

(314) "自化" here means "naturally live and propagate (自然化
育)", as in *The Classic of Rites - Yue Ji* (《禮記‧樂記》)："樂者,
天地之和也, ...和, 故百物皆化. 鄭玄注：化, 猶生也." See 中央研
究院《搜詞尋字》.

(315) See footnote 313.

(316) This "unidentifiable and nameless (無名)" is Tao. See
Chapter 1 Line 1.

(317) "亦" here is "merely just (祇是)", as in:
　　I. "亦者, 不過之義" in *Jing Ci Yan Shi* (《經詞衍釋》).
　　II. "寡人之從君而西也, 亦晉之妖夢是踐" in *The Commen-
　　　tary of Zuo - The Fifteenth Year of Duke Xi* (《左傳‧僖
　　　公十五年》).
　　III. "王亦不好士也, 何患無士" in *Strategies of the Warring
　　　States - Strategies of Qi IV* (《戰國策‧齊策四》).
　　Source: 中央研究院《搜詞尋字》.

(318) "將" here is "adhere to (遵奉/秉承)", as in:
　　I. "束帛將命于朝. 鄭玄注: 將, 猶奉也" in the *Book of
　　　Etiquette and Ceremonial - Rites of Courtesy Calls* (《
　　　儀禮‧聘禮》).

II. "人之所以貴於禽獸者, 智慮; 智慮之所將者, 禮義" in
Liezi - Yang Zhu (《列子•楊朱》).
Source: 中央研究院《搜詞尋字》.

(319) See footnote 313.

(320) "定" here is "settle in serenity (安)", as indicated in *Shuowen Jiezi* (《說文解字》).

(321) This "德" here is Confucian "moral virtue (德行)" not Laozi's "Manifestation of Tao (Te, 德)". This is because:
I. This entire chapter (Lines 108-111) focuses on criticizing Confucian values like "benevolence (仁)", "righteousness (義)", and "propriety (禮)".
II. Manifestation of Tao (德) does not exist in high (上 德) or low (下德) levels . In fact, Manifestation of Tao nurtures all things (Chapter 51 Line 139: 德畜之) and so exists without different levels.
III. If "德" here means "Manifestation of Tao", then the subsequent phrase "失道而後德" in Line 110 makes no sense. "Manifestation of Tao" is a display of Tao's action, and so losing Tao would simultaneously lose its Manifestation as well. How then can Manifestation of Tao (德) independently exist without Tao (道)?

(322) "下德不失德, 是以無德" provides one of the sharpest rebukes of Confucius teaching. Laozi reasoned that it is those who inherently lack "morals" will fear losing "morals". Accordingly, those who espouse not to lose "morals", like Confucius, are actually the ones inherently without "morals".
The correct interpretation in vernacular Chinese of "上德不 德, 是以有德; 下德不失德, 是以無德" should be:
"上等德行的人無需德行, 因此亦正顯示他本已具有德行; 下 等德行的人不想失去德行, 因此反顯露他本來就是沒甚德 行."

(interpreted by Kwok Kin Poon)

(323) "以" here is "reason (因也)", as in *The Book of Odes - Odes Of Bei* (《詩經•邶風》): "何其久也, 必有以也." See *Kangxi Dictionary* (《康熙字典》).

(324) Why is there actually no reason for those with benevolence to act? This is because the Universe does not follow the concept of being benevolent (Chapter 5 Line 13: 天地不仁, 以萬物為芻狗), and so ultimately, all their efforts are in vain. There is then actually no point for them to do anything.

(325) "攘臂" here means "rolling up one's sleeves and bare one's arms (捋起袖子, 伸出胳膊)", as in *Mengzi - Jin Xin II* (《孟子•盡心下》): "馮婦攘臂下車, 眾皆悅之." See 《重編國語辭典修訂本》.

(326) "扔" here means "coercively drag (引也)", as indicated in *Kangxi Dictionary* (《康熙字典》).

(327) See footnote 321.

(328) In *Zhuangzi - The Way of Heaven* (《莊子•天道》), Laozi was recorded to have chastised Confucius, a chief proponent of propriety, in a similar manner: "Ah! Master, you are introducing disorder into the nature of man! (意！夫子亂人之性也！)" See James Legge's *The Sacred Books of China, The Texts of Taoism*.

(329) "前識" here is "the ability to foresee (先見之明)", as annotated by Wang Bi (王弼):
"前識者, 前人而識也."
Source: 王弼《老子王弼注》. 台北: 新興書局, 1964, p.048.

(330) "大丈夫" here is "those who have great aspirations (有志氣而勇敢剛毅的男子)", as in *Mengzi - Teng Wen Gong II* (《孟子•滕文公下》) :「富貴不能淫, 貧賤不能移, 威武不能屈, 此之謂大丈夫." See《重編國語辭典修訂本》.

(331) See Chapter 42 Line 119 for more elaboration on "One".

(332) "貞" here is "proper order (正)" as in:
  I. "貞, 正也" in *Guangya - Shigu I* (《廣雅•釋詁一》).
  II. "一人元良, 萬邦以貞" in the *Book of Documents - Tai Jia III* (《書經•太甲下》).
  Source：中央研究院《搜詞尋字》.

(333) "恐" is "perhaps (恐怕)", as in:
  I. "恐, 疑也" in *Guangyun* (《廣韻•用韻》).
  II. "學如不及, 猶恐失之" in *The Analects - Tai Bo* (《論語•泰伯》).
  Source：中央研究院《搜詞尋字》.

(334) "發" here is "shake and quake (動)", as annotated in *Kangxi Dictionary* (《康熙字典》): "《老子•道德經》地無以寧, 將恐發. 發, 動也."

(335) "貴高" here means "noble (高貴)", as in the *Book of Song - Biography of Wang Jingwen* (《宋書•王景文傳》)："貴高有危殆之懼, 卑賤有溝壑之憂." See 《漢語大詞典》.

(336) "蹶" here means "overthrow (顛覆)", as in in *Xunzi - Cheng Xiang* (《荀子•成相》)："主之孽, 讒人達, 賢能遁逃國乃蹶. 楊倞注：蹶, 顛覆也." See 中央研究院《搜詞尋字》.

(337) "Lowly and primitive (下)" can be considered to be "One", for it is the foundation of all things. See Chapter 39 Line 113.

(338) "不穀" here means "incapable (不善)", with which ancient

rulers humbly designate themselves. This can be seen in *The Commentary of Zuo - the Fourth Year of Duke Xi* (《左傳•僖公四年》)："齊侯曰：豈不穀是為？先君之好是繼, 與不穀同好, 如何？" See 《重編國語辭典修訂本》.

(339) "致" here means "possess (取得)", as in *The Analects - Zi Zhang* (《論語•子張》)："君子學以致其道." See 中央研究院《搜詞尋字》.

(340) "輿" literally means "a carriage (車)". See *Kangxi Dictionary* (《康熙字典》).

"數輿", hence, refers to the number (數) of horses pulling a carriage (輿). In the Shang-Zhou era (商周時代), the number of horses pulling one's carriage reflected one's social status. The greater the number of horses, the higher the social status. Such custom is recorded in the *Book of Song - Li V - Wan Du Ji* (《宋書•禮五•王度記》): "天子駕六, 諸侯駕五, 卿駕四, 大夫三, 士二, 庶人一." See 沈約, 《宋書》卷十八禮五. 北京: 中華書局, 1974 , p.495.

(341) "璖" here should mean "the appearance of a jade stone (玉貌)", as indicated in *The Comprehensive Dictionary of Ancient and Contemporary Rhymes* (《古今韻會》). See *Kangxi Dictionary* (《康熙字典》).

Accordingly, "璖璖如玉" can be interpreted as "appear as a precious jade".

In the past, many interpreted "璖璖" as "rare and precious (稀少珍貴)" by quoting an annotation by Heshang Gong (河上公):

"璖璖喻少, 落落(珞珞)喻多. 玉少故見貴, 石多故見賤. 言不欲如玉為人所貴, 如石為人所賤, 當處其中也."
Source: 《漢語大詞典》.

Heshang Gong was incorrect, for "the middle ground (其中)" is never the ideal position, but the very bottom is. See Chapter 66 Line 178: "江海所以能為百谷王者, 以其善下之, 故能為百谷王."

See footnote 342 for more elaborations on "琭琭如玉".

(342) "珞" here means "a necklace (瓔珞/頸飾)" as indicated in *Yupian* (《玉篇》). See *Kangxi Dictionary* (《康熙字典》).

Accordingly, "珞珞如石" can be interpreted as "appearing as conspicuous gemstones on a necklace".

Some incorrectly contended "珞珞如石" means "one should be as strong as stones in holding one's principles". This is incorrect, for this directly contradicts Laozi's assertion of the strong shall come to its end very soon. See Chapter 30 Line 91: "物壯則老, 是謂不道, 不道早已."

"不欲琭琭如玉, 珞珞如石" advises one not to pursue being showy and conspicuous, even if one is superior or noble. Hence, "wise sages wear rags as their clothing while bearing jades within them" (Chapter 70 Line 191: 是以聖人被褐懷玉). As such, Wang Bi (王弼) also wrote:

> "玉石琭琭珞珞, 體盡於形, 故不欲也."
>
> Source: 王弼《老子王弼注》. 台北: 新興書局, 1964, p.051.

(343) The correct interpretation in vernacular Chinese of "故致數輿無輿. 不欲琭琭如玉, 珞珞如石" should be:

> "所以, 那些擁有數馬拉動車子的王侯公卿的高貴, 本就是建築在連車子也沒有的貧困平民的低賤之上. 他們當不想自己耀目如珍貴的寶玉, 顯眼如頸上項鏈的寶石."
>
> (interpreted by Kwok Kin Poon)

(344) 反 is "返", which is "restore/return back (返回)", as in:

I. "吾自衛反魯, 然後樂正,《雅》《頌》各得其所" in *The Analects - Zi Han* (《論語•子罕》).

II. "悔相道之不察兮, 延佇乎吾將反" in *Verses of Chu - Li Sa* (《楚辭•離騷》).

III. "寒暑易節, 始一反焉" in *Liezi - Tang Wen* (《列子•湯問》).

Source: See 中央研究院《搜詞尋字》.

(345) "動" here means "action (行動)", as in:
    I. "動, 作也" in *Erya - Shigu II* (《爾雅•釋詁下》).
    II. "擬之而後言, 議之而後動" in the *Book of Changes -
    The Great Treatise I* (《易經•繫辭上》).
    Source: See 中央研究院《搜詞尋字》.

(346) The correct interpretation in vernacular Chinese of "反者道
之動" should be:
    "使一切復返於道, 這就是道的力量和行動."
    (interpreted by Kwok Kin Poon)

(347) "建言" here means "a saying from the past (古語/古諺)", as
in Yan Fu's (嚴復) *On Our Salvation* (《救亡決論》) : "建言有
之：天不變, 地不變, 道亦不變." See《漢語大詞典》.

(348) See footnote 31.

(349) "纇纇" here means "rough and uneven (不平)". See《漢語
大字典》.

(350) See Chapter 28 Line 83.

(351) 辱 here is "污濁", as indicated in *Guangya - Shigu III* (《廣
雅•釋詁三》) : "辱, 污也." See 中央研究院《搜詞尋字》.

(352) "廣" here is "generous and magnanimous (寬廣)", as in:
    I. "廣，闊也。" in *Zihui* (《字彙》).
    II. "漢之廣矣，不可泳思。" in *The Book of Odes -
    Odes Of Zhou And The South -* (《詩經•周南•漢廣》).
    Source: 中央研究院《搜詞尋字》.

(353) "建" here is "steadfast and sturdy (健)", as annotated by
Yu Yue (俞樾) in *Zhuzi Pingyi - Laozi* (《諸子平議•老子》): "建
德若偷. 建, 當讀為健.《釋名•釋言語》曰：健, 建也. 能有所建為
也. 是建、健音同而義亦得通. 健德若偷, 言剛健之德, 反若偷惰

也, 正與上句廣德若不足一律." See《漢語大詞典》.

(354) "偷" here is "weak and frail (薄也)". See *Kangxi Dictionary* (《康熙字典》).

(355) "質" here is "primitive and simple (樸實/樸素)", as in:
  I. "原始要終, 以爲質也" in the *Book of Changes - The Great Treatise* (《易經•繫辭》). See *Kangxi Dictionary* (《康熙字典》)
  II. "質, 樸也" in *Yupian* (《玉篇》). See 中央研究院《搜詞尋字》.
  III. "夫君子取情而去貌, 好質而惡飾" in *Hanfeitzu - Explaining Laozi* (《韓非子•解老》). See 中央研究院《搜詞尋字》.

(356) "真" here is "pure and unadulterated (純正/不虛假)", as in *Zhuangzi - Tian Zifang* (《莊子•田子方》)："其為人也真." See 《重編國語辭典修訂本》.

(357) "渝" here is "become tainted (變汙)", as indicated in *Shuowen Jiezi* (《說文解字》).

(358) "方" here is "rectangular (矩)", as indicated in *Jiyun* (《集韻》). See 中央研究院《搜詞尋字》. For more elaborations on "大方", please see footnote 359.

(359) "隅" here is "corner (角)", as indicated in *Yupian* (《玉篇》). See *Kangxi Dictionary* (《康熙字典》).
   Why "the most rectangular shape has no corners (大方無隅)"? In calculus, countless infinitely small rectangular edges join up to form a circle, which has no corner.

(360) "器" here means "worldly tangible objects (有形的具體事物)", as in the *Book of Changes - The Great Treatise I* (《易經•繫辭上》): "形而上者謂之道, 形而下者謂之器." See 中央研究院

《搜詞尋字》. Also, see "神器" in Chapter 29 Line 86.

(361) The correct interpretation in vernacular Chinese of "大器晚成" should be:

"最大的具體事物(德), 是需要長時間來漸漸完成的."

(interpreted by Kwok Kin Poon)

(362) See footnote 297.

(363) "隱"is "unimaginably and wonderfully (微妙/不可見)", as in:
   I. "隱, 微也" in *Erya - Shigu* (《爾雅•釋詁》). See 中央研究院《搜詞尋字》.
   II. "探賾索隱, 鉤深致遠, 以定天下之吉凶" in the *Book of Changes - The Great Treatise I* (《易經•繫辭上》). See 中央研究院《搜詞尋字》.
   III. "隱, 小則不可見" in *Shuowen Jiezi Zhu* (《說文解字注》). See *Kangxi Dictionary* (《康熙字典》).

(364) See Chapter 1 Line 1.

(365) "唯" here is "without exception/only (衹有/衹是)", as in:
   I. "唯, 獨也" in *Guangya - Shigu III* (《廣雅•釋詁三》).
   II. "惟, 獨. 或作唯" in *The Book of Expletives* (《經傳釋詞》).
   III. "盈天地之間者唯萬物" in the *Book of Changes - Xu Gua* (《易經•序卦》).
   IV. "芳與澤其雜糅兮, 唯昭質其猶未虧" in *Verses of Chu - Li Sa* (《楚辭•離騷》).
   Source: 中央研究院《搜詞尋字》.

(366) "貸" here means "supplying and furnishing (施予/給予)", as in:
   I. "貸, 施也. 謂我施人曰貸也" in *Shuowen Jiezi Zhu* (《說文解字注》).
   II. "貸, 予也" in *Guangya - Shigu III* (《廣雅•釋詁三》).

III. "宋公子鮑禮於國人, 宋饑, 竭其粟而貸之" in *The Commentary of Zuo - the Sixteenth Year of Duke Wen* (《左傳•文公十六年》).

Source: 中央研究院《搜詞尋字》.

(367) For more elaborations on "One", see Chapter 14 Line 43, footnote 90, Chapter 22 Line 66, and Chapter 39 Line 112.

(368) "Two" can be thought of as a pair of complementary opposing forces, be it negative and positive or male and female. In Chinese, these two opposing forces are usually represented as "Yin (陰)" and "Yang (陽)".

(369) "Three" can be thought of as a third entity that is generated by the interactions between the "Two" opposing forces.

(370) See footnote 11.

(371) "強梁" here is "the brutal and the strong (強勁有力/剛強橫暴)", as in Kuan Huan's (桓寬) Yan Tie Lun《鹽鐵論》: "剛者折, 柔者卷. 故季由以強梁死, 宰我以柔弱殺." See《漢語大詞典》.

(372) "不得其死" here means "do not reap a natural and pleasant death (不得善終)", as in *The Analects - Xian Jin* (《論語•先進》) : "若由也, 不得其死然. 何晏集解, 孔曰 : 不得以壽終." See《重編國語辭典修訂本》.

(373) "父" here is "甫", See *Kangxi Dictionary* (《康熙字典》).
This "甫 is " starting point/point of origin (始/起初)", as in:
  I. "甫, 始也" in *Yupian* (《玉篇•用部》).
  II. "甫, 以男子始冠之偶, 引伸為始也" in *Shuowen Jiezi Zhu* (《說文解字注》).
  Source: 中央研究院《搜詞尋字》.

(374) The correct interpretation in vernacular Chinese of Line

121 should be:

"人們所教化的, 我也用它來教化人. '剛強橫暴的人不得善
終', 我必用它作為教化的開始."
(interpreted by Kwok Kin Poon)

(375) "馳騁" here is "runs/gallops freely (自由遊走)", as in *Huainanzi - Jingshen* (《淮南子•精神》)︰ "血氣滔蕩而不休, 則精神馳
騁於外而不守矣." See 《重編國語辭典修訂本》.

(376) "無有" here is "something without shape nor form (不見形
相的東西)", as in *Master Lu's Spring and Autumn Annals - Shen Fen* (《呂氏春秋•審分》)︰ "清靜以公, 神通乎六合, 德耀乎海外,
意觀乎無窮, 譽流乎無止, 此之定性於大湫, 命之曰無有. 高誘注︰
無有, 無形也. 道無形, 無形言得道也." See 《漢語大詞典》.

(377) "無閒 (無間)" here is "infinitely small spaces (無間/沒有空
隙/極微小處)" as in *Selections of Refined Literature - Yang Xiong - Jie Chao* (《文選•揚雄•解嘲》)︰ "大者含元氣, 細者入無間. 李
善注︰無間, 言至微也." See 《漢語大詞典》.

(378) See footnote 10.

(379) See footnote 11.

(380) "及" here means "attained (至也)", as indicated in
Guangyun (《廣韻》). See *Kangxi Dictionary* (《康熙字典》).

(381) "多" here means "important (重)", as indicated in *Shuowen Jiezi* (《說文解字》).

(382) "病" here is "suffering (苦)", as in *The Commentary of Zuo - the Sixteenth Year of Duke Xiang* (《左傳•襄二十四年》)︰ "范
宣子為政, 諸侯之幣重, 鄭人病之." See *Kangxi Dictionary* (《康熙字典》).

(383) See footnote 283.

(384) "長久" here means "living long (長壽)", as in:

I. "敢問治身, 奈何而可以長久" in *Zhuangzi - Letting Be and Exercising Forbearance* (《莊子•在宥》).

II. "臣獨何人, 以堪長久, 常恐先朝露, 填溝壑" in Cao Zhi's (曹植) *Qiu zi shi biao* (《求自試表》).

Source: 《漢語大詞典》.

(385) See footnote 31. Laozi had always cherished acting in one's natural way and would have never asked one to be pretending or disingenuous.

(386) "弊" here means "exhausted (竭/盡)", as in *Guanzi - Chi Mi* (《管子•侈靡》)："澤不弊而養足. 尹知章注：弊, 竭也." See 中央研究院《搜詞尋字》.

(387) "沖" here is "hollow and empty (空虛)", as in:

I. "沖, 沖虛" in *Yupian* (《玉篇》).

II. "原流泉淳, 沖而徐盈. 高誘注：沖, 虛也" in *Huainanzi - Yuan Tao* (《淮南子•原道》).

Source: 中央研究院《搜詞尋字》.

(388) "大成若缺, 其用不弊; 大盈若沖, 其用不窮" describes Tao, while subsequent "大直若屈, 大巧若拙, 大辯若訥" applies to humans.

Applying Tao's way to discuss human social norms and behaviours is a key feature in Laozi's arguments.

(389) "直" here is "strict and proper (正見)", as indicated in *Shuowen Jiezi Zhu* (《說文解字注》)："(直)正見也. 左傳曰: 正直為正, 正曲為直. 其引申之義也. 見之審則必能矯其枉, 故曰正曲為直."

(390) "屈" here is "submissive and yielding (屈服/屈從)", as in

The Commentary of Zuo - the Twenty-ninth Year of Duke Xiang (《左傳•襄公二十九年》) : "直而不倨, 曲而不屈." See 中央研究院《搜詞尋字》.

It is important to note one should only be "submissive and yielding" to Tao, not to any person or ruler. "大直若屈" is in fact related to "曲則全" in Chapter 22 Line 66. For further elaborations, please see footnote 172.

(391) The correct interpretation in vernacular Chinese of "大直若屈" should be:

"最大的正直, 乃是屈折(於道)."

(interpreted by Kwok Kin Poon)

(392) Why "the sharpest and the most brilliant is actually dim-witted"? This is because the truly brilliant ones only follow Tao without their acquired intellects or personal wits.

Those who act with their acquired intellects are actually fools that create chaos in the world. See Chapter 18 Line 55: "慧智出, 有大偽", and Chapter 38 Line 111: "前識者, 道之華, 而愚之始."

(393) "訥" here means "inarticulate (言語遲鈍)", as indicated in *Shuowen Jiezi* (《說文解字》): "訥, 言難也." See 中央研究院《搜詞尋字》.

Nature, which is the most eloquent, enlightens us without any word. Hence, "the most eloquent is inarticulate".

(394) The correct interpretation in vernacular Chinese of "躁勝寒, 靜勝熱" should be:

"疾動或稍克服寒涼, 惟清靜卻終可克服苦熱."

(interpreted by Kwok Kin Poon)

(395) "正" here means "true guiding principle (常例/常法/準則)", as in *Guanzi - Bai Guan* (《管子•八觀》) : "江海雖廣, 池澤雖博, 魚鱉雖多, 罔罟必有正." See 中央研究院《搜詞尋字》.

(396) Why tranquillity is the true guiding principle? Tranquillity preserves the true essences of all things, while rash fierceness offends the fundamental natures of all things. Hence, tranquillity trumps all, as annotated by Wang Bi (王弼):

> "躁罷然後勝寒, 靜無為以勝熱. 以此推之, 則清淨為天下正也. 靜則全物之真, 躁則犯物之性, 故惟清淨乃得如上諸大也."
>
> Source: 王弼《老子王弼注》. 台北: 新興書局, 1964, p.056-057.

(397) "卻" here is "retreat/reclaim (返回)", as in:

  I. "金龜換酒處, 卻憶淚沾巾" in Li Ba's (李白) *Dui Jiu Yi He Jian* (《對酒憶賀監》).

  II. "百川尚有西流日, 一老曾無卻少時" in Duan Keji's (段克己) *Zhe Gu Tian - Qing Yang Xia Dui Jiu* (《鷓鴣天•青陽峽對酒》).

  Source: 中央研究院《搜詞尋字》.

(398) "欲得" here means "selfish greed to possess (貪得)", as in *Hanfeitzu - Explaining Laozi* (《韓非子•解老》): "聖人衣足以犯寒, 食足以充虛, 則不憂矣. 眾人則不然, 大為諸侯, 小餘千金之資, 其欲得之憂不除也." See 《漢語大詞典》.

(399) "彌" here is "further (程度加深)", as in:

  I. "彌, 益也" in *Xiao Erya - Expanding Old Words* (《小爾雅•廣詁》).

  II. "其曲彌高, 其和彌寡" in *Selections of Refined Literature - Song Yu - Dui Chu Wang Wen* (《文選•宋玉•對楚王問》).

  Source: 中央研究院《搜詞尋字》.

(400) As one travels outside and gains more acquired knowledge, one is more likely to be tainted with artificial social norms and concepts. This drives one to be further away from Tao.

(401) "名" here is "comprehend (明)". See *Kangxi Dictionary* (《康熙字典》).

(402) "益" here means "increasing (增加)", as in:
  I. "益, 加也" in *Guangya - Shigu II* (《廣雅•釋詁二》).
  II. "益, 增也" in *Guangyun* (《廣韻》).
  III. "子木懼, 言諸王, 益其祿爵而復之" in *The Commentary of Zuo - the Twenty-sixth Year of Duke Xiang* (《左傳•襄公二十六年》)
  Source: 中央研究院《搜詞尋字》.

(403) "損" here is "diminish (減少/虧損)", as in:
  I. "損, 減也" in *Shuowen Jiezi* (《說文解字》).
  II. "損, 減少也" in *Yupian* (《玉篇》).
  III. "損下益上, 其道上行" in the *Book of Changes - Sun* (《易經•損》).
  Source: 中央研究院《搜詞尋字》.

(404) Why is that "there is nothing that one cannot do"? By acting without any personal differentiation and intent, one has united with Tao. For Tao, there is nothing that it cannot do (Chapter 37 Line 106: "道常無為而無不為").

(405) "取" here is "rule (治)", as in:
  I. "取, 為也" in *Guangya - Shigu III* (《廣雅•釋詁三》).
  II. "成侯嗣公, 聚斂計數之君也, 未及取民也. 俞樾平議：此取字, 亦當訓治, 取民言治民也" in *Xunzi - Wang Zhi* (《荀子•王制》).
  Source: 中央研究院《搜詞尋字》.

(406) "事" here means "great accomplishments (偉立之功)", as indicated in *Kangxi Dictionary* (《康熙字典》): "《釋名》事, 偉也. 偉立也. 凡所立之功也. "

"無事" is not "do nothing" or "not do anything". Laozi only asked one to leave behind selfish achievements in order to follow Tao to govern properly. This concept is akin to "無為". See footnote 10.

(407) "不善者, 吾亦善之" cannot be "those who are not benevolent (or kind), I am also benevolent (or kind) to them". This is because wise sages do not follow the concept of being benevolent (Chapter 5 Line 13: 聖人不仁, 以百姓為芻狗).

(408) "德" here is "attain (得)", as in :
　　I.　"德, 得也" in *Guangya - Shigu III* (《廣雅•釋詁三》).
　　II.　"是故用財不費, 民德不勞, 其興利多矣" in *Mo Yze - Economy of Expenditures I* (《墨子•節用上》).
　　Source: 中央研究院《搜詞尋字》.
　"德" here is not "virtue". Since wise sages treat all people with no mercy as if they are straw-made dogs (Chapter 5 Line 13: 聖人不仁, 以百姓為芻狗), they do not follow the human concept of having "good virtue (善德)".

(409) The correct interpretation in vernacular Chinese of Line 134 should be:
　　"聖人沒有既定不變的私心, 祗以百姓的心作為自己的心.
　　百姓喜好的, 我也喜好他們所喜好的; 百姓不喜好的, 我也
　　喜好他們這個不喜好. 這才得到與百姓完全一樣的喜(與不
　　喜)."
　　(interpreted by Kwok Kin Poon)

(410) "不信者, 吾亦信之" cannot be "those who are not trustworthy, I also trust them". Trusting someone who is not trustworthy is very much against the nature of Tao, for Tao always delivers what one sows. See Chapter 37 Line 71 and footnote 183. Further, wise sages only make the mindset of the people as their own (聖人無常心, 以百姓心為心), and so they distrust what others distrust. See Chapter 49 Line 134.

(411) See footnote 408.

(412) The correct interpretation in vernacular Chinese of Line 135 should be:

"百姓信服的，我也信服他們所信服的; 百姓不信服的，我也信服他們這個不信服. 這才得到與百姓完全一樣的信(與不信)."

(interpreted by Kwok Kin Poon)

(413) "歙歙" here means "the appearance of no prejudice (無所偏執貌)", as annotated by Wang Bi (王弼):

"聖人之于天下，歙歙焉，心無所主也."

Source: 王弼《老子王弼注》. 台北: 新興書局, 1964, p.060.

(414) "渾" here means "primitive simplistic nature (質樸)", as in Sikong Tu's (司空圖) *Xiong Hun* (《雄渾》) : "返虛入渾，積健為雄." See 中央研究院《搜詞尋字》.

(415) What does "become newborn babies (孩)" mean? Wang Bi (王弼) annotated:

"皆使和而無欲，如嬰兒也."

"(The wise sages) make all become harmonious and without any selfish desire, just like newborn babies."

(interpreted by KS Vincent Poon)

Source: 王弼《老子王弼注》. 台北: 新興書局, 1964, p.059.

(416) "十有三" is literally "thirteen", which here actually refers to "the four limbs and nine orifices (四肢九竅)".

"有" here is "and (又)", as in *The Book of Odes - Odes Of Bei - Zhong Feng* (《詩經•邶風•終風》): "終風且曀，不日有曀. 鄭玄箋：有，又也." See中央研究院《搜詞尋字》.

Hence, "十有三" is "ten (十) and three (三)", which is "thirteen". Such usage is often seen in other classics, for instance, "At thirteen, he learned music (十有三年學樂)", in the *Book of Rites - The Pattern of the Family* (《禮記•內則》). See James

Legge's *The Sacred Books of China, The Texts of Confucianism*.

"Thirteen" then refers to the numerical sum of the four limbs and the nine orifices (四肢九竅) of the human body, as annotated by Hanfeitzu (韓非子) :

> "四肢與九竅十有三者."
>
> Source: *Hanfeitzu - Explaining Laozi* (《韓非子•解老》) .

The nine orifices (九竅) are the two nostrils, the two ear canals, the two eyes, the mouth, the urethral opening, and the anus.

Many scholars of the past and present, including Wang Bi (王弼) and Gao Heng (高亨), mistakenly took "十有三" as "three out of ten (十分有三分)". See 王弼《老子王弼注》. 台北: 新興書局, 1964, p.061, and 高亨《老子正詁》. 上海: 開明書店, 1949, p.106.

(417) "動" here is "often (每每)", as in:

I. "且兵兇器, 雖克所願, 動亦耗病" in *Records of the Grand Historian - Bells* (《史記•律書》).

II. "車輪動盈箱, 舟載輒連柂" in Wang Anshi's (王安石) *Gan Tang Li* (《甘棠梨》).

Source: 中央研究院《搜詞尋字》.

(418) "之" here is "go into (往)", as in:

I. "之, 往也" in *Erya - Shigu I* (《爾雅•釋詁上》).

II. "百爾所思, 不如我所之" in *The Book of Odes - Odes Of Yong - Zai Chi* (《詩經•鄘風•載馳》).

III. "滕文公為世子, 將之楚, 過宋而見孟子" in in *Mengzi - Teng Wen Gong I* (《孟子•滕文公上》).

Source: 中央研究院《搜詞尋字》.

(419) "死地" here is "in dire and deadly position (必死之地)", as in *Records of the Grand Historian - Biography of Marquis of Huaiyin* (《史記•淮陰侯傳》): "其勢非置之死地, 使人人自為戰." See 《重編國語辭典修訂本》.

(420) "厚" here is "high regard (看重)", as in *Mo Yze - Exaltation of the Virtuous II* (《墨子•尚賢中》): "厚於貨者, 不能分人以祿." See 中央研究院《搜詞尋字》.

(421) The first "生" here is "possessions (財物/生計)", as in *Discourses of the States - Discourses of Zhou III* (《國語•周語下》): "若積聚既喪, 又鮮其繼, 生何以殖? 韋昭注: 生, 財也." See 中央研究院《搜詞尋字》.

The second "生" here is "life (生命)", as in *Xunzi - Wang Zhi* (《荀子•王制》): "水火有氣而無生, 草木有生而無知." See 中央研究院《搜詞尋字》.

The two interpretations above are further support by the *Book of Documents - Pan Geng II* (《書經•盤庚中》): "往哉生生! 今予將試以汝遷, 永建乃家." See 《重編國語辭典修訂本》.

(422) The correct interpretation in vernacular Chinese of Line 137 should be:

"從出生到死亡期間, 生的人, 有四肢九竅的身軀; 死的人, 也有四肢九竅的身軀; 人在生時, 每每往赴必死絕地來犯險, 亦同樣有著此四肢九竅的身軀. 這是件什麼事情呢? 就是為了這身軀而令人太看重自己的財物和性命啊!"

(interpreted by Kwok Kin Poon)

(423) "攝" here is "maintaining (保養)", as in Yuan Hongdao's (袁宏道) *Qi Gai Gao Yi* (《乞改稿一》): "或者斷緣謝事, 靜攝數月, 庶其有瘳." See 中央研究院《搜詞尋字》.

(424) "被" here is "come into (及/到達)", as indicated in:

I. "被, 及也" in *Yupian* (《玉篇》).

II. "光被四表. 蔡沈《集傳》: 被, 及." in the *Book of Documents - Yao Dian* (《書經•堯典》).

III. "北盡塞表, 東被海涯" in Sima Guang's (司馬光) *Ying Zhao Yan Chao Zheng Que Shi Shi* (《應詔言朝政闕失事》).

Source: 中央研究院《搜詞尋字》.

(425) "容" is "to lay/ to apply (用)", as in :

    I.   "容, 用也, 合事宜之用" in *Shiming* (《釋名》).

    II. "是以人稼之容足, 耨之容耨, 據之容手, 此之謂耕道" in *Master Lu's Spring and Autumn Annals - Shen Shi* (《呂氏春秋•審時》).

    Source: 中央研究院《搜詞尋字》.

(426) "育" here means "cultivate (培養)", as in:

    I.   "育, 養子使作善也" in *Shuowen Jiezi* (《說文解字》).

    II. "育, 養也" in *Yupian* (《玉篇》).

    III. "君子以果行育德. 王弼注 : 育德者, 養正之功也" in the *Book of Changes - Meng* (《易經•蒙》).

    IV. "尊賢育下, 以彰有德" in *Mengzi - Gao Zi II* (《孟子•告子下》).

    Source: 中央研究院《搜詞尋字》.

(427) "亭" here is "cultivate (化育)", as annotated in *Kangxi Dictionary* (《康熙字典》): "《老子•道德經》亭之毒之. 註: 亭謂品其形, 毒謂成其質. 毒, 徒篤反. 今作育."

(428) "毒" here is "develop (育)", as annotated in *Kangxi Dictionary* (《康熙字典》). See footnote 427.

(429) "覆" here is "return (回復)" as in the *Book of Changes - Gan* (《易經•乾》): "終日乾乾, 反復道也." 王弼注作"覆". 阮元校勘記 : "《釋文》復, 本亦作覆." See 中央研究院《搜詞尋字》.

(430) See footnote 13.

(431) Ibid.

(432) See footnote 67

(433) "宰" here means "that which dominates (主宰者)", as in:

    I.   "宰, 凡為事物之主者亦曰宰" in *Zhengzitong* (《正字

通》).

II. "若有真宰, 而特不得其眹" in *Zhuangzi - The Adjustment of Controversies* (《莊子•齊物論》).

See 中央研究院《搜詞尋字》.

(434) See Chapter Line 1 and Chapter 25 Line 74.

(435) "兌" here refers to "the senses of the ears, eyes, noses, and mouths (耳目鼻口)", as annotated by Gao You (高誘) in *Huainanzi - Tao Ying* (《淮南子•道應》) : "王若欲久持之, 則塞民於兌. 高誘注：兌, 耳目鼻口也. 《老子》曰：塞其兌也." See 中央研究院《搜詞尋字》.

(436) "勤" here means "exhausted (盡)", as in *Huainanzi - Zhu Shu Xun* (《淮南子•主術訓》) : "力勤財匱. 任繼愈注： 勤, 即盡." See 《漢語大字典》.

(437) "濟" here means "to achieve (成就)" as in:

I. "濟, 成也" in *Erya - Shiyan* (《爾雅•釋言》).

II. "必有忍, 其乃有濟; 有容, 德乃大" in the *Book of Documents - Jun Chen* (《書經•君陳》).

Source: 中央研究院《搜詞尋字》.

(438) See footnote 221.

(439) This "Small (小)" is Tao, for Tao is so small that it can even penetrate infinitely small space (無有入無閒). See Chapter 43 Line 122.

(440) Tao is the gentlest yet oversees the toughest (天下之至柔, 馳騁天下之至堅). See Chapter 43 Line 22. Therefore, the gentlest is the source of true strength.

(441) "遺" here "retain (留)", as in:

I. "寧王遺我大寶龜" in the *Book of Documents - Da Gao*

(《書經•大誥》).

II. "古之遺愛也" in *The Commentary of Zuo - the Nineteenth year of Duke Zhao* (《左傳•昭十九年》).

Source: *Kangxi Dictionary* (《康熙字典》).

(442) "殃" here is "harm (災禍)", as indicated in *Guangya - Shiyan* (《廣雅•釋言》) : "殃，禍也." See 中央研究院《搜詞尋字》.

(443) "習" here is "comprehend (瞭解/熟悉)", as in:

I. "是皆習民數者也" in *Discourses of the States - Discourses of Zhou I* (《國語•周語上》).

II. "嘗無師傅所教學, 不習於誦. 高誘注：習, 曉" in *Strategies of the Warring States - Strategies of Qin V* (《戰國策•秦策五》).

Source: 中央研究院《搜詞尋字》.

For further elaborations on this "Immutable (常)", see Chapter 16 Lines 50 and 51.

(444) "介然" here means "unwaveringly (堅定不動搖)", as in *Xunzi - Xiushen* (《荀子•修身》) : "善在身, 介然必以自好也." See 《漢語大詞典》.

(445) "徑" here is "narrow paths (小路)", as indicated in *Yupian* (《玉篇》): "徑, 小路也." See *Kangxi Dictionary* (《康熙字典》).

(446) "除" here is "construct (修治)", as in the *Book of Han - Biography of Dongfang Shuo* (《漢書•東方朔傳》) : "舉籍阿城以南, 盩厔以東, 宜春以西, 提封頃畝, 及其賈直, 欲除以為上林苑, 屬之南山." See 《重編國語辭典修訂本》.

(447) "朝" here is "mansions (宮室)", as annotated by Wang Bi (王弼): "朝, 宮室也." See 王弼《老子王弼注》. 台北: 新興書局, 1964, p.064.

The correct interpretation in vernacular Chinese of "朝甚除" should be:

"宮室建造太多."

(interpreted by Kwok Kin Poon)

(448) "文綵" is "elegant and colourful dresses (華美的衣服)", as indicated in *Records of the Grand Historian - Biographies of Usurers* (《史記•貨殖列傳》) : "齊帶山河, 膏壤千里, 宜桑麻, 人民多文綵布帛魚鹽." See 《漢語大詞典》.

(449) "厭" here is "indulge with food (飽/飫)", as in:
   I.   "厭, 足也" in *Jiyun* (《集韻》).
   II. "萬年厭于乃德. 陸德明釋文, 馬云 : 厭, 飫也" in the *Book of Documents - Luo Gao* (《書經•洛誥》).
   III. "原憲不厭糟糠, 匿於窮巷. 司馬貞索隱 : 饜, 飽也" in *Records of the Grand Historian - Biographies of Usurers* (《史記•貨殖列傳》).
   Source: 中央研究院《搜詞尋字》.

(450) "財貨" here means "wealth and possessions (財物)", as in *Records of the Grand Historian - Annals of Xiang Yu* (《史記•項羽本紀》) : " 沛公居山東時, 貪於財貨, 好美姬." See 《漢語大詞典》.

(451) "盜夸" here is "great robbers (盜魁)", as indicated in *Hanyu Da Cidian* (《漢語大詞典》). "夸" here is "great (大)", as seen in *Kangxi Dictionary* (《康熙字典》).

(452) "建" here means "institute (樹立)", as in Liu Zongyua's (柳宗元) *Treatise on Feudalism* (《封建論》): "予以為周之喪久矣, 徒建空名於公侯之上耳." See《重編國語辭典修訂本》.

(453) "以" here is "thus (因)", as indicated in *Kangxi Dictionary* (《康熙字典》).

(454) "於" here is "for (為了)", as in *Records of the Grand Historian - House of Duke Tai of Qi* (《史記•齊太公世家》) : "齊使管

仲平戎於周." See 中央研究院《搜詞尋字》.

(455) "德" here is not Confucius's "moral virtues (德行)". Instead, it is the resulting outcome (i.e., manifestation) of following Tao. Laozi abhorred Confucius's "moral values". See Chapter 38 Line 108 and footnote 322.

(456) "Pure and genuine (真)" here refers to "original simplicity (樸)" as in Chapter 24 Line 84 "常德乃足, 復歸於樸". This is because cultivating Tao for oneself results in one returning to the pure and original simplicity (樸). See also footnote 356.

(457) The correct interpretation in vernacular Chinese of Line 147 should be:

> "為了自身而修養道, 他的德乃就真樸; 為了家庭而修養道,
> 他的德乃就豐足; 為了家鄉而修養道, 他的德乃就更為增長;
> 為了國家而修養道, 他的德乃就更為豐厚; 為了天下而修養
> 道, 他的德乃就更為全面而普及."
>
> (interpreted by Kwok Kin Poon)

(458) "觀" here is "examine others with one's understanding (以我所了解的來觀察事物)", as in *Shuowen Jiezi Zhu* (《說文解字注》): "凡以我諦視物曰觀." Here "one's understanding" refers to "one's understanding of Tao".

(459) The "above rationale" refers to Chapter 54 Line 147.

(460) "含德" here is "harbouring the Manifestation of Tao (懷藏道德)", as in Xiao Tong's (蕭統) *Preface to The Collected Works of Tao Yuanming* (《陶淵明集序》): "含德之至, 莫踰於道; 親己之切, 無重於身." See 《漢語大詞典》.

(461) "比" here is "the same as (同/齊同)", as in:

> I. "比, 齊也" in *Zihui* (《字彙》).
> II. "比物四驪, 閑之維則. 陸德明釋文 : 比, 齊同也" in *The*

Book of Odes - Minor Odes of the Kingdom - Liu Yue (
《詩經•小雅•六月》).
Source: 中央研究院《搜詞尋字》.

(462) "赤子" here is "newborn babies (初生的嬰兒)", as in the
Book of Documents - Kang Gao (《書經•康誥》) : "若保赤子, 惟
民其康乂. 孔穎達疏: 子生赤色, 故言赤子." See《漢語大詞典》.

(463) Those who richly harbour the Manifestation of Tao only
live by their natures and pay no attention to concepts and values
set by humans. Accordingly, they are the same as newborn
babies.

(464) "據" here means "seize (抓)", as in *Records of the Grand
Historian - Annals of Empress Dowager Lu* (《史記•呂太后本
紀》) : "呂后祓, 還過軹道, 見物如蒼犬, 據高后掖, 忽弗復見." See
中央研究院《搜詞尋字》.

(465) "攫鳥" here is "fierce birds of prey (鷙鳥/兇猛的鳥)", as
annotated by Cheng Xuanying (成玄英): "攫鳥, 鷹鸇類也." See
《漢語大詞典》.

(466) Why do fierce animals not attack newborn babies? This
is because newborn babies only live by Tao and do not offend
anything in nature, as annotate by Wang Bi (王弼):
"赤子無求無欲, 不犯眾物, 故毒蟲之物無犯之人也. 含德之
厚者, 不犯於物, 故無物以損其全也."
Source: 王弼《老子王弼注》. 台北: 新興書局, 1964,
p.066.

(467) "全" here is "perfectly (完整/完好)", as in:
I. "全, 完也" in *Shuowen Jiezi* (《說文解字》).
II. "得此六材之全, 然後可以為良. 鄭玄注 : 全, 無瑕病"
in *The Rites of Zhou - Record of Trades* (《周禮•考工
記》).

III. "純粹全犧, 獻之公門. 李善注引孔安國曰：體完曰全"
　　in *Selections of Refined Literature - Mei Sheng - Qi Fa*
　　(《文選•枚乘•七發》).

IV. "耄期身未病, 貧困氣猶全" in Lu You's (陸游) *Zi Yi* (《
　　自貽》).

Source: 中央研究院《搜詞尋字》.

(468) "作" here means "grows and develops (長)", as annotated
by Wang Bi (王弼):

"作, 長也. 無物以損其身, 故能全長也."
Source: 王弼《老子王弼注》. 台北: 新興書局, 1964,
p.067.

(469) See footnote 161.

(470) The correct interpretation in vernacular Chinese of
"未知牝牡之合而全作, 精之至也" should be:

" (嬰兒)不曉得陰氣陽氣相調合, 卻能完好無損地成長, 這可
說是真氣的極致了."
(interpreted by Kwok Kin Poon)

(471) "嗄" here is "a voice that has become hoarse (聲音嘶啞)",
as indicated in *Yupian* (《玉篇》)："嗄, 聲破." See 中央研究院《
搜詞尋字》.

(472) For further elaborations on this "Immutable (常)", see
Chapter 16 Lines 50 and 51.

(473) "益" here means "increase/prolong (增加)", as in:

I. "益, 加也" in" *Guangya - Shigu II* (《廣雅•釋詁二》).
II. "益, 增也" in *Guangyun* (《廣韻•昔韻》).
III. "子木懼, 言諸王, 益其祿爵而復之" in *The Commentary
　　of Zuo - the Twenty-sixth Year of Duke Xiang* (《左傳•
　　襄公二十六年》).

Source: 中央研究院《搜詞尋字》.

(474) "祥" here is "ominous omens (凶的徵兆)", as in:

    I. "亳有祥, 桑、穀共生于朝. 孔穎達 《正義》: 祥是 惡事先見之徵" in the *Book of Documents - Common Possession of Pure Virtue* (《書經•咸有一德》). See 《重編國語辭典修訂本》.

    II. "妖孽自外來謂之祥" in the *Book of Han - Treatise on the Five Elements* (《漢書•五行志》). See *Kangxi Dictionary* (《康熙字典》).

Note "祥" does mean "fortuitous and ominous omens (吉凶之兆)". See *Kangxi Dictionary* (《康熙字典》). In our context, however, it should be interpreted as "ominous omens" only.

(475) "使氣" here is "headstrong and assertive (恣逞意氣)", as in Su E's (蘇鶚) *Du Yang Za Bian* (《杜陽雜編》): "魚朝恩專權使氣, 公卿不敢仰視." See 《漢語大詞典》.

(476) See footnote 256.

(477) See footnote 261 and Chapter 30 Line 91.

(478) See footnote 262.

(479) See Chapter 30 Line 91.

(480) This is because Tao cannot be described in words. See Chapter 1 Line 1.

(481) See footnote 435.

(482) "分" here is "chaos (紛亂貌)", as in *Gui Gu Zi - Di Xi* (《鬼谷子•抵巇》): "天下分錯." See 中央研究院 《搜詞尋字》.

    See also Chapter 4 Line 11.

(483) "以" here is "rely on". See footnote 165.

(484) "正" here is "proper (合規範/合標準)", as in *The Analects - Zi Han* (《論語•子罕》): "吾自衛反魯, 然後樂正, 《雅》、《頌》各得其所." See 中央研究院《搜詞尋字》.

(485) "以" here is "consider (認為/以為)", as in
    I.   "以, 猶謂也" in *The Book of Expletives* (《經傳釋詞》).
    II. "告臧孫, 臧孫以難; 告郈孫, 郈孫以可" in *The Commentary of Zuo - the Twenty-fifth Year of Duke Zhao* (《左傳•昭公二十五年》).
    III. "人人自以得上意" in the *Book of Han - Annals of Emperor Yuan* (《漢書•元帝紀》).
    Source: 中央研究院《搜詞尋字》.

(486) "奇" here means "evil and ominous (奇邪/詭異不正)", as in Liu Zongyuan's (柳宗元) *Shi Ling Lun Xia* (《時令論下》) : "必言其中正, 而去其奇衺." See 中央研究院《搜詞尋字》.
    Accordingly, employing troops is a sign of bad omen (兵者不祥之器). See Chapter 31 Line 92.

(487) See footnote 405.

(488) See Chapter 48 Line 133 and footnote 406.

(489) The correct interpretation in vernacular Chinese of "以正治國, 以奇用兵, 以無事取天下" should be:
    "治國依仗正道, 用兵認為不祥, 治天下憑藉不做大事."
    (interpreted by Kwok Kin Poon)

(490) This corresponds to "when one aims to accomplish anything great, one is unqualified to rule all under Heaven (及其有事, 不足以取天下)" in Chapter 48 Line 133.

(491) "利器" here refers to "instruments that benefit people individually", such as currency, trade, and other social policies.

(492) "滋" here means "increasing (增長)", as indicated in *Shuowen Jiezi* (《說文解字》): "滋, 益也."

(493) "昏" here means "chaos (亂)", as in the *Book of Documents - Speech at Mu* (《書經•牧誓》): "昏棄厥肆祀弗答. 傳: 昏, 亂也. 疏: 昏闇於事必亂, 故昏爲亂也." See *Kangxi Dictionary* (《康熙字典》).

(494) The correct interpretation in vernacular Chinese of "民多利器, 國家滋昏" should be:

"百姓得到更多有利自己的工具(例如貨幣、貿易等), 國家便益增混亂了."

(interpreted by Kwok Kin Poon)

(495) See footnote 314.

(496) See Chapter 48 Line 133 and footnote 406.

(497) See footnote 148.

(498) "淳淳" here means "simple and honest (淳樸篤厚)", as in Zhang Shao's (張紹) *Chong You Guan* (《沖佑觀》): "皇風蕩蕩, 黔首淳淳." See 《重編國語辭典修訂本》.

(499) "察察" here is "tactful and discerning (分別辨析)", as in the *New Book of Tang - Biography of Tutu Chengcui* (《新唐書•吐突承璀傳》) : "以黃門直東宮, 為掖廷局博士, 察察有才." See 《重編國語辭典修訂本》.

(500) "缺缺" here means "slick and cunning (詐僞貌/具小聰明的)", as in Liu Zongyuan's (柳宗元) *Tong Ye Feng Di Bian* (《桐葉封弟辨》) : "是直小丈夫缺缺者之事, 非周公所宜用, 故不可信." See 《重編國語辭典修訂本》.

(501) "極" here means "ultimate (頂點)" as indicated in *Shuowen*

Jiezi Zhu (《說文解字注》): "極, 凡至高至遠皆謂之極."

(502) "正" here should be interpreted as "good/agreeable (完善/美好)", as in *Yili - Shi Guan Li* (《儀禮•士冠禮》)："三加曰, 以歲之正, 以月之令, 咸加爾服. 鄭玄注： 正, 猶善也." See 中央研究院《搜詞尋字》.

(503) The correct interpretation in vernacular Chinese of "孰知其極？其無正" should be:

> "誰曉得這禍這福最終會是怎麼樣呢？這實在沒有所謂美善的呀!"
>
> (interpreted by Kwok Kin Poon)

(504) See footnote 486.

(505) "方" here is "duly (正直)", as in the *Book of Han - Biography of Dong Zhongshu* (《漢書•董仲舒傳》)："悼王道之不昭, 故舉賢良方正之士." See 《重編國語辭典修訂本》.

(506) See footnote 237.

(507) "廉" here means "uncorrupted with integrity (廉潔)", as in:
   I. "廉, 清也" in *Yupian* 《玉篇•閭部》.
   II. "貧者見廉, 富者見義" in *Mo Yze - Xiushen* (《墨子•修身》).
   Source: 中央研究院《搜詞尋字》.

(508) "劌" here means "hurt (傷)", as in Yu Ji's (虞集) *Yue Sheng Tang Ji* (《悅生堂記》)："內劌其心, 外伐其形." See 《重編國語辭典修訂本》.

(509) "直" here means "honestly (正直)", as in *The Commentary of Zuo - the Twenty-eighth Year of Duke Xi* (《左傳•僖公二十八年》): "師直為壯, 曲為老." See 《重編國語辭典修訂本》.

(510) "肆" here means "conflict (衝突)", as in *The Book of Odes*

- *Greater Odes of the Kingdom - Huang Yi* (《詩經•大雅•皇矣》)
："是伐是肆, 是絕是忽. 鄭玄箋：肆, 犯突也." See 中央研究院《
搜詞尋字》.

(511) "治" here means "cultivate (修養)", as in:
  I. "仁者之思也恭，聖人之思也樂，此治心之道也" in *Xun-zi - Jiebi* (《荀子•解蔽》).
  II. "或問治己. 曰：治己以仲尼" in *Fayan - XiuShen* (《法言•修身》).
  Source: 中央研究院《搜詞尋字》.
  "人" here means "self (自己)", as in *Nineteen Old Poems -Marching On and On* (《古詩十九首•行行重行行》)："思君令人老，歲月忽已晚." See 中央研究院《搜詞尋字》.

(512) "事" here means "to pursue/serve (奉行/從事)", as in *Han-feitzu - Nan Yi* (《韓非子•難一 》): "今管仲不務尊主明法, 而事增寵益爵." See 《漢語大字典》.

(513) "嗇" here is "farmer (農夫)", as in:
  I. "嗇, 農人" by Wang Bi (王弼). See 王弼《老子王弼注》. 台北: 新興書局, 1964, p.071.
  II. "田夫謂之嗇夫" in *Shuowen Jiezi Zhu* (《說文解字注》).

(514) "德" here is not "virtue" but is "attainment/yield (得)", as in:
  I. "德, 得也" in *Guangya - Shigu III* (《廣雅•釋詁三》).
  II. "是故用財不費, 民德不勞, 其興利多矣. 孫詒讓《閒詁》：德與得通" in *Mo Yze - Economy of Expenditures I* (《墨子•節用上》).
  Source: 中央研究院《搜詞尋字》.
  Wang Bi (王弼) further annotated:
  "唯重積德不欲銳速, 然後乃能使早服其常, 故曰早服謂之重積德者也."
  "It is solely because the farmer focuses on amassing yield without the desire to rush that the farmer can obey

Nature from the very beginning. Hence, this is why 'Having obeyed Nature from the very beginning can be called as focusing on gradually amassing one's yield'."
(interpreted by KS Vincent Poon)
Source: 王弼《老子王弼注》. 台北: 新興書局, 1964, p.072.

"Without the desire to rush" and "gradually" are important, for "the most magnificent worldly entity evolves gradually and requires a long time to become established (大器晚成)". See Chapter 41 Line 117.

(515) "克" here means "competent (勝任)", as in *Shuowen Jiezi* (《說文解字》): " 克, 肩也. 徐鍇曰：肩, 任也. 負何之名也. 與人肩膊之義通, 能勝此物謂之克."

(516) "極" here means "limit (盡頭)", as in:
   I.   "極, 已也" in *Guangya - Shigu IV* (《廣雅•釋詁四》).
   II. "極, 終也" in *Guangyun* (《廣韻•職韻》).
   III. "悠悠蒼天, 曷其有極. 鄭玄箋：極, 已也" in *The Book of Odes - Odes Of Tang - Bao Yu* (《詩經•唐風•鴇羽》).
   Source: 中央研究院《搜詞尋字》.

Why is it that "there is no task in which one is not competent" and "one's limit cannot be known"? If one obeys Nature from the very beginning, then one is with the limitless Tao. As Wang Bi (王弼) annotated here:

"道無窮也."
Source: 王弼《老子王弼注》. 台北: 新興書局, 1964, p.072.

(517) The correct interpretation in vernacular Chinese of Line 160 should be:

"在修養自己事奉大自然的事情上, 大家就比不上農夫了. 祇有農夫, 才可稱做起初就已服從了大自然(德). 起初就已服從大自然, 乃可稱之為重視慢慢累積而得到收穫. 能重視

慢慢累積而得成果, 那就無所不能勝任了. 無所不能勝任,
人們便不知道你能力的極限了."

(interpreted by Kwok Kin Poon)

(518) "有" is "為", as in:
  I. "有, 猶為也. 為、有一聲之轉, 故為可訓為有, 有亦可訓
      為" in *The Book of Expletives* (《經傳釋詞》).
  II. "眇能視, 不足以有明也" in the *Book of Changes - Lu* (
      《易經•履》).
  Source: 中央研究院《搜詞尋字》.
  This "為" means "rule (治理)", as in:
  I. "為, 治也" in *Xiao Erya - Expanding Old Words* (《小
      爾雅•廣詁》).
  II. "為政以德" in *The Analects - Wei Zheng* (《論語•為
      政》).
  Source: 中央研究院《搜詞尋字》.

(519) "之" here is "apply (用)", as in *Strategies of the Warring
States - Strategies of Qi III* (《戰國策•齊策三》) : "故物舍其所
長, 之其所短, 堯亦有所不及矣. 高誘注 : 之, 猶用也." See 中央研
究院《搜詞尋字》.

(520) "母" here is "motherly root of all (根源)", as in *Huainanzi -
Chu Zhen* (《淮南子•俶真》) : "涅非緇也, 青非藍也. 茲雖遇其
母, 而無能復化已. 高誘注 : 母, 本也." See 中央研究院《搜詞尋
字》.

Accordingly, in our context, this "母" can then be interpreted
as "motherly Nature" or even "Manifestation of Tao (德)". See
Chapter 1 Line 1.

(521) The correct interpretation in vernacular Chinese of "莫知其
極, 可以有國. 有國之母, 可以長久" should be:
  "人們不知道你能力的極限, 你便可以治理國家了. 用德來
  治理國家, 那就可以長久了."
  (interpreted by Kwok Kin Poon)

(522) "長生久視" here means "長生久活", as in *Master Lu's Spring and Autumn Annals - Zhong Ji* (《呂氏春秋•重己》 : "世之人主貴人, 無賢不肖, 莫不欲長生久視. 高誘注 : 視, 活也." See 《漢語大詞典》.

(523) Why should one be as mindful as cooking a small fish in governing? Laozi had always cherished the benefit of allowing Tao to act naturally with no human interference. Such is like cooking a small fish: avoid meddling for the best result. As such, Wang Bi (王弼) annotated:

"不擾也, 躁則多害, 靜則全真."
"Do not disturb, for rashness delivers much harm, while tranquillity bears the full nature of all things."
(interpreted by KS Vincent Poon)
Source: 王弼《老子王弼注》. 台北: 新興書局, 1964, p.072.

(524) "莅" here means "govern (治理)", as in *Mengzi - Liang Hui Wang I* (《孟子•梁惠王上》): "莅中國而撫四夷也." See 《漢語大字典》.

(525) "鬼" here means "wit (敏慧)", as in:
I. "虔、儇, 慧也…自關而東, 趙、魏之間謂之黠, 或謂之鬼" in *Fangyan - Volume I* (《方言•卷一》).
II. "鬼, 慧也" in *Guangya - Shigu I* (《廣雅•釋詁一》).
Source: 中央研究院《搜詞尋字》.

(526) "亦" here means "surely (確實)", as in the *Book of the Later Han - Elaboration on Biography of Dou Rong* (《後漢書•竇融傳贊》): "悃悃安豐, 亦稱才雄. 李賢注 : 亦, 猶實也." See 中央研究院《搜詞尋字》.

(527) For Line 162, many incorrectly took "鬼" as "ghosts" or "evil spirits" and "神" as "gods" or "deities". Laozi had only asked one to follow Tao and had never addressed the existence

of supernatural entities.

"Ghosts" or "Deities" may be consistent with some branches of Taoist religion (道教), but these are certainly not consistent with *Tao Te Ching*, the canon of Taoism (道家).

Wise sages inherently do not harm anyone, for they follow Tao, which benefits all without doing any harm (Chapter 81 Line 219: "天之道, 利而不害").

The correct interpretation in vernacular Chinese of Line 162 should be:

"治理大國如烹煮小魚(務必留神, 切勿傷害魚身的完好). 用道來治理天下的人, 他的敏慧不會是他的精神. 並不是因為他的敏慧不是他的精神, 而是他的精神不會傷害人. 並不是因為他的精神不傷害人, 而是遵道的聖人確實本來就是不會傷害人啊!"

(interpreted by Kwok Kin Poon)

(528) "交" here means "come together (俱/共)", as in:

　I.　"交, 俱也" in *Xiao Erya - Guang Yan* (《小爾雅•廣言》.

　II.　"交, 共也" in *Yupian* (《玉篇•交部》).

　Source: 中央研究院《搜詞尋字》.

(529) See footnote 528. If a great and powerful state humbles itself to a lowly position, it will then be able to draw everyone to it. Hence, all shall come together, as Wang Bi (王弼) annotated:

　"天下所歸會也."

　Source: 王弼《老子王弼注》. 台北: 新興書局, 1964, p.073.

(530) "取" here means "acceptance (接受)", as in:

　I.　"取, 受也" in *Guangyun* (《廣韻•麌韻》).

　II.　"取衣者亦以篋. 鄭玄注：取, 猶受也" in *The Classic of Rites - Sang Da Ji* (《禮記•喪大記》).

　Source: 中央研究院《搜詞尋字》.

(531) "或" here is "is/are/have (有)", as in:

    I. "或, 有也" in *Guangya - Shigu I* (《廣雅•釋詁一》).

    II. "有一於此, 未或不亡" in the *Book of Documents - Songs of the Five Sons* (《書經•五子之歌》).

    Source: 中央研究院《搜詞尋字》.

(532) The correct interpretation in vernacular Chinese of Line 165 should be:

"故此, 大國若以謙下來對待小國, 則取得小國的信服; 小國以謙下來接待大國, 則取得大國的信任。所以, 他們有些憑謙下以取得信服, 有些憑謙下而取得信任."

(interpreted by Kwok Kin Poon)

(533) "兼畜" here means "subjugate (兼并/并吞)". See《漢語大詞典》.

(534) "入" here means "adopt (采納)", as in:

    I. "入, 納也" in *Yupian* (《玉篇》).

    II. "諫而不入, 則莫之繼也" in *The Commentary of Zuo - the Second Year of Duke Xuan* (《左傳•宣公二年》).

    Source: 中央研究院《搜詞尋字》.

(535) "事" here means "serve (侍奉)", as in:

    I. "事, 奉也" in *Yupian* (《玉篇》).

    II. "事父母, 能竭其力; 事君, 能致其身" in *The Analects - Xue Er* (《論語•學而》).

    Source: 中央研究院《搜詞尋字》.

(536) In "大者", "大" is "important (重要/重大)", as in Zhuge Liang's (諸葛亮) *Chu Shi Biao* (《出師表》): "故臨崩寄臣以大事也." See 《漢典》.

"者" here is "an auxiliary word used at the end of a sentence as an intonation (語氣助詞)", as seen in *Mengzi - Li Lou II* (《孟子•離婁下》) : "大人者, 不失其赤子之心者也." See 中央研究院《搜詞尋字》.

(537) "奧" here is "a safe haven (庇蔭之所)", as indicated in *Zhengyun* (《正韻》): "奧, 室西南隅, 人所安息也." See *Kangxi Dictionary* (《康熙字典》).

"奧" here should not be taken as "deep" nor "mysterious", for Line 167 emphasizes that Tao is a safe haven for all.

(538) The correct interpretation in vernacular Chinese of "道者萬物之奧" should be:

"道是萬物安棲的地方."

(interpreted by Kwok Kin Poon)

(539) "保" here is "safeguard (安)", as in:
  I. "保, 定也" in *Guangya - Shigu IV* (《廣雅•釋詁四》).
  II. "保民而王, 莫之能禦也. 趙岐注 : 保, 安也" in *Mengzi - Liang Hui Wang I* (《孟子•梁惠王上》).
  Source: 中央研究院《搜詞尋字》.

(540) "尊" here is "according to (遵/依照)", as in *Mo Yze - Fortification of the City Gate* (《墨子•備城門》) : "然則守者必善, 而君尊用之, 然後可以守也. 俞樾平議 : 尊當為遵, 古字通也." See 中央研究院《搜詞尋字》.

(541) "加" here is "to gift and benefit others (施及/施加)", as in:
  I. "加, 施也" in *Zihui* (《字彙》).
  II. "此所謂勸賞不必遍加乎天下, 而天下從焉者也" in Han Yu's (韓愈) *Shang Zai Xiang Shu* (《上宰相書》).
  Source: 中央研究院《搜詞尋字》.

(542) In the Zhou era, "三公 (Three Chief Mentors)" refers to "the most honourable titles among all officials (人臣中最尊崇的三個官銜)", as in the *Book of Documents - Officers of Zhou* (《書經•周官》): "立太師、太傅、太保, 茲惟三公, 論道經邦, 燮理陰陽." See 《重編國語辭典修訂本》. Also see KS Vincent Poon and Kwok Kin Poon, *English Translation of Classical Chinese Calligraphy Masterpieces*, Cao Quan Stele, footnote 68, pp. 36-

37. Toronto: The SenSeis, 2019.

(543) "拱璧" here is "a grand piece of jade (大璧)", as in *The Commentary of Zuo - the Twenty-eighth Year of Duke Xiang* (《左傳•襄公二十八年》) : "與我其拱璧, 吾獻其柩. 孔穎達疏：拱, 謂合兩手也, 此璧兩手拱抱之, 故為大璧." See 《漢語大詞典》.

(544) "以" here is "have/carry (有)", as in:
  I.   "君之門以九重" in *Verses of Chu - Jiu Bian* (《楚辭•九辯》).
  II. "今楚國雖小, 絕長續短, 猶以數千里, 豈特百里哉" in *Strategies of the Warring States - Strategies of Chu IV*(《戰國策•楚策四》).
  Source: 中央研究院《搜詞尋字》.

(545) "先" here is "honour (尚/尊)", as in *Master Lu's Spring and Autumn Annals - Xian Ji* (《呂氏春秋•先己》): "五帝先道而後德. 高誘注: 先, 猶尚也." See 《漢語大字典》.

(546) "Four-horse carriages (駟馬)" refers to the high social status of a minister (including the Three Mentors), who had the privilege of having his carriage pulled by four horses (卿駕四). See footnote 340.

(547) "坐" here is "naturally (自然而然的)", as in:
  I.   "坐, 猶自也" in Zhang Xiang's (張相) *Annotations to Words and Phrases in Poems and Verses - Volume IV* (《詩詞曲語辭匯釋•卷四》).
  II. "墮肢體黜聰明, 離形去知, 同於大通, 是謂坐忘" in *Zhuangzi - The Great and Most Honoured Master* (《莊子•大宗師》).
  Source: 中央研究院《搜詞尋字》.

(548) "進" here is "progress to (行)", as in:
  I.   "進, 行也" in *Guangya - Shigu I* (《廣雅•釋詁一》).

II. "徒銜枚而進. 鄭玄注：進, 行也" in *The Rites of Zhou - Offices of Summer* (《周禮•夏官》).

III. "進而視之, 欲其微至也. 鄭玄注：進, 猶行也." in *Record of Trades - Lun Ren* (《考工記•輪人》).

Source: 中央研究院《搜詞尋字》.

(549) The correct interpretation in vernacular Chinese of Line 168 should be:

"對於不喜好道的人, 道又怎會丟棄他們呢? 故此, 確立天子設置三公, 雖則天子有拱璧之大的財寶, 三公有駟馬之車的尊崇, 倒不如自然而然地實踐此道."

(interpreted by Kwok Kin Poon)

(550) "德" here is not Confucius's "moral virtue (德行)" nor "kindness". Since wise sages treat all people with no mercy (Chapter 5 Line 13: 聖人不仁, 以百姓為芻狗), they do not follow the human concept of having "good virtue (善德)" nor "kindness".

Wise sages merely manifest themselves by following Tao, which dictates that one reaps what one sows (Chapter 23 Line 71: "同於道者, 道亦樂得之; 同於德者, 德亦樂得之; 同於失者, 失亦樂得之"). Accordingly, wises sages respond with fair retribution and so will answer "enmity" with "enmity". Indeed, Tao excels in responding (Chapter 73 Line 197: "不言而善應").

As such, "報怨以德" here has nothing to do with Confucius's contention of "return kindness for injury (以德報怨)" seen in *The Classic of Rites - Biao Ji* (《禮記•表記》): "以德報怨, 則寬身之仁也." See James Legge's *The Sacred Books of China, The Texts of Confucianism.*

Many scholars of the past and present have mistakenly interpreted Laozi's "報怨以德" as Confucius's "以德報怨". One example is renowned late Qing scholar Kang Youwei (康有為), who wrote:

"以德報怨, 其學出於老子."

"Return kindness for injury; such thought is derived from Laozi."

(interpreted by KS Vincent Poon)

Source: *A Study of Confucius as a Reformer* (《孔子改制考》), 卷二, 周末諸子並起創教考之道家創教.

(551) The correct interpretation in vernacular Chinese of Line 170 should be:

"幹那沒有私慾的行為; 做那沒有大功的事情; 嚐那沒有好壞的味道. 無分大小多少, 我僅用大自然的規律(德)來回應仇怨."

(interpreted by Kwok Kin Poon)

(552) "作" here means "originate (始)", as in:
I. "作, 始也" in *Guangya - Shigu I* (《廣雅•釋詁一》).
II. "烝民乃粒, 萬邦作乂" in the *Book of Documents - Yi and Ji* (《書經•益稷》).
Source: 中央研究院《搜詞尋字》.

(553) "終" here is "ultimately (終究/畢竟)", as in:
I. "不矜細行，終累大德" in *Book of Documents - Lu Ao* (《書經• 旅獒》).
II. "騰蛇乘霧，終為土灰" in Cao Cao's (曹操) *Steps through the Illustrious Gate - Gui Sui Shou* (《步出夏門行•龜雖壽》).
Source: 中央研究院《搜詞尋字》.

(554) "安" here is "calm and tranquil (安靜)", as in:
I. "安, 靜也" in *Shuowen Jiezi* (《說文解字》).
II. "君子安其身而後動. 孔穎達疏： 故先須安靜其身而後動" in the *Book of Changes - The Great Treatise II* (《易經•繫辭下》).
Source: 中央研究院《搜詞尋字》.

(555) "持" here is "grasp (掌握)", as in *Lunheng - Gu Xiang* (《論衡•骨相》)："君後三歲而入將相, 持國秉." See 中央研究院《搜詞尋字》.

(556) "兆" here is "begin/rise (開始)", as in *The Commentary of Zuo - the First Year of Duke Ai* (《左傳•哀公元年》) : " (少康) 能布其德, 而兆其謀, 以收夏眾, 撫其官職...遂滅過、戈, 復禹之績. 杜預注 : 兆, 始也." See 中央研究院《搜詞尋字》.

(557) "泮" here is "break apart (分開/分別)", as in *Records of the Grand Historian - Biography of Lu Jia* (《史記•陸賈傳》) : "自天地剖泮未始有也." See 《重編國語辭典修訂本》.

(558) "散" here means "break up (開裂)", as in:
   I. "淩澗尋我室, 散帙問所知" in Xie Lingyun's (謝靈運) *Chou Cong Di Hui Lian* (《酬從弟惠連》).
   II. "香草已堪回步履, 午風聊復散衣襟" in Wang Anshi's (王安石) *Ci Yu He Ji Cheng Bei Hui Shang Zhu You* (《 次御河寄城北會上諸友》).
   Source: 中央研究院《搜詞尋字》.

(559) A sturdy tree (木) of one's entire embrace is not favourable, for "wood that is strong will be quickly chopped down (木強則兵)". See Chapter 76 Line 205.

(560) As such, one should not allow any sprout to rise in the first place.

(561) This "overly lavished elevated terrace (高臺)" is not favourable, for constructing too many luxurious buildings shall lead to ill-cultivated fields and empty granaries (朝甚除, 田甚蕪, 倉甚虛). See Chapter 53 Line 145.

(562) "起" here means "rises from (開始)", as in:
   I. "起, 引伸之為凡始事、凡興作之偁" in *Shuowen Jiezi Zhu* (《說文解字注》).
   II. "明法度, 定律令, 皆以始皇起" in *Records of the Grand Historian - Biography of Li Si* (《史記•李斯列傳》).
   Source: 中央研究院《搜詞尋字》.

(563) As such, one should not even accumulate any soil to build the terrace in the first place.

(564) This "journey (行/外遊)" of thousands of miles is not favourable, for as one walks further away from home and exhausts oneself, the less one knows about Tao (其出彌遠, 其知彌少). See Chapter 47 Line 130.

(565) "足下" here means "at one's foot (腳下)", as in Yue Fu Shi Ji - *Jiao Zhong Qing Qi* (《樂府詩集‧焦仲卿妻》): "足下躡絲履, 頭上玳瑁光." See 《重編國語辭典修訂本》.

As such, one should not even make a single step to start any journey in the first place.

(566) The correct interpretation in vernacular Chinese of Line 173 should be:

"靜態的事情易於掌握, 未發生的事情易於謀策. 脆弱的事情易於擊碎, 微小的事情易於破散. 在事情未發生前要預先治理, 在事情未紛亂前要預先整治. 給人砍伐的粗如合抱的巨樹, 生長自極細的幼苗; 甚費人力物力的九層巨大高臺, 開始於堆積第一筐的泥土; 令人疲累的千里外遊, 開始於你提起腳掌走的第一步."

(interpreted by Kwok Kin Poon)

(567) "從" here means "conduct a matter (為/從事)", as in *Guanzi - Zheng Shi* (《管子‧正世》): "知得失之所在, 然後從事. 尹知章注：從, 為." See 中央研究院《搜詞尋字》.

(568) "過" here means "lost (失掉)", as in *Discourses of the States - Discourses of Zhou I* (《國語‧周語上》): "夫天地之氣, 不失其序; 若過其序, 民亂之也. 韋昭注：過, 失也." See 中央研究院《搜詞尋字》.

In our context, this "lost" refers to the people losing their inherent simplicities bestowed by Tao while living in a sophisticated society.

(569) The correct interpretation in vernacular Chinese of "復衆人之所過" should be:

"讓人們復得所失掉的道."

(interpreted by Kwok Kin Poon)

(570) "以" here is "merely (惟/祇)", as in *Strategies of the Warring States - Strategies of Qi IV* (《戰國策•齊策四》) : "君家所寡有者, 以義耳." See 中央研究院《搜詞尋字》.

(571) "輔" here is "to facilitate (佐助)", as in:
I.   "輔, 助也" in *Guangya - Shigu III* (《廣雅•釋詁二》).
II. "爾尚輔予一人" in the *Book of Documents - Speech of Tang* (《書經•湯誓》).
Source: 中央研究院《搜詞尋字》.

(572) "以" here is "because (因為/由於)", as in *The Analects - Wei Ling Gong* (《論語•衛靈公》) : "君子不以言舉人, 不以人廢言." See 中央研究院《搜詞尋字》.

(573) "賊" here means "vandalize (毀)", as in:
I.   "賊, 敗也. 段玉裁注 : 敗者, 毀也. 毀者, 缺也" in *Shuowen Jiezi Zhu* (《說文解字注》).
II. "毀則為賊. 杜預注 : 毀則, 壞法也" in *The Commentary of Zuo - the Eighteenth Year of Duke Wen* (《左傳•文公十八年》).
Source: 中央研究院《搜詞尋字》.

(574) "稽" here means "the same (同)", as annotated by Wang Bi (王弼): "稽, 同也."See 王弼《老子王弼注》. 台北: 新興書局, 1964, p.079.

(575) "與" here is "engage in (參與)", as in:
I.   "與, 參與也" in *Guangyun* (《廣韻•御韻》).
II. "非天下之至變, 其孰能與於此" in the *Book of Changes - The Great Treatise I* (《易經•繫辭上》).

Source: 中央研究院《搜詞尋字》.

(576) See footnote 114

(577) "言" here is "oneself (我)", as in:
   I.   "言，我也" in *Erya - Shigu I* (《爾雅•釋詁上》).
   II. "彤弓弨兮，受言藏之. 毛傳：言，我也" in *The Book of Odes - Minor Odes of the Kingdom - Tong Gong* (《詩經•小雅•彤弓》).
   III. "弋言加之，與子宜之. 鄭玄箋：言，我也" in *The Book of Odes - Odes Of Zheng - NueYue Ji Ming* (《詩經•鄭風•女曰雞鳴》).
   Source: 中央研究院《搜詞尋字》.

(578) The correct interpretation in vernacular Chinese of "是以欲上民, 必以言下之" should be:
   "故此, 若想居於百姓之上, 那就必須我先處於百姓之下."
   (interpreted by Kwok Kin Poon)

(579) "先" here is "lead (引導/倡導)", as in:
   I.   "明智禮, 足以教之, 上身服以先之. 尹知章注：所以率先於下也" in *Guanzi - Da Kuang* (《管子•權修》).
   II. "躬以簡儉為天下先" in Wang Anshi's (王安石) *Ben Chao Bai Nian Wu Shi Zha Zi* (《本朝百年無事札子》).
   Source: 中央研究院《搜詞尋字》.

(580) "重" here is "burdensome (負累)", as in *The Book of Odes - Minor Odes of the Kingdom - Wu Jiang Da Che* (《詩經•小雅•無將大車》)："無思百憂, 祇自重兮. 鄭玄箋：重, 猶累也." See 中央研究院《搜詞尋字》.

(581) The correct interpretation in vernacular Chinese of "是以聖人處上而民不重, 處前而民不害" should be:
   "故此聖人居於高位而百姓不覺得他是一重負擔, 居於領導而百姓也不覺得他會帶來傷害."
(interpreted by Kwok Kin Poon)

(582) "樂推" here means "willing to endorse (樂意擁戴)", as in the *Book of Song - Annals of Emperor Wu II* (《宋書•武帝紀中》) : "自非百姓樂推, 天命攸集, 豈伊在予, 所得獨專." See 《漢語大詞典》.

(583) Tao is indescribable (Chapter 1 Line 1), for it is infinitely great without limit. If an entity can be described by humans and appears as great, it must thus be describable and so cannot be infinitely great without limit. Hence, it must be small, as Wang Bi (王弼) annotated:
> "肖則失其所以為大矣."
> Source: 王弼《老子王弼注》. 台北: 新興書局, 1964, p.080.

The correct interpretation in vernacular Chinese of Line 181 should be:
> "世人都認為我說道大, 但它卻全不似大. 正因為大, 故此它才全不似大呢. 假若似大, 它老早就是細啦!"
> (interpreted by Kwok Kin Poon)

(584) "持" here means "uphold (握住)", as in:
I.   "持, 握也" in *Shuowen Jiezi* (《說文解字》).
II. "媼之送燕后也, 持其踵為之泣" in *Strategies of the Warring States - Strategies of Zhao IV* (《戰國策•趙策四》).
Source: 中央研究院《搜詞尋字》.

(585) "保" here is "rely on (恃/憑藉)", as in *The Commentary of Zuo - the Twenty-third Year of Duke Xi* (《左傳•僖公二十三年》) : "保君父之命而享其生祿, 於是乎得人. 杜預注：保, 猶恃也." See中央研究院《搜詞尋字》.

(586) "慈" here is "earnest adoration (篤愛)", as in *The Com-*

mentary of Zuo - the Twenty-seventh year of Duke Zhuang (《左傳•莊公二十七年》)：“夫禮樂慈愛, 戰所畜也. 孔穎達疏：慈謂愛之深也.” See中央研究院《搜詞尋字》.

“慈” here is not Confucius's “benevolence and kindness (仁慈)”. This is because wise sages do not follow the concept of being benevolent or having kindness (Chapter 5 Line 13: 聖人不仁, 以百姓為芻狗).

Accordingly, “慈” only applies to a wise sage's attitude towards Tao, which is “earnest adoration”.

(587) “儉” here is “frugality (節省/簡樸)”, as in:
   I.   “儉, 省節也” in *Pianhai Leibian* (《篇海類編•人物類•人部》).
   II. “禮, 與其奢也, 寧儉. 皇侃注：去奢從約謂之儉” in *The Analects - Ba Yi* (《論語•八佾》).
   Source: 中央研究院《搜詞尋字》.

(588) See footnote 579.

(589) Why should one dare not to lead and be the most preeminent? This is because “if one wishes to be positioned above the people, then one must put oneself below the people”. See Chapter 69 Line 179.

(590) The correct interpretation in vernacular Chinese of “我有三寶, 持而保之：一曰慈, 二曰儉, 三曰不敢為天下先” should be:
   “我有三寶, 常緊握而依仗著它：一稱為篤愛於道, 二稱為節儉素樸, 三稱為不敢做天下的領導.”
   (interpreted by Kwok Kin Poon)

(591) “廣” here means “prosper (增多/增強)”, as in the *Book of Han - Treatise on Food and Money I* (《漢書•食貨志上》)：“薄賦斂, 廣畜積.” See 中央研究院《搜詞尋字》.

(592) “且” here means “adopt (取)”, as annotated by Wang Bi (

王弼): "且, 猶取也." See 王弼《老子王弼注》. 台北: 新興書局, 1964, p.081.

(593) See footnote 313.

(594) See Chapter 28 Line 80 and footnote 221.

(595) See footnote 104.

(596) "士" here means "the commander-in-chief of soldiers (帥)", as annotated by Wang Bi (王弼): "士, 卒之帥也." See 王弼《老子王弼注》. 台北: 新興書局, 1964, p.081.

(597) "與" here means "to battle (戰)", as in *The Commentary of Zuo - the Ninth year of Duke Ai* (《左傳•哀公九年》) : "宋方吉, 不可與也. 杜預注 : 不可與戰." See 中央研究院《搜詞尋字》.

(598) See footnote 408.

(599) See Chapter 66 Line 180.

(600) See footnote 325.

(601) "扔" here means "defeat (摧)", as in the *Book of the Later Han - Biography of Ma Rong* (《後漢書•馬融》): "竄伏扔輪. 註: 言爲輪所摧也." See *Kangxi Dictionary* (《康熙字典》).

(602) "無敵" here means "being defeated (不敵)", for "無" can be "不" according to *Kangxi Dictionary* (《康熙字典》): "無, 猶不也."

(603) Line 187 does not mean Laozi had recommended one to be pretending, scheming, or calculating. Rather, Laozi here advised one should always be cautious and consider oneself to be at a disadvantage. See Line 188.

(604) "幾" here means "will then (則)" as in:

   I. "幾, 猶則也" in *A Collection of the Annotations of Functional Words in Ancient Books - Volume V* (《古書虛字集釋•卷五》).

   II. "其無乃廢先王之訓, 而王幾頓乎" in *Discourses of the States - Discourses of Zhou I* (《國語•周語上》).

   Source: 中央研究院《搜詞尋字》.

(605) For Laozi's treasures (寶), see Chapter 67 Line 182.

(606) "抗" here means "raises (舉)", as in:

   I. "抗, 舉也" in *Guangya - Shigu I* (《廣雅•釋詁一》).

   II. "大侯既抗, 弓矢斯張. 毛傳：抗, 舉也" in *The Book of Odes - Minor Odes of the Kingdom - Bin Zhi Chu Yan* (《詩經•小雅•賓之初筵》).

   Source: 中央研究院《搜詞尋字》.

(607) "加" here is "to counter an enemy (抵擋敵人)", as in:

   I. "加, 當也" in 王弼《老子王弼注》. 台北: 新興書局, 1964, p.082.

   II. "當, 敵也" in *Yupian* (《玉篇》). See 中央研究院《搜詞尋字》.

   III. "然則君請當其君, 臣請當其臣. 何休注：當, 猶敵也" in *Gongyang Zhuan - the Twenty-third Year of Duke Zhuang* (《公羊傳•莊公十三年》). See 中央研究院《搜詞尋字》.

(608) The sorrowful side considers itself to be at a disadvantage and so never underestimates its enemies. Hence, it is more likely to prevail.

(609) Why most are unable to understand and carry out Laozi's words? This is because many are tainted with selfish desires and lusts for glory, as annotated by Wang Bi (王弼):

"惑於躁欲, 故曰莫之能知也; 迷於榮利, 故曰莫之能行也."

Source: 王弼《老子王弼注》. 台北: 新興書局, 1964, p.083.

(610) "言" here means "narratives (言論/見解)", as in:
  I. "如何昊天？辟言不信" in *The Book of Odes - Minor Odes of the Kingdom - Yu Wu Zheng* (《詩經•小雅•雨無正》).
  II. "言無二貴, 法不兩適. 故言行而不軌於法令者必禁" in *Hanfeitzu - Wen Bian* (《韓非子•問辯》).
  Source: 中央研究院《搜詞尋字》.

(611) "宗" here means "foundational basis (根本)", as in:
  I. "宗, 本也" in *Guangya - Shigu III* (《廣雅•釋詁三》).
  II. "禮賓矜窮, 禮之宗也. 韋昭注：宗, 本也" in *Discourses of the States - Discourses of Jin IV* (《國語•晉語四》).
  Source: 中央研究院《搜詞尋字》.

(612) See footnote 208. The "lord (君)" here refers to Manifestation of Tao.

(613) The correct interpretation in vernacular Chinese of Line 190 should be:
  "言論要有個根本, 事物總有個主宰(德). 祇因人們不懂得這道理, 所以才不了解我."
  (interpreted by Kwok Kin Poon)

(614) "希" here is "rare (罕/少)", as in *Erya - Shigu II* (《爾雅•釋詁下》) : "希, 罕也." See 中央研究院《搜詞尋字》.

(615) "則" here is "model after (效法)", as in:
  I. "惟天為大, 惟堯則之" in *Mengzi - Teng Wen Gong I* (《孟子•滕文公上》).
  II. "皋陶於是敬禹之德, 令民皆則禹" in *Records of the Grand Historian - Annals of Xia* (《史記•夏本紀》).

Source: 中央研究院《搜詞尋字》.

(616) The correct interpretation in vernacular Chinese of Line 191 should be:

"了解我的人極少, 效法我的更屬難能可貴. 故此也證明了聖人身上穿的是卑賤的麻衣, 心內藏的卻是無價的寶玉呀!"

(interpreted by Kwok Kin Poon)

(617) "知不知, 上" should not be taken as "understand yet pretend not to understand is superior". This is because Laozi had always opposed dishonesty.

"知不知, 上" should also not be taken as "understand that one does not understand is superior". Even those who follow and understand Tao can only be considered as enlightened, not superior. Merely understanding that one does not understand Tao certainly does not qualified to be called superior.

Line 192 should be interpreted along with the previous "知我者希" in Line 191. This "知" in Line 192 "知不知, 上" carries the same implication of understanding Laozi "知我" in Line 191.

Remarkably, Laozi's teaching of "understanding (知)" and "not understanding (不知)" was nicely borrowed by Tang Calligrapher Sun Guoting (孫過庭) in his *A Narrative on Calligraphy* (書譜):

"門生獲書機, 父削而子懊. 知與不知也. 夫士屈于不知己, 而申於知己. 彼不知也, 曷足怪乎?! ... 老子云: '下士聞道, 大咲之; 不咲之則不足以為道也.'"

"...the story of a disciple (of Wang Xizhi) who first acquired Wang Xizhi's calligraphy scribed on his long table but later lost it for his father scraped it off, leaving the son shocked and remorseful. Such stories illustrate the difference between truly comprehending and not comprehending the art. Alas, an intellect grieves when others do not comprehend him and becomes free and at ease when others comprehend him. For those who do not comprehend, why should we bother to blame or criticize them?! ... as Laozi once stated, 'Scholars of the lowest class, when they have heard about Dao, laugh greatly at it. If it were not (thus) laughed at, it would not be fit to be the Dao.'"

Source: KS Vincent Poon & Kwok Kin Poon, *A Narrative on Calligraphy by Sun Guoting, Revised and Enhanced Edition* 英譯書譜增訂版, pp.61-62.

(618) "病" here is "suffering from exhaustion (苦/疲憊)", as in:

    I.   "人極于病. 傳: 欲使惡人極于病苦, 莫敢犯者" in the *Book of Documents - Marquis of Lu on Punishments* (《書經•呂刑》). See *Kangxi Dictionary* (《康熙字典》).

    II. "今日病矣, 予助苗長矣！趙岐注：病, 罷也" in *Mengzi - Gong Sun Chou I* (《孟子•公孫丑上》). See 中央研究院《搜詞尋字》.

    III. "此恐吾攻己, 故示我不病. 請為戮千乘, 卒三萬, 與分吳地也" in *Shuo Yuan - Quan Mou* (《說苑•權謀》).

    Source: 中央研究院《搜詞尋字》.

"病" here cannot be "diseased" nor "sick". All humans, including those who understand Tao, can contract diseases and become sick.

(619) The correct interpretation in vernacular Chinese of Line 192 should be:

"能知曉那些不懂道的, 此乃優尚; 沒能知曉那懂道的, 可就疲苦了."

(interpreted by Kwok Kin Poon)

(620) The correct interpretation in vernacular Chinese of Line 193 should be:

"因為了解疲苦之所以成為疲苦, 所以才會不疲苦. 聖人不疲苦, 因為他了解疲苦之所以成為疲苦, 所以就不疲苦了."

(interpreted by Kwok Kin Poon)

(621) "狎" here means "alter (易)", as in *Yupian* (《玉篇》): "狎, 易也." See *Kangxi Dictionary* (《康熙字典》).

(622) "厭" here means "inflict harm (損害/迫害)", as in *The Commentary of Zuo - the Second Year of Duke Wen* (《左傳•文公二年》): "及晉處父盟以厭之. 註: 厭猶損也." See *Kangxi Dictionary* (《康熙字典》).

(623) The correct interpretation in vernacular Chinese of Line 194 should be:

> "當百姓再不懼怕君主的威嚇時, 他們天大的怒威便即來臨了. 不要遷移人們居住的地方, 也不要傷害人們維生的生計. 因為你不迫害百姓, 故此百姓才不會傷害你."
> (interpreted by Kwok Kin Poon)

(624) "自知" here means "understand oneself (了解自身)", as in Su Shi's (蘇軾) *Yu Ye Jin Shu Shu*《與葉進叔書》: "僕聞有自知之明者, 乃所以知人." See 《重編國語辭典修訂本》. See also Chapter 33 Line 98.

(625) "敢" here means "aggressive (進取)", as indicated in *Shuowen Jiezi* (《說文解字》).

(626) "殺" here means "caused to have an unnatural death (致死)" as in:

> I.   "殺, 戮也" in *Shuowen Jiezi* (《說文解字》).
> II. "志士仁人, 無求生以害仁, 有殺身以成仁" in *The Analects - Wei Ling Gong* (《論語•衛靈公》).
> Source: 中央研究院《搜詞尋字》.

(627) The correct interpretation in vernacular Chinese of Line 196 should be:

> "勇於進取的那就喪命; 勇於不進取的那就活命. 這兩者, 有利也有害. 大自然之所厭惡, 誰曉得箇中的原故呢? 所以就聖人尚且覺得這是很困難的呀!"

(interpreted by Kwok Kin Poon)

(628) "繟" here is "at ease (舒緩/舒坦)", as indicated in *Shuowen Jiezi* (《說文解字》): "繟, 帶緩也."

(629) "恢恢" here is "wide and far apart (寬闊廣大的樣子)", as in *Selections of Refined Literature - Lu Ji - Han Gao Zu Gong Chen Song* (《文選•陸機•漢高祖功臣頌》) : "恢恢廣野, 誕節令圖." See 《重編國語辭典修訂本》.

(630) See footnote 486.

(631) "常" refers to Tao. See footnote 1.

(632) "司" here is "administrate (掌管/主持)", as in:
  I. "司, 主也. 盜賊司目, 民無所放" in *Guangya - Shigu III* (《廣雅•釋詁三》).
  II. "彼其之子, 邦之司直. 毛傳：司, 主也" in *The Book of Odes - Odes Of Zheng - Gao Qiu* (《詩經•鄭風•羔裘》).
  Source: 中央研究院《搜詞尋字》.

(633) The correct interpretation in vernacular Chinese of "常有司殺者殺. 夫代司殺者殺, 是謂代大匠斲" should be:
  "然而, 常道自有掌管殺戮的去殺. 你替代掌管殺戮的去殺, 這就叫做替代技藝高超的木匠來伐木了."
  (interpreted by Kwok Kin Poon)

(634) See footnote 614.

(635) See footnote 421.

(636) See footnote 365.

(637) "為" here means "seek (謀求)", as in *Mengzi - Jin Xin I* (《

183

孟子•盡心上》) : "雞鳴而起, 孳孳為利者, 跖之徒也." See 中央研究院《搜詞尋字》.

(638) The correct interpretation in vernacular Chinese of Line 202 should be:

> "唯獨不貪求財物的君主, 才肯定遠勝那些視財如命、徵收重稅的君主哩!"
> (interpreted by Kwok Kin Poon)

(639) "兵" here is "kill or inflict injury by a weapon (用兵器殺傷)", as in *Records of the Grand Historian - Biography of Bo Yi* (《史記•伯夷列傳》) : "左右欲兵之." See 中央研究院《搜詞尋字》.

In our context, since "兵" is applied to wood, it should be interpreted as "chop down by a tool".

(640) "奉" here means "to gift to (送/給予)", as in:

I. "奉, 與也" in *Guangyun* (《廣韻•腫韻》).

II. "秦違蹇叔, 而以貪勤民, 天奉我也. 杜預注 : 奉, 與也" in *The Commentary of Zuo - the Thirty-third Year of Duke Xi* (《左傳•僖公三十三年》).

III. "比奉書, 即蒙寵答, 以感以怍" in Wang Anshi's (王安石) *Yu Ma Yun Pan Shu* (《與馬運判書》).

Source: 中央研究院《搜詞尋字》.

(641) "者" here is "an auxiliary word that is used at the end of a sentence as an intonation (語氣助詞)". See footnote 536.

(642) Wise sages do not depend on others; they only rely on Tao. Tao also does not depend on others; it only relies on Tao itself. See footnote 13.

(643) "勝" here means "better than (優過之)", as in *Master Zhou's Almanac* (《周子通書》): "實勝善也, 名勝恥也." See *Kangxi Dictionary* (《康熙字典》).

(644) "以" here is "therefore (因此)", as in:

I. "以, 因也 " in *Zhengzitong* (《正字通•人部》).

II. "孝公得商君, 地以廣, 兵以強" in *Hanfeitzu - Jian Jie Shi Chen* (《韓非子•姦劫弒臣》).

Source: 中央研究院《搜詞尋字》.

(645) "易" here is "replace (替代)", as in *The Commentary of Zuo - the Thirtieth Year of Duke Xi* (《左傳•僖公三十年》): "因人之力而敝之, 不仁; 失其所與, 不知; 以亂易整, 不武." See 中央研究院《搜詞尋字》.

(646) "受" here is "accept (容納)", as in:

I. "受, 容納也" in *Kangxi Dictionary* (《康熙字典》).

II. "君子以虛受人" in the *Book of Changes - Xian* (《易經•咸》). See 中央研究院《搜詞尋字》.

(647) "垢" here is "shame (恥辱)", as in:

I. "國君含垢, 天之道也. 杜預注：忍垢恥" in *The Commentary of Zuo - the Fifteenth Year of Duke Xuan* (《左傳•宣公十五年》). See《漢語大字典》.

II. "忍垢苟全, 則犯詩人胡顏之譏" in *Selections of Refined Literature - Cao Zhi - Shang Ze Gong Ying Zhao Shi Biao* (《文選•曹植•上責躬應詔詩表》). See 《重編國語辭典修訂本》.

(648) "社稷" originally means "god of the land and god of the crops (土神和穀神)", but later refers to "state (國)", as in:

I. "能執干戈以衛社稷, 雖欲勿殤也, 不亦可乎" in *The Classic of Rites - Tan Gong II* (《禮記•檀弓下》).

II. "食人之祿, 當分人之憂, 苟利社稷, 死生以之" in Wang Shizhen's (王世貞) *Ming Feng Ji* (《鳴鳳記》).

Source: 《重編國語辭典修訂本》.

(649) "不祥" here means "misdeeds (不善)", as in *Strategies of the Warring States - Strategies of Qi IV* (《戰國策•齊策四》) : "

寡人不祥，被於宗廟之崇，沉於諂諛之臣." See 《重編國語辭典修訂本》.

(650) "正言" here is "proper narratives (合於正道的言論)", as in Kuan Huan's (桓寬) *Yan Tie Lun* (《鹽鐵論》): "藥酒, 病之利也; 正言, 治之藥也." See 《漢語大詞典》.
　"言" is "言論", see footnote 610.

(651) "若" here is "is/are/does(乃)", not "seemingly" or "as if". See footnote 31.

(652) "正言若反" cannot be "proper narratives appear to be pointing towards the opposite" nor "proper narratives are seemingly improper". If these interpretations were true, then *Tao Te Ching* would have narrated "one should not follow Tao" in order to tell "one should follow Tao"; such is clearly not the case.
　Tao embraces and includes all human points of views, for there is actually nothing that is absolutely agreeable nor disagreeable (Chapter 58 Line 158: "正復為奇, 善復為妖"). A wise ruler, therefore, merely focuses on returning all back to Tao by accepting the existence of countering ways manifested by Tao (Chapter 40 Line 115: 反者道之動). Such is the gist of Line 211.
　Accordingly, the correct interpretation in vernacular Chinese of "正言若反" is:
　　"合於正道的言論, 乃是容納一切相反面而同返於道的言論."
　　(interpreted by Kwok Kin Poon)
　Note "反" in "正言若反" can take the meaning of "countering ways", "restoring back to Tao", or both.

(653) "左契" here is "notes or documents that provide evidence of proof (證明文件/證明書)", such as "land deeds (田契)" or "contracts (契約)".
　"左" carries the meaning of "evidence of proof (佐證/憑證)", as in:
　　I.　"左, 證左也" in *Shiya - Shi Xun II* (《拾雅•釋訓中》).

II. "廷尉定國考問, 左驗明白. 顏師古注：左, 證左也. 言
當時在其左右見此事者也" in the *Book of Han - Biography of Yang Chang and Yang Jun* (《漢書•楊敞傳附楊惲》).

Source: 中央研究院《搜詞尋字》.

"契" here is "notes or documents (券)", as in:

I. "契, 券也" in *Yupian* (《玉篇•大部》).

II. "掌稽市之書契. 鄭玄注：書契, 取予市物之券也" in
The Rites of Zhou - Offices of Earth (《周禮•地官》).

Source: 中央研究院《搜詞尋字》.

An example of "左契" as "notes or documents that provide evidence of proof" can be seen in Du Mu's (杜牧) *Hang Zhou Xin Zao Nan Ting Zi Ji* (《杭州新造南亭子記》)："今權歸於佛, 買福賣罪, 如持左契, 交手相付." See 《漢語大詞典》.

"Notes or documents that provide evidence of proof", such as contracts, are generally made based upon willing mutual consents. Accordingly, grievances can be minimized if all parties follow these documents devotedly, as Wang Bi (王弼) annotated:

"左契防怨之所由生也."

Source: 王弼《老子王弼注》. 台北: 新興書局, 1964, p.089.

(654) "責" here means "demand (索取)", as indicated in *Shuowen Jiezi* (《說文解字》): "責, 求也."

(655) "德" here is not Confucius's "moral virtues (德行)". Rather, it is the resulting outcome (i.e., manifestation) of following Tao. Laozi abhorred Confucius's "moral values". See Chapter 38 Line 108 and footnote 322.

(656) See footnote 632.

(657) "(契)" here refers to "documents that provide evidence of proof (左契)". See footnote 653.

(658) "Che (徹)" here refers to "the land taxation system (田稅制度)" under Zhou Dynasty's Well-field system (井田制度), as elaborated in:

I. "徹, 稅也" in *Guangya - Shigu II* (《廣雅•釋詁二》).

II. "夏后氏五十而貢, 殷人七十而助, 周人百畝而徹, 其實皆什一也. 趙岐注：家耕百畝者徹, 取十畝以為賦. 名雖異而多少同, 故曰皆什一也" in *Mengzi - Teng Wen Gong I* (《孟子•滕文公上》).

III. "夫十一而稅, 周謂之徹" in the *Book of the Later Han - Biography of Lu Kang* (《後漢書•陸康傳》).

Source: 中央研究院《搜詞尋字》.

(659) Wise sages never demand anything from the people (Line 212: "不責於人"). Therefore, they only focus on adhering to agreements and documents (有德司契). Only those without the Manifestation of Tao will focus on demanding taxes from the people (無德司徹).

(660) "與" here means "support (助)", as in *Mengzi - Gong Sun Chou I* (《孟子•公孫丑上》): "取諸人以為善, 是與人為善者也. 朱熹集注：與, 猶助也." See 中央研究院《搜詞尋字》.

(661) "善" here should be distinguished from its usual meaning of "good", "nice", or "kind". Here, it refers to those who are "well-acquainted with Tao" or "rich in Tao". See footnote 35.

(662) The correct interpretation in vernacular Chinese of Line 213 should be:

"有德的人祇掌管田地約契, 無德的人掌管的是用稅制徹法來徵稅. 大自然之道可沒什麼親或不親的, 祇常常幫助那些喜好於道的人."

(interpreted by Kwok Kin Poon)

(663) "使" here is "makes/results in (讓/致使)", as in :

I. "維子之故, 使我不能餐兮" in *The Book of Odes -*

Odes Of Zheng - Jiao Tong (《詩經•鄭風•狡童》).

II. "出師未捷身先死, 長使英雄淚滿襟" in Du Fu's (杜甫) *Shu Xiang* (《蜀相》).

Source: 中央研究院《搜詞尋字》.

(664) "什伯" here means "more than a tenfold or a hundredfold (超過十倍百倍)", as in *Mengzi - Teng Wen Gong I* (《孟子•滕文公上》): "夫物之不齊, 物之情也. 或相倍蓰, 或相什伯, 或相千萬." See 《漢語大字典》.

(665) Why no contact with other states? This is because people living by Tao do not possess any selfish desire, and so all are content with whatever their circumstances. Accordingly, it is unnecessary to deal with any other state. Hence, Wang Bi (王弼) annotated these people as "having nothing to desire for themselves (無所欲求)". See 王弼《老子王弼注》. 台北: 新興書局, 1964, p.091.

(666) "既以" here is "since already (既然已經)", as in *Xunzi - Fu Guo* (《荀子•富國》) : "既以伐其本, 竭其原, 而焦天下矣." See 《漢語大詞典》.

(667) "為" here is "to gift (施/給與)", as in *The Commentary of Zuo - the Twenty-third Year of Duke Xiang* (《左傳•襄公二十三年》 : "齊侯將為臧紇田. 杜預注 : 與之田邑." See 中央研究院《搜詞尋字》.

(668) Why do they possess plenty? Since wise sages gift themselves to all, everyone reveres and endorses them, as annotate by Wang Bi (王弼):

"物(人)所尊也."

Source: 王弼《老子王弼注》. 台北: 新興書局, 1964, p.091.

(669) "與" here means "bestow (給予)", as in:

I. "天子不能以天下與人" in *Mengzi - Wan Zhang I* (《孟

子•萬章上》).

II. "此明君且常與, 而賢臣且常取也" in *Hanfeitzu - Zhong Xiao* (《韓非子•忠孝》).

Source: 中央研究院《搜詞尋字》.

(670) Why are they more affluent? Since wise sages bestow themselves upon all, everyone follows them, as annotated by Wang Bi (王弼):

"物所歸也."

Source: 王弼《老子王弼注》. 台北: 新興書局, 1964, p.091.

(671) The correct interpretation in vernacular Chinese of Line 218 should be:

"聖人不會為自己積聚財貨. 既然已經把自己的施予他人, 那麼自己就愈為富裕; 既然已經把自己的贈與他人, 那麼自己就愈為豐餘."

(interpreted by Kwok Kin Poon)

(672) "利" is "benefit (利益)", as in:

I. "利, 所得而喜也" in *Mo Yze - Canon I* (《墨子•經上》).

II. "利, 害之反" in *Zhengzitong* (《正字通》).

III. "是能容之, 以保我子孫黎民, 亦職有利哉" in the *Book of Documents - Tai Shi* (《書經•泰誓》).

Source: 中央研究院《搜詞尋字》.

(673) "為" here should be "to gift (施)". See line 218 and footnote 667.

"為" here should not be taken as "act", for "為而不爭" serves as a direct elaboration on "既以為人己愈有" in Line 218. Further, a wise sage focuses on "無為", not "為". See Chapter 2 Line 6.

(674) The correct interpretation in vernacular Chinese of Line 219 should be:

"大自然之道, 乃利於萬物而不會傷害; 聖人之道, 是施與大眾而不會相爭."

(interpreted by Kwok Kin Poon)

SECTION THREE

Translated Text Only

Pursue to nullify oneself - *Tao Te Ching*

草書 Cursive Script   130x34cm 2000AD
Source: *A Collection of Kwok Kin Poon's Calligraphy*

Laozi's Tao Te Ching (老子道德經)

Translated Text Only

KS Vincent POON (潘君尚) & Kwok Kin POON (潘國鍵)

Chapter 1

1. The Tao (The Tao, The Path, or The Way) that can be spoken or described is not the "Immutable and Everlasting Tao". The Name that can be named or spelt out is not the "immutable and everlasting Name". That which is "unidentifiable and nameless" is the Originator of the Universe, whereas that which is "identifiable and with names" is the Mother of all things.

2. Therefore, the "immutable and everlasting Tao" and the "unidentifiable and nameless" can hopefully be used to examine the unimaginable underlying wonders of Tao; whereas, the "immutable and everlasting Name" and the "identifiable and with names" can hopefully be used to examine the fundamental path that all things follow.

3. Both the "unidentifiable and nameless" and the "identifiable and with names" stem from the same source, but we merely labelled them differently. Similarly, both are regarded as great mysteries. Mysteries upon mysteries, such are the doors and gates to all wonders of Tao and the Universe.

Chapter 2

4. All under Heaven recognize the beauty of the beautiful, and in doing this, they have the idea of what ugliness is; they all recognize the goodness of the good, and in doing this, they have the idea of what not good is.

5. Hence, the idea of "existence" and "non-existence" emerge from each other; "difficult" and "easy" give rise to each other; "long" and "short" compare with each other; "high" and "low" contrast each other; "notes" and "tones" harmonize each other; "front" and "back" accompany each other.

6. This is why a wise sage deals with all matters by "not acting with any personal differentiation and intent" and implements enlightenment of others through the wordless. All things spring up naturally without diction. Tao begets all without anything and acts without relying on any other. Tao accomplishes but never claims any achievement. Alas, it is precisely because it does not claim any achievement that its achievements shall never depart away from all things.

Chapter 3

7. Not honouring distinguished individuals keeps the people away from rivalry among themselves; not prizing goods that are difficult to procure keeps the people away from becoming thieves; not presenting anything that can provoke selfish desires keeps the people's minds away from unrest.

8. Therefore, the wise sage governs to empty the people's minds (to rid their minds of narcissistic and arrogant ideas), to fill their bellies (to rid their thoughts of unnecessary greed), to weaken their wills (to prevent them from carrying out conceited acts), and to strengthen their bones (to maintain their natural healthy bodies).

9. The wise sage constantly seeks to keep the people without acquired knowledge and without selfish desire; this will make those who are clever with acquired intelligence have no place nor condition to apply their skills. If one acts to not act with any personal differentiation and intent, then there is nothing

that one cannot govern or manage well.

Chapter 4

10. Tao is inherently "void and empty" and utilizes this to apply itself; since it is infinitely "void and empty", it is everywhere and invariably never exhaust itself. Deep and unfathomable indeed, it is the most revered fundamental root of all things.

11. Tao dims all brilliance. Tao disintegrates all chaos. Tao harmonizes all light. Tao adapts and merges with the muddy and obscure surroundings. Indeed, Tao is so profound and buried within that it always exists.

12. I do not know whose offspring it is; I imagine it existed before Heaven.

Chapter 5

13. The Universe does not follow the concept of being benevolent. It treats all things with no mercy as if they are straw-made dogs. The wise sages also do not follow the concept of being benevolent; they treat all people with no mercy as if they are straw-made dogs, no different from all other things.

14. Isn't the dynamic realm of our Universe like that of a bellows? When it is left idle, it keeps its original nature of endless emptiness; when operated, the air is expelled, and it becomes more agitated.

15. Accordingly, speaking too much invariably results in the loss of all arguments; hence, it is better to follow and keep one's original idle tranquillity.

Chapter 6

16. The Valley Spirit never dies. Thus, it is known as "The Mysterious Motherly Channel of All Things".

17. The valve of "The Mysterious Motherly Channel" is the root of the Universe.

18. This valve indeed does exist without end and applies itself without any laborious effort.

Chapter 7

19. The Universe is long-enduring and lasts for ages. The reason why the Universe can endure and last thus long is because it does not live of, or for, itself. This is how it can last and endure for so long.

20. Hence, the wise sages put their own selves last and thus find their own selves in the most foremost place; they abandon their own selves and thus find their selves well-preserved.

21. Is this not because of their selflessness? Due to their selflessness, they are able to bring about their own selves.

Chapter 8

22. The most well-versed in Tao is water. Water excels in benefiting all things without competing with others and is always willing to occupy any low place that everyone dislikes. Hence, water resembles Tao.

23. The distinguished ones reside themselves at places that are rich in Tao; their minds settle in the abyssal niches where

Tao rests; they befriend those who are passionate with Tao; their words are with the trustworthiness of Tao; their governances follow the principles of Tao; they employ talents that are well-versed in Tao, and they always act following the timing that is dictated by Tao.

24. Alas, it is because the distinguished ones do not compete with others that no one can thus blame them for anything.

Chapter 9

25. Those who hold and also accumulate are inferior to those who abandon. Those who hammer to become acute and sharpen themselves cannot be preserved for too long.

26. Those who are abundantly wealthy never keep and secure their wealth forever. Those who are conceited because of their wealth are delivering themselves into misfortunes and tragedies.

27. Accordingly, when one's work has been accomplished and one's name has become distinguished, withdrawing into seclusion is the way of Nature.

Chapter 10

28. Resting one's mind to embrace the singular Tao, how can the mind and Tao not be separated in the first place? Holding one's inherent natural forces to become the most gentle, how can one's gentleness match that of a baby? Cleansing ones' mind of imperfection, how can there not be any imperfection in the first place?

29. Loving the people and ruling the state, how can one not use acquired intelligence? Monitoring the opening and closing

of the valve of Motherly Nature, how can one not apply one's motherly way? Achieving a thorough understanding that reaches all corners of the Universe, how can one not first study and learn acquired knowledge?

30. Tao begets all things and nurtures them. It begets them without anything and acts without relying on any other; it oversees all without dominating over them. Such is known as the "Most Mysterious Manifestation of Tao".

Chapter 11

31. In a wooden wheel, thirty spokes assemble around the hub; it is at the empty space of the hub that grants the usefulness of the entire cart.

32. When the clay is fashioned into vessels, it is at the empty space that grants them their usefulness.

33. The door and windows are chiselled out from the walls to form a habitable room; it is at the empty space within the doors and windows that grants the room to be useful and habitable.

34. Hence, a solid entity merely facilitates the application of the void; ultimately, the void is where one finds usefulness and utility.

Chapter 12

35. Feeding one's eyes with all the five colours (i.e., all the different colours) excessively will make one go blind; delivering one's ears with all the five musical notes (i.e., all types of music) immoderately will make one go deaf;

36. Providing one's tongue with all the five flavours (i.e., all the different tastes) exorbitantly will impair one's sense of taste; riding horses and hunting obsessively will make one lose sanity; rare and treasured valuables will motivate one to act towards harming and taking advantage of others.

37. This is why the wise sages only seek to satisfy the bare necessity of their bellies and choose not to be enslaved by what can be seen. Hence, the wise sages leave behind the former mindset of indulgence and choose to take this latter mindset of frugality.

Chapter 13

38. Honour and humiliation are one's anxieties; great tragedies are regarded so high that they have become one's own self.

39. What is "honour and humiliation are one's anxieties"? Honour, which is regarded as superior, ultimately becomes humiliation, which is regarded as lowly. Having honour brings about anxiety, losing it also brings about anxiety. Such is "honour and humiliation are one's anxieties".

40. What is "great tragedies are regarded so high that they have become one's own self"? The reason why I face great tragedies is because I highly regard my precious self. If I do not regard my own self, how then can tragedies be bestowed upon me?

41. Hence, for those who highly regard all under Heaven as themselves, all under Heaven can be entrusted to them; for those who cherish all under Heaven as themselves, all under Heaven can be confided to them.

Chapter 14

42. For an entity that cannot be seen, we name it Yi (The Big); for an entity that cannot be heard, we name it Xi (The Tranquil Silence); for an entity that we cannot hold or grasp, we name it Wei (The Without).

43. These three qualities cannot be thoroughly examined nor inquired, and so they can be together regarded as One. The very top of One is not bright, clear, nor distinct, while the very bottom of One is not dull. The One is endless, cannot be named, and eventually returns to the state of no matter.

44. This One is hence called the form of the formless, phenomenon of the matter-less. It can also be said it is in a state of uncertainty of existence. When one faces it, one cannot see its front; when one chases after it, one cannot see its back.

45. Grasping the ancient way of Tao can thus empower one to oversee and command any realm of the present day. If one is able to comprehend the origin of the ancient Tao, then one can be said as having retained the rules and principles mandated by Tao.

Chapter 15

46. Those in the past who were adept at following Tao to deal with all matters were deeply profound and extraordinary as well as connected themselves with Nature. They were so profound that they were beyond our comprehension. Alas, for they could not be fully comprehended, I can only barely attempt to provide some description of them here:

47. reluctant indeed, they were stepping on frozen streams; cautious indeed, they were fearful of their surroundings; solemn

indeed, they were respectful of rules and principles; scattering indeed, they were melting ices which were evanescent and hard to define; sincere, plain, and honest indeed, they were living solely by their primitive simplicities; brilliant and vast indeed, they were open valleys; murky indeed, they were obscure.

48. What can induce cloudiness, by applying tranquillity, to consequentially and gradually be cleared up? What can make stillness, by applying perpetual dynamic actions, to consequentially and gradually emerge? (Only Tao, nothing else.) Those who understand this rationale never like to be overfilled in any aspect. Alas, for they are not overfilled in any aspect, they are then able to be inconspicuous and take no accomplishment as their own.

Chapter 16

49. Those who follow Tao pursue to nullify themselves to the utmost degree and safeguard their inherent tranquilities with absolute diligence. All things dynamically generate and develop together, and I observe them all inevitably return to their eventualities. Alas, there are so many diverse things, yet every one of them always returns to its respective root (i.e., Tao).

50. Returning to the root is known as being Tranquil, which is otherwise known as returning to the Natural Destiny. Returning to the Natural Destiny is known as adhering to the Immutable. Understanding this Immutable is known as Enlightenment. If one does not know nor understand this Immutable and acts rashly without due consideration, then one shall face ominous outcomes.

51. Knowing this Immutable empowers one to forbear all. Forbearing all means one is unselfish and selfless; being unselfish and selfless means one is the most desirable for all; being the most desirable for all means one is following the way of Nature; following the way of Nature means one is walking the path of Tao. Tao is everywhere, exists all the time, and never ends. Accordingly, walking the path of Tao shall enable one to be free from all peril in one's entire life.

Chapter 17

52. For the finest of superior rulers, their subjects only know of their existences but do not realize their governances. For the lesser rulers, their subjects are close to them and so commend them. For the even lesser rulers, their subjects fear them. For the least of the least rulers, their subjects openly insult and despise them.

53. Are the words above not enough to be credible? How can they not be credible! With this concern in mind, indeed, rulers should weigh heavily when they give speeches or decrees.

54. When the state has accomplished an enormous undertaking, all its people shall hence only say, "We are as we are, of our natural selves!"

Chapter 18

55. When the great and ultimate Tao is not followed, benevolence and righteousness appear. When acquired wisdom and intellect come about, great hypocrisy appears.

56. When there is no harmony among the six kinships, filial piety and parental devotion appear. When the state is in chaos, loyal subordinates appear.

Chapter 19

57. If a society abandons living by the examples of the so-called sages as well as leaving behind acquired wisdom, then its people will benefit a hundredfold. If a society abandons living by benevolence and righteousness, then true filial piety will be revived among its people. If a society abandons living by clever schemes and renounces cherishing personal gains, then there will be no thieves or robbers.

58. As the three narrations above are insufficient to completely illustrate my contentions, so allow me to pen further: one should acknowledge one's pure inherent nature and embrace primitive simplicity, deride selfishness and minimize selfish desires.

Chapter 20

59. If one insulates oneself from acquiring knowledge and not follow scholarly disciplines, then one shall be free from worries. The uttering of a polite "Yes!" and the exclamation of an angry "Ah!", how different are they? What is defined as "good" and what is defined as "bad", how different are they? Nonetheless, one should fear or respect anything that everyone fears or respects.

60. Tao is indeed so vast and spacious that it has no limit, of course! The masses form jolly crowds, feeling happy, hurried and excited; they all seem to be attending a full banquet dining on meat from sacrificial ceremonies or have ascended upon an elevated terrace on a beautiful spring day. It is just me alone, however, who appears to be tranquil indeed and yet to surface; I seem to be as primitive as a baby who has yet to smile and as laid-back indeed as a person who has no direction or goal.

61. Everyone has lots to spare, while I alone am the one who has lost everything. Indeed, I am a foolish man with a senseless mind! How ignorant and foolish indeed I am! Other people are brilliant and conspicuous, while I alone am obtuse and undiscerning. They all are so intelligent and discerning, while I alone am dim-witted.

62. Tranquil indeed, I am the still sea; restless as the high winds indeed, I am without any restraint. Everyone is acting for a reason, while I alone appear to be dim-witted and inferior. I alone am different from all others and value the nurturing Mother Nature.

Chapter 21

63. The rules and principles of the great yet vacuous Manifestation of Tao only follow Tao. When Tao manifests to become objects, it is in a state of uncertainty. A state of uncertainty indeed, within it, there are phenomena. A state of uncertainty indeed, within it, there are matters. Unfathomable depth indeed, within it, there are minuscule essences of all things.

64. These minuscule essences are genuine in existence and can be observed and tested. From the long past to the present, Tao's Name (Manifestation of Tao) has never departed away and is relied upon to endow the birth of all things.

65. How do I know the physical forms of the birth of all things? Solely by the above rationale.

Chapter 22

66. It is the ones that are humble and submissive to Tao that can be fully preserved; it is the ones that are crooked that can be straightened; it is the ones that are dented that can

be filled; it is the ones that are worn that can become new; it is the ones that are deficient that can attain; it is the ones that are rich that can become unsettled. Thus, the wise sages embrace the singular Tao as the principle of all under Heaven.

67. Not showing one's brilliance thus enables one to become enlightened; not being self-assertive and arrogant thus enables one to be celebrated by all others; not being boastful of one's accomplishment thus enables one's merits to be recognized; not being complacent thus enables one to acquire growth and supremacy.

68. Alas, it is because if a person does not compete with others, then no one under Heaven can compete with that person. People of the past once said only those who are humble and submissive to Tao can be preserved; how can that be just empty words! Indeed, complete preservation belongs to those who do not compete with others.

Chapter 23

69. Words that cannot be heard are a fundamental nature of the Manifestation of Tao. Therefore, sounds from violent winds do not last for a whole morning, and noises from sudden torrential rains do not last for an entire day. What directs all these? The Universe. Even the Universe cannot make its own act last forever, let alone mere humans!

70. Hence, from the point of those who follow and serve under Tao: those with Tao shall act the same way as Tao; those with the Manifestation of Tao shall act the same way as the Manifestation of Tao; those who fail both shall act the same way as failing both.

71. Those who act the same way as Tao shall have Tao happily embracing them; those who act the same way as the Manifestation of Tao shall have the Manifestation of Tao happily embracing them; those who act the same way as failing both shall have the way that fails both happily embracing them. Are the words above not enough to be credible? How can they not be credible!

Chapter 24

72. Those who lift their heels can never stand firm; those who crouch down can never walk; those who show their brilliance can never be enlightened; those who are self-assertive and arrogant are never celebrated by all others; those who are boastful of their accomplishments are never recognized for their merits; those who are complacent can never acquire any growth or supremacy.

73. All these impulsive and ostentatious behaviours, from the standpoint of Tao, are known as rotten leftover delicacies as well as bodies of ugly tumours, which are always loathed by the people. Hence, those who have grasped the way of Tao never put themselves to act in such manners.

Chapter 25

74. There is a certain entity that is homogenously turbid yet natural and born before the birth of the Universe. Formless indeed, it singularly exists, never changes, cycles periodically, and never grows tired. Hence, it can manifest itself to become the Mother of all under Heaven.

75. I do not know its name, so I shall designate it as Tao; if one wants to be more specific, we can only barely call it great. It is great; hence, it flows everywhere in all directions. It flows

everywhere in all directions; hence, it can reach the ultimate limit. It can reach the ultimate limit; hence, it must return back to the great Tao. Therefore, Tao is great, Nature is great, Earth is great, and the most desirable for all is also great.

76. In our realm, there are then four greats, and the most desirable for all takes up one of them. Yet, humankind takes its law from Earth; Earth takes its law from Nature; Nature takes its law from the Tao. Tao takes its law naturally from itself (i.e., Tao is what it is).

Chapter 26

77. Gravity and prudence are the foundational roots of frivolity and imprudence. Tranquil stillness is the lord of rash actions. Accordingly, the wise sages, night and day, do not leave behind their heavy supplies to walk with frivolity and imprudence. Even though they are honourable and distinguished, their minds are still unmoved and at ease, taking prudence and tranquillity to transcend above the mundane world .

78. Why then would the rulers of great states, for their own sakes, take all under Heaven lightly with imprudence? If they take the path of imprudence, they shall then lose their foundations to rule. If they act rashly, they shall lose their thrones.

Chapter 27

79. Those who are well acquainted with Tao carry out their tasks without leaving any trace; those who are well acquainted with Tao speaks without any fault; those who are well acquainted with Tao calculate without the need of any instru-

ment; those who are well acquainted with Tao use no bolts or bars to shut a door that can never be thus opened; those who are well acquainted with Tao use no tie with ropes or strings to make knots that can never be thus loosened.

80. Therefore, the wise sages are invariably adept at exclusively using Tao to assist all kinds of people, for their very own original natures do not leave anyone behind; the wise sages are invariably adept at exclusively using Tao to assist in facilitating all kinds of affairs, for their very own original natures do not leave any affair unattended. Such is called "Catching the Enlightenment".

81. Accordingly, those who are well acquainted with Tao are teachers of those who are not well acquainted with Tao; those who are not well acquainted with Tao are resources and materials for those who are well acquainted with Tao.

82. If one does not value one's teachers and not treasure one's resources, then one is still greatly baffled in the way of Tao, even if one is extremely intelligent. Such is called "The Most Profound and Wonderful Mystery of Tao".

Chapter 28

83. Understanding one's masculine strength yet upholding to act with feminine tenderness enables one to become the lowest point of the valley, which is the most desirable place for all under Heaven. If one becomes the lowest point of the valley for all under Heaven, then the everlasting Manifestation of the immutable Tao shall never leave one, and so one returns to the state of a newborn baby, original and simple. Accordingly, knowing the clean and clear aspect of the Manifestation of Tao yet upholding its obscure and muddy aspect is the principle of all under Heaven.

84. If one applies the principle of all under Heaven, then one shall never stray from the everlasting Manifestation of the immutable Tao and so is able to return all back to the "limitless infinity" (i.e., Tao). Knowing how to achieve high glory yet upholding humiliation is assuming the role of the lowest point of the valley of all under Heaven. If one assumes the role of the lowest point of the valley of all under Heaven, then one shall reach upon the everlasting Manifestation of the immutable Tao and so is able to return all back to the original simplicity.

85. When this original simplicity disperses and manifests itself in the physical world, it becomes all sorts of worldly entities. When wise sages administrate these entities and become the leader of all officials, they, therefore, administrate via Tao without any personal discernment.

Chapter 29

86. For those who wish to oversee all under Heaven under their rule, I do not see they will succeed; all under Heaven collectively is an entity of extraordinary nature and cannot be ruled. Those who rule it with their own differentiations and intents shall eventually fail, while those who tightly take hold of it with absolute dominance shall eventually lose it.

87. After all, there are some people who are emphatic and assertive, while some who are mild and submissive; some who blow through their noses, while some who blow through their mouths; some who are strong and sturdy, while some who are weak and frail; some who humble themselves to Tao, while some who (refuse to humble and so) wreck themselves by Tao.

88. This is why the wises sages deal away with indulgence, deal away with conceitedness, and deal away with pride and arrogance.

Chapter 30

89. Those who use Tao to assist rulers never use military might to violently suppress all under Heaven. Such a matter of violent suppression shall easily produce counter results. Wherever the military is, weeds and thorns shall rise. After a major military operation, there will certainly be bad and ominous years to come.

90. Accordingly, one should only prefer securing favourable results but not dare to adopt violent suppression. Securing favourable results should not be accompanied by vanity; securing favourable results should not be accompanied by boastfulness; securing favourable results should not be ac-companied by arrogance; securing favourable results should be seen by all as something that is absolutely necessary with no other option; securing favourable results should not be done with violent suppression nor should it be used to justify violent suppression.

91. Indeed, if one is mighty and fierce, one will frail and wither, and so it can be said as not following Tao. Whatever that is not following Tao will come to its end very soon!

Chapter 31

92. Alas, even the finest army is a worldly entity of bad omen. People always despise it, and so those who have grasped the way of Tao never employ it. The honourable ones, during peaceful times, highly regard the left (i.e., good omen), while, during war times, the right (i.e., bad omen).

Hence, the military is considered an entity of bad omen and not a tool for the honourable ones; they only utilize it when there is no other option. One should always hold simplicity and tranquillity in the highest regard.

93. A military victory is never wonderful. If one does proclaim it to be wonderful, then one is seeing killing others as desirable. Alas, those who desire to kill others shall not have their aspirations realized under Heaven.

94. Good and auspicious matters honour the left, while evil and calamitous matters honour the right. The second in command of the army is to be positioned on the left; the commanding general-in-chief is to be positioned on the right. This means wars should be treated as rites of mourning. For those who have killed many, they should thus weep with great sorrows. Even if they are victorious, they should treat their victories as rites of mourning.

Chapter 32

95. Tao is immutable, has no name, and is primordially original and simple. Although it appears to be puny as well as humble, nothing under Heaven can subjugate it. If rulers can uphold Tao in their governances, then all shall naturally submit to their reigns. As Nature and Earth work together, refreshing dew naturally forms. Likewise, the people shall naturally follow the rulers without any command or decree.

96. The Originator manifests and generates the "identifiable and with names" (i.e., Te). Since the Name is already identifiable and thus limited, one should know where to reach and when to stop. Knowing where to reach and when to stop shall allow one to be free from all peril.

97. One should understand Tao to all under Heaven is like that of streams from valleys to rivers and seas.

Chapter 33

98. Knowing and understanding others is only intelligent; knowing and understanding oneself is true enlightenment. Overcoming others is only being more powerful; overcoming oneself is true strength.

99. Those who are satisfied with whatever their circumstances are always wealthy; those who steadfastly act by Tao always have their aspirations realized. Not losing one's way in following Tao enables one to last long; to die but not perish enables one to have true longevity.

Chapter 34

100. The great Tao flows and permeates everywhere indeed; it influences all. All things rely on it to spawn and flourish, yet it does not proclaim itself to be so. It claims no credit in its accomplishments. Tao embraces and nurtures the physical beings of all but never claims to be their master.

101. This immutable Tao of no selfish desire can be named as puny; however, all things follow and adhere to it, yet it never claims to be their master; so, it can be named as great. As it never claims itself to be great, it is thus able to accomplish its greatness.

Chapter 35

102. Those who grasp the great phenomenon manifested by Tao shall have all under Heaven follow them. Such following ensures all under Heaven not to be harmed, and great

peace and ease shall arise. Offering people good music and delicacies can merely attract them as passing guests only.

103. When Tao is expressed in or described with words, it is so bland and dull that it is not distinct. When one sees it, it cannot be seen. When one listens to it, it cannot be heard. However, when one applies it, it can never be exhausted.

Chapter 36

104. If one plans to diminish something, one must first expand it; if one plans to weaken something, one must first strengthen it; if one plans to ruin something, one must first raise and establish it; if one plans to acquire something, one must first give it away. This principle is known as the "Enlightenment from Wei".

105. The gentle and weak is better than the bold and strong. A fish should not leave its abyssal niche. Instruments that benefit the state should not be displayed to the people.

Chapter 37

106. Tao immutably has no personal differentiation and intent to do anything, yet there is nothing that it cannot do. If rulers of states can uphold Tao in their governances, all things shall naturally live and propagate on their own. As selfish desires do arise during natural propagations, I will counter and repress them with the original simplicity of the "unidentifiable and nameless".

107. Applying the original simplicity of the "unidentifiable and nameless" is just allowing everything to adhere to having no selfish desire. If all leave behind selfish desires to

return to their state of inherent tranquillity, then all under Heaven shall naturally settle themselves in serenity.

Chapter 38

108. Those with high virtue do not need any virtue, thus indicating they, in fact, already have virtues. Those with low virtue fear the loss of their virtues, thus indicating they, in fact, do not inherently have any virtue. Those with high virtue do not need to do anything to be virtuous, and so there is no reason for them to act; those with low virtue need to act to cultivate their virtues, and so they do have a reason to act;

109. Those with high benevolence act to cultivate benevolence, but there is actually no reason for them to act. Those with high righteousness act to cultivate righteousness, and so they do have a reason to act. Those with high propriety act and expect others to follow suit: if others do not respond to them with propriety, they shall bare their arms and coercively drag the nonconformists to comply.

110. Accordingly, when Tao is lost in a society, virtues appear; when virtues are lost, benevolence appears; when benevolence is lost, righteousness appears; and when righteousness is lost, propriety appears.

111. Alas, propriety is poor in honesty and the main culprit of chaos. Having acquired knowledge and being able to foresee is actually the most superficial in the realm of Tao and the beginning of stupidity. Thus, those who have great aspirations in following Tao put themselves where Tao is most rich and sturdy but not where Tao is poor and thin. They reside themselves at the very solid and genuine core of Tao but not the superficial exterior of it. This is why

those who have great aspirations in following Tao leave behind the former of foreseeing and choose the latter of following Tao.

Chapter 39

112. Those that have obtained One since the past are: Nature, which carry One to become pure and clear; Earth, which carries One to become settled and established; the spirits, which carry One to obtain their vitalities; the valleys, which carry One to become filled with abundant diversity; all things, which carry One to live and exist; the rulers of states, who carry One to rule all under Heaven in proper order. The One fulfils and realizes all their corresponding characteristics.

113. If Nature does not have One to become pure and clear, it shall perhaps fracture; if Earth does not have One to become settled and calmed, it shall perhaps shake and quake; if the spirits do not have One to obtain their vitalities, they shall perhaps become exhausted and die; if the valleys do not have One to become filled with abundant diversity, they shall perhaps dry up and become barren; if all things do not have One to live and exist, they shall perhaps become extinct; if the rulers of states do not have One to become noble, their thrones shall perhaps be overthrown.

114. Accordingly, one should know that anything noble and distinguished is based on something lesser and unrefined, while anything superior is rooted in something lowly and primitive. Hence, rulers of states call themselves "The Orphaned", "The Forsaken", or "The Incapable". Isn't this a demonstration of the distinguished is based on the lesser and unrefined? Isn't this true? Therefore, the honour of possessing many horses to pull one's carriage relies on the

inferiority of not possessing any carriage. The honourable should thus never desire to be as dazzling as jades nor as conspicuous as gemstones on a necklace.

Chapter 40

115. Restorative countering forces are Tao's actions. The weak and the puny are Tao's apparatus. All under Heaven sprang from the entity that can be conceived and named, and the entity that can be conceived and named originates from the one that cannot be conceived nor named (i.e., Tao).

Chapter 41

116. Scholars of the highest calibre, when they hear about Tao, earnestly act according to it. Scholars of the average calibre, when they hear about Tao, sometimes keep it and sometimes lose it. Scholars of the lowest calibre, when they hear about Tao, laugh greatly at it; if it were not laughed at by them, it would not be fit to be Tao.

117. Thus, there was a saying from the past: Tao's clear and bright way is elusive and obscure; Tao's way to advance forward is to retreat backwards; Tao's flat and even path is rough and uneven; the supreme Manifestation of Tao is rudimentary and lowly as the bottom of a valley; the cleanest and clearest aspect of the Manifestation of Tao is obscure and muddy; the most generous and magnanimous aspect of the Manifestation of Tao is still insufficient; the most steadfast and sturdy aspect of the Manifestation of Tao is weak and frail; those of primitive and simple pureness are tainted with many impurities; the most rectangular shape has no corners; the most magnificent worldly entity evolves gradually and requires a long time to become established;

the most astounding sound is not audible; the great phenomenon manifested by Tao has no shape nor form; Tao, hence, is unimaginably and wonderfully "unidentifiable and nameless".

118. Alas, hence, it is only Tao that excels in supplying and furnishing all as well as accomplishing all things.

Chapter 42

119. Tao spawned One; One spawned Two; Two spawned Three; Three spawned all things. All things possess the negative (Yin) and embrace the positive (Yang), and the interactions between these two countering forces make all things to exist in harmony.

120. People surely dislike "The Orphaned", "The Forsaken", and "The Incapable"; yet, these are the very descriptions that rulers of states call themselves. Accordingly, that which diminishes is actually favoured, that which favours is actually diminished.

121. What all other people use to enlighten others, I also use it to enlighten others. "The brutal and the strong do not reap a natural and pleasant death", I shall take this admonition as the starting point to enlighten others.

Chapter 43

122. The gentlest under Heaven gallops freely within the toughest. Tao is without shape nor form, and so it can penetrate even the toughest object under Heaven that has countless infinitely small spaces within it. I, therefore, know that it is the most beneficial to act in the gentlest manner, which is not to act with any personal differentiation and intent.

123. Enlightenment through the wordless and the benefits of not acting with any personal differentiation and intent are rarely recognized and attained by those under Heaven.

Chapter 44

124. Fame or life, which one is dearer to you? Life or wealth, which one is more important to you? Attainment of wealth or losing your life, which one is actually suffering? Accordingly, securing what one prizes shall cost one dearly, while treasuring too many shall invariably lead to an enormous loss.

125. Knowing to be satisfied with whatever the circumstances shall never bring shame to oneself; while knowing where to reach and when to stop shall never bring peril to oneself. Able to do both shall make one live long.

Chapter 45

126. The most accomplished is actually still deficient, but its applications are inexhaustible; the most abundant is actually hollow and empty, but its applications are limitless. The strictest and the most proper is actually submissive and yielding to Tao; the sharpest and the most brilliant is actually dim-witted; the most eloquent is actually inarticulate.

127. Rash and fiery actions may temporarily overcome icy and hostile situations, yet it is tranquillity that shall ultimately and inexhaustibly overcome boiling fierceness. Pristine tranquillity is the true guiding principle of all under Heaven.

Chapter 46

128. When all under Heaven embrace Tao, the people reclaim their distinguished running horses to work and fertilize the fields. When the world rejects Tao, war horses give birth in the wild.

129. There is no calamity greater than being dissatisfied with one's circumstances and no fault greater than selfish greed to possess. Accordingly, the satisfaction from being satisfied with whatever the circumstances is everlasting satisfaction indeed.

Chapter 47

130. One can understand all under Heaven without leaving one's home, and one can realize Nature's way without peeking out of a single window. If one walks further away from one's home, the lesser one knows about the true nature of the world.

131. Accordingly, the wise sages do not travel yet know all under Heaven, do not peek out of a single window yet comprehend Tao, and do not act with any personal differentiation and intent yet accomplish everything.

Chapter 48

132. Pursue learning knowledge day by day increases one to act with personal differentiations and intents. Pursue following Tao day by day diminishes one to act with personal differentiations and intents: diminishing upon diminishing, one shall eventually not act with any personal differentiation and intent. As there is no personal differentiation and

intent to do anything, there is nothing that one cannot do.

133. When ruling all under Heaven, one should always never aim to accomplish anything great. When one aims to accomplish something great, one is unqualified to rule all under Heaven.

Chapter 49

134. The wise sages do not have a fixed and distinct mindset of their own; they make the mindset of the people as their own. Anything that the people find good, I also favour it to be good. Anything that the people find not good, I also favour it to be not good. Such is attaining what should be favoured from the people.

135. Anything that the people find trustworthy, I believe it to be trustworthy. Anything that the people find untrustworthy, I also believe it to be untrustworthy. Such is acquiring what should be trusted from the people.

136. The wise sages living under Heaven have no prejudice of their own and turn the minds of all under Heaven back to their primitive simplistic natures. The wise sages make all become newborn babies.

Chapter 50

137. From birth to death, those who are alive have a body of four limbs and nine orifices (i.e., the bodily self); those who are dead have a body of four limbs and nine orifices; while living, those who often risk themselves to go into dire and deadly situations also have a body of four limbs and nine orifices. Why is this so? It is because the body brings about too much regard to one's possessions and bodily life!

138. Alas, I have heard that those who are well acquainted with maintaining their lives never face any fierce rhinoceros or tiger when travelling on land and never come into contact with any armed soldier when marching into enemy camps: the rhinoceros finds no place in them into which to thrust its horn, the tiger finds no place in them in which to fix its claws, and the armed soldier finds no spot in them at which to lay his weapons. Why is that so? For they never put themselves in dire and deadly situations.

Chapter 51

139. Tao begets all things, the Manifestation of Tao nurtures all things. All things take their shapes and forms according to their natures, and the manners of all things are then established accordingly. Therefore, all things honour Tao and exalt its Manifestation.

140. Although Tao should be honoured and its Manifestation exalted, all things do not need to be directed by them to invariably follow their own natures. Tao begets all, and its Manifestation nurtures all; they both rear all, raise all, cultivate all, develop all, feed all, and return all back to Tao. Tao begets all without anything, acts without relying on any other, and oversees all without dominating over them. Such is known as "Most Mysterious Manifestation of Tao".

Chapter 52

141. All under Heaven comes from the Originator (i.e., Tao), which manifests itself to become the Mother of all under Heaven (i.e., Te or Manifestation of Tao). As we know the Manifestation of Tao is the mother of all, we can conceive that all matters are the offsprings of the Manifestation of Tao; since we know all matters are the offsprings of the

Manifestation of Tao, we should thus dedicate ourselves to pursue the motherly way of the Manifestation of Tao but not its offspring, the materialistic matters. Doing this shall allow one to be free from perils in one's entire life.

142. If one closes off all senses and shuts the door (between physical matters and one's mind), then one shall never be exhausted. If one advances the senses to achieve personal accomplishments, then one shall never be assisted by Tao and eventually become tired and exhausted.

143. Being able to perceive the Small is known as Enlightenment; being able to sustain abiding by the most gentle is known as true strength. Applying the light of Tao to restore one's inherent inner enlightenment shall thus not retain any harm for oneself. Such is known as "Comprehending the Immutable".

Chapter 53

144. Suppose I understand and am unwaveringly following the great Tao, I still surely fear that I will go astray as I apply myself through this great path of Tao. The great path of Tao is very smooth and level; yet, people prefer to take alternative narrow paths that deviate from the way of Tao.

145. They construct too many mansions, which leads to ill-cultivated fields and empty granaries. Further, they wear elegant and colourful dresses, carry sharp swords, indulge themselves with food and drinks, and have excessive wealth and possessions; such people are great robbers and certainly not following the way of Tao!

Chapter 54

146. Those who are adept at instituting Tao never have Tao
     pulled out from themselves. Likewise, those who are adept
     in embracing Tao never drop Tao from themselves. Their
     descendants shall thus perpetually celebrate their prede-
     cessors.

147. Cultivating Tao for oneself makes one's manifestation
     pure and genuine; cultivating Tao for one's family makes
     one's manifestation plentiful; cultivating Tao for one's
     county makes one's manifestation flourish; cultivating Tao
     for one's state makes one's manifestation rich; cultivating
     Tao for all under Heaven makes one's manifestation to be
     universal.

148. Accordingly, the cultivation of Tao for the self can be
     applied to examine the self, the cultivation of Tao for the
     family can be applied to examine the family, the cultiva-
     tion of Tao for the county can be applied to examine the
     county, the cultivation of Tao for the state can be applied
     to examine the state, the cultivation of Tao for all under
     Heaven can be applied to examine all under Heaven. How
     do I know all under Heaven is like this? Solely because of
     the above rationale.

Chapter 55

149. Those who richly harbour the Manifestation of Tao are the
     same as newborn babies. Poisonous insects like bees
     and scorpions, as well as venomous snakes like serpents,
     will not sting or bite them; fierce beasts will not seize them;
     vicious birds of prey will not strike them. The bones and
     ligaments of an infant are soft and tender, yet infants can
     hold their fists firmly.

150. A newborn baby does not yet know the harmonization between the positive and the negative, but it perfectly grows and develops: it epitomizes the greatest essence of Tao. A newborn baby cries all day without its voice becoming hoarse, for it demonstrates the greatest harmony with Tao. Understanding this natural harmony is known as understanding the Immutable. Understanding this Immutable is known as possessing Enlightenment.

151. Those who try to deliberately prolong their own natural lives are known to eventually face ominous omens. Minds that are headstrong and assertive are known as being violent. If one is mighty and fierce, one will frail and wither, and so it can be said as not following Tao. Whatever that is not following Tao will come to its end very soon.

Chapter 56

152. Those who understand Tao do not speak of it; those who speak of Tao do not understand it. One should close off one's senses, shut one's door connecting the outer world to the inner mind, conceal one's brilliance, embrace one's simplicity to disintegrate all chaos, harmonize one's splendour to make it agreeable, and adapt and merge with one's muddy and obscure surroundings. Such is known as "The Deep and Mysterious Unification with Tao and the Universe".

153. Accordingly, within Tao, one cannot find anything to be familiar with nor distant from; one cannot find anything favourable nor harmful; one cannot find anything honourable nor dishonourable. As a result, one becomes the most honourable under Heaven.

Chapter 57

154. A ruler should rely on the correct way (i.e., the way of Tao) to govern and consider employing troops as an evil and ominous measure. One should take and govern all under Heaven without relying on accomplishing anything great. How do I know this is so? Solely because of the above rationale.

155. When all under Heaven have more prohibitions or censorships, its people tend to be more poor and stagnant; when the people have more tools to benefit themselves, the state becomes increasing chaotic; when the people increasingly have more wits and craftiness, more evil ploys and contrivances will appear; many laws shall then require to be legislated and enacted, yet more criminals and robbers shall spawn.

156. This is why the wise sages once said, "I do not act with any personal differentiation and intent, and so the people shall naturally live and propagate peacefully by themselves; I favour tranquillity, and so the people shall naturally right themselves in accordance with Tao; I never aim to accomplish anything great, and so the people shall naturally become rich by themselves; I empty myself of any selfish desire, and so the people shall naturally retain their original simplicity."

Chapter 58

157. When the governing is undiscerning and dim-witted, the people shall be simple and honest; when the governing is tactful and discerning, the people shall be slick and cunning.

158. Tragedies indeed have good fortunes sitting next to them, while good fortunes indeed have tragedies lurking beneath them. Who knows which one is the actual ultimate? Tao itself does not have any so-called agreeable side! What is now considered agreeable can return to be recognized as evil and ominous; what is now considered good can return to be recognized as ominous.

159. The people's confusion surrounding Tao has subsisted for a long time. Hence, wise sages behave duly according to Tao without any discernment, act with integrity without hurting any other, behave honestly without creating conflicts, and apply their brilliance without dazzling anyone.

Chapter 59

160. In cultivating the self to serve Nature, there is no one more proficient than a farmer. Alas, only a farmer can be called to have obeyed Nature from the very beginning. Having obeyed Nature from the very beginning can be called as focusing on steadily amassing one's yield. If one focuses on steadily amassing one's yield, then there is no task in which one is not competent. Since there is no task in which one is not competent, one's limit cannot be known.

161. Since one's limit cannot be known, one can then rule the state; ruling the state by applying motherly Nature shall make one's rule to last long. Such is like a tree with deep and firm roots, which illustrates the principle of longevity and long-lasting vitality.

Chapter 60

162. In governing a great state, one should be as mindful as cooking a small fish. If one applies the principles of Tao

in governing all under Heaven, then one's wit appears not so sound in the mind; not that one's wit is not sound in the mind, but one's mind does not harm anyone. Not that one's mind does not harm anyone, but the wise sages surely, by their very natures, never harm anyone!

163. Alas, both parties, the rulers and their people, will then not harm each other. Thus, all can come together to attain the outcome of returning to the way of Tao.

Chapter 61

164. A great and powerful state should situate itself at a lowly position like that of the downstream of a river, which is the place of all under Heaven coming together, and the feminine way of all under Heaven. Feminine always uses tranquillity to win over masculine and applies tranquillity to be in a lowly and humbled position.

165. Hence, if a stronger state humbles itself towards a weaker state, it shall then earn the acceptance of the weaker state. If a weaker state humbles itself towards the stronger state, it shall then earn the acceptance from the stronger state. Hence, there are those who humble themselves to acquire the faith of the weaker state, and there are those who humble themselves to gain the trust of the stronger state.

166. The stronger state only wishes to subjugate the weaker ones; the weaker state only wishes to adopt serving the stronger ones. Alas, as such, this ensures both the strong and the weak will get what they desire. The most important is being humble, regardless of the size of the state.

Chapter 62

167. Tao is a safe haven for all things. Those who are well acquainted with Tao treasure it, and those who are not well acquainted with it rely on it to safeguard themselves. Those who speak nice words can apply themselves only in the marketplace, but those who act according to Tao can gift and benefit all people.

168. For those who are not acquainted with Tao, why would Tao abandon them? Thus, establishing the role of a Son of Heaven (i.e., the supreme ruler) and designating the positions of the Three Chief Mentors, even though the Son of Heaven possesses the priceless treasure of a grand jade as large as one's embrace and the Mentors carry the great honour of having four-horse carriages, are no match for a society that naturally progresses to reside in Tao.

169. Why did the wise from the past prize Tao so much? Did they not all say "all wishes shall be granted if one applies Tao; all faults shall be stripped away if one returns to follow Tao"? Hence, Tao is the most valuable under Heaven.

Chapter 63

170. Those who follow Tao act to not act with any personal differentiation and intent, conduct all matters without aiming to accomplish anything great, and taste all things without distinguishing any flavour. Great, small, few, many, they do not consider them as such; they merely respond to any enmity according to their manifestations from following Tao.

171. Wise sages tackle a difficult issue when it is still easy to manage, and they deal with a great matter when it is still

trivial and small; all difficult issues under Heaven always originate from issues that are initially easy to manage, and all great matters under Heaven always stem from matters that are initially trivial and small.

172. Therefore, the wise sages ultimately do not do anything great; as such, they can accomplish their greatness. Alas, those who make promises lightly surely lack trustworthiness, while those who find many things easy shall surely find many difficulties ahead. Hence, even wise sages find all matters difficult to address. As such, they never do anything great, and so they ultimately never face anything difficult.

Chapter 64

173. When an issue is still calm and tranquil, it is easy to grasp it. When an issue has not risen, it is easy to take measures against it; when a matter is weak, it is easy to break it apart; when a matter is still extremely small, it is easy to break it up. Actions should be taken before any issue develop, and good governance should occur before any chaos begin. A sturdy tree of one's entire embrace that is destined to be chopped down grows from the tiniest sprout; an overly lavished elevated terrace of nine levels rises from the first pile of accumulated soil; an exhaustive journey of thousands of miles starts by lifting a single foot.

174. Those who act with personal differentiations and intents shall eventually fail, and those who hold shall eventually lose hold. This is why the wise sages do not act with any personal differentiation and intent and so never fail; they do not hold and thus never lose hold. People conduct their business and often fail on the eve of success. If they were as meticulous in following the way of Tao at the end as

they were at the beginning, they would not have failed.

175. Accordingly, a wise sage desires no selfish desires and does not treasure rare valuables. A wise sage learns not to learn and restores all people back to their inherent simplicities that they had once lost. A wise sage merely acts to facilitate the natures of all things and dares not act to serve one's personal intents and purposes.

Chapter 65

176. Those in the past who are well-acquainted with Tao act not to make the people more intelligent but rather to make them less intelligent. The people become difficult to govern because they have too much acquired intelligence. Those who use acquired intelligence to govern are vandals to the state, while those who do not are blessings to the state. One should know both cases originate from the same norm governed by Tao.

177. Being always mindful of this norm is known as the "Most Mysterious Manifestation of Tao". This "Most Mysterious Manifestation of Tao" is so deep and far-reaching indeed that it engages in reverting all worldly matters to their respective inherent simplicities. Eventually, all then shall reach to the "Great Conformity to Tao".

Chapter 66

178. The reason why the rivers and seas are able to be the most desirable for waters from all valleys is because they are proficient at being positioned below all valleys. This is why they are able to be the most desirable for waters from all valleys.

179. As such, if one wishes to be positioned above the people, then one must put oneself below the people; if one wants to lead the people, then one must put oneself at a position behind all people.

180. Therefore, although the wise sages are situated above the people, the people do not find them burdensome; although the wise sages are situated in front leading the people, the people will not find them injurious. Hence, all under Heaven are willing to endorse them and do not grow weary of and despise them. Since the wise sages do not compete with others, no one under Heaven can compete with them.

Chapter 67

181. All under Heaven say although my so-called Tao is great, it appears not to be so. Alas, it is only because of its unlimited greatness that it appears not to be so. If it appears to be great, it would indeed be small long long time ago!

182. I have three treasures that I always uphold and rely on: the first is earnest adoration of Tao, the second is frugality, and the third is not daring to lead and be the most preeminent among all under Heaven. When one adores Tao, one can thus be courageous; when one is frugal, one can thus flourish; when one dares not to lead and be the most preeminent among all under Heaven, one can thus become a distinguished and talented leader among all.

183. Today, many abandon earnest adoration of Tao yet adopt blind courage, abandon frugality yet adopt raw prosperity, abandon placing oneself behind all others yet adopt preeminence. They shall all perish indeed! Alas, applying earnest adoration of Tao in battles shall ensure one's victory, while applying it in defending shall make one's garrison

firm; Nature will then surely come to one's aid and utilize one's earnest adoration of Tao to protect one's safety.

Chapter 68

184. Those who are skilled at being commanders never show their valour; those who are skilled at battles never show their might and anger; those who are skilled at overwhelming their enemies never need to battle their enemies; those who are skilled at delegating responsibilities to their subordinates always humble themselves below their subordinates.

185. Such is known as the attainment of being not competitive, the genuine way to unleash the true capabilities of one's subordinates, and being compatible with the pinnacle of the long-established Nature.

Chapter 69

186. Those who commanded troops once said, "I do not dare to be on the offensive; I rather prefer to be on the defensive; I dare not advance an inch; I prefer to retire a foot."

187. This is known as advancing as if one cannot advance; baring one's arms to fight as if one does not have any arm to bare; defeating the enemy as if one is being defeated by the enemy; holding one's weapon as if one has no weapon to hold.

188. There is no greater tragedy than underestimating or disregarding one's enemy. Doing so will then lose all my treasures that I mentioned previously. Thus, when one raises an army to counter an enemy, the side who is in sorrow

shall prevail.

Chapter 70

189. My words are quite easy to understand and quite easy to carry out. Yet, most under the Heaven is unable to understand and carry them out.

190. All narratives should have a foundational basis supporting them, and all things have a lord behind them. Alas, it is solely because not understanding these that people thus do not comprehend me.

191. Those who understand and acknowledge me are extremely rare; those who model after me are to be treasured. Therefore, the wise sages are the people who wear rags as their outer coverings yet bear jades buried deep within themselves!

Chapter 71

192. Understanding why many not understand Tao is superior, not understanding why some understand Tao suffers from exhaustion.

193. Alas, because understanding why suffering is suffering shall then make one not suffer. Wise sages do not suffer because they know why suffering is suffering, and so they never suffer.

Chapter 72

194. If the people no longer fear the ruler's might and oppression, then the people's great might shall arrive. A ruler should not arbitrarily alter the whereabouts of the people's

dwellings nor inflict harm to their livelihoods. Alas, it is only if you do not inflict harm on the people, then the people will not inflict harm on you.

195. Accordingly, the wise sages understand themselves yet do not show their brilliance to others; they care for themselves but do not elevate themselves above others. Thus, the sages leave behind the former path of suppression and choose to follow these latter paths.

Chapter 73

196. Those who are audacious in being aggressive shall face horrendous and unnatural deaths; those who are audacious in being not aggressive shall live their natural lives. Considering these two scenarios, one is advantageous while the other injurious. Nature has its own dislikes, who knows why? Hence, even wise sages find it so difficult to address!

197. Nature's way is not competitive yet proficient at overcoming, does not speak yet is proficient at responding, does not need to be called upon yet shows up by itself, and is at ease yet excels in scheming. The meshes of the great net deployed by Nature are wide and far apart, but nothing is missed.

Chapter 74

198. When the people do not fear death, what is the point of threatening them with death? Suppose the people were always inherently afraid of dying, and if there existed those who were evil and ominous, I could simply seize and execute them. Who then would dare to become like them?

199. Yet, the Immutable already has its way to administrate executions. Alas, anyone who executes in place of the way administrated by the Immutable can be said to be an unqualified person chopping up wood instead of the master carpenter. Indeed, those who chop up wood in place of the master carpenter rarely not hurt their own hands.

Chapter 75

200. The people starve because of the heavy reliance on taxes consumed by their rulers; it is through this that they starve.

201. The people are difficult to govern because their rulers act with personal differentiations and intents; it is through this that they become difficult to govern. The people take death lightly because their rulers hold their own personal posses- sions and livelihoods in too high of a regard; it is through this that the people take death lightly.

202. Alas, without exception, rulers who do not seek to pursue their personal possessions and livelihoods are certainly far more distinguished than those who draw heavy taxes and highly regard their own possessions and livelihoods.

Chapter 76

203. When alive, a person's body is soft, gentle, and fragile; at death, rigid, stiff, and sturdy. All things, including plants, are soft and brittle when they are alive; at death, they are all dried-up and withered.

204. Therefore, rigidity, stiffness, and sturdiness belong to those of the dead, while softness, gentleness, and fragility belong to those that are alive.

205. Hence, those who rely only on raw military might will never secure a true victory, a sturdy tree will be quickly chopped down to be used as fine lumber. Therefore, being strong and mighty is at inferior, while being gentle and weak is at the superior.

Chapter 77

206. Is it not Nature's way like drawing a bow and arrow? If one draws too high, then one shall depress it; if one draws too low, then one shall raise it. One diminishes the abundant while supplements the insufficient.

207. Nature's way diminishes the abundant while supplements the insufficient. Not so with the way of humans, which diminishes the insufficient to gift to the abundant.

208. Who then can take from the abundant to gift to all under Heaven? Only Tao, of course! Hence, wise sages act without relying on others and accomplish without claiming any credit. They never wish to show that they are distinguished.

Chapter 78

209. There is nothing under Heaven gentler and weaker than water, yet there is nothing better than it to attack the mighty and strong; therefore, in this respect, nothing can replace it.

210. The weak is better than the strong, and the gentle is better than the bold. Everyone under Heaven knows this, but no one can carry it out in practice.

211. Thus, the wise sages once said, "A person who can accept all the shame of a state can be called the master of the state; a person who can accept all the misdeeds of a state can be called the leader of all under the Heaven." Proper narratives of Tao are countering ways to restore all back to Tao.

Chapter 79

212. Even when a great grievance has been reconciled, there still must be some grievance remaining. How then can reconciliation be a good solution? Thus, wise sages conduct their businesses only by holding documents that provide evidence of proof and never demand anything from the people.

213. Those with the Manifestation of Tao administrate by adhering to documents; those without the Manifestation of Tao administrate by demanding land taxes with the system of Che. Nature's way devotes to no one, yet it always supports those who are well acquainted with Tao.

Chapter 80

214. An ideal state is small, with very few people living in it. The ideal governance should result in instruments of more than a hundredfold not to be applied. It also makes people regard death as a grave matter and choose not to emigrate to places far away. Although there are boats and carriages, they find no need to ride on them; although there is an army, there is no need to display it.

215. The ideal governance makes people return to using string knots to count and communicate. The people enjoy their primitive food and cherish their plain clothes; they are

content with their simple dwellings and are happy with their native habits and customs.

216. Neighbouring states observe each other, and the cries of fowls and dogs among the neighbouring states can also be heard. Yet, till their deaths, people from different states shall have no contact with each other.

Chapter 81

217. True and honest words are never nice, while nice words are never true and honest. Those who are well acquainted with Tao do not argue, while those who argue are not well acquainted with Tao. Those who understand Tao do not understand a wide range of acquired knowledge, while those who understand a wide range of acquired knowledge do not understand Tao.

218. The wise sages never amass anything for themselves. Since they already gift themselves to others, they already possess plenty; since they already bestow themselves upon others, they are already affluent.

219. The way of Nature benefits all without doing any harm; the way of a wise sage gifts all without competing with others.

SECTION FOUR

Correct Interpretation in Vernacular Chinese

《道德經》艱深句子正解並白話對譯

Humankind takes its law from Earth- Tao Te Ching

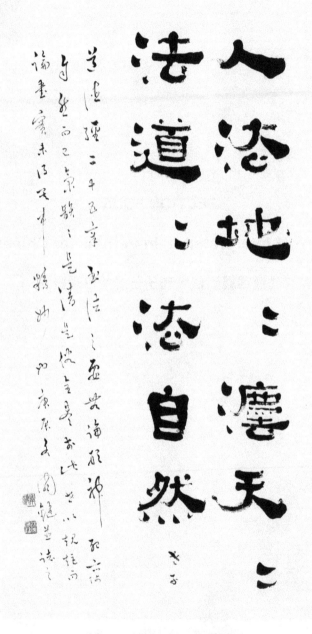

隸書 Clerical Script   68x34cm 2000AD
Source: A Collection of Kwok Kin Poon's Calligraphy

《道德經》艱深句子正解並白話對譯
(註釋見英譯相關條目)

潘國鍵

第一章

2. 故常無, 欲以觀其妙; 常有, 欲以觀其徼。
故此, 姑且用這個「常道」和「無名」, 希望能夠探索一下道的玄奧深妙; 也姑且用這個「常名」和「有名」, 希望能夠觀察一下德的萬物規迹。

第二章

6. 生而不有, 為而不恃。
全無實質而獨自產生, 毫不依仗而獨自作為。

第四章

11. 湛兮似或存!
(道)極其深厚啊! 它是常常存在的!

12. 吾不知誰之子, 象帝之先。
我不知曉這道是誰所生的, 猜想在天出現前便已存在了吧。

第五章

15. 多言數窮, 不如守中。
太多說話終會辭窮, 倒不如保持虛靜。

第八章

23. 居善地; 心善淵; 與善仁; 言善信; 正善治; 事善能; 動善時。
身住在喜好道的地方; 心宿在深藏道的靜淵; 結交修養道的人們;
說話則本於道的誠信; 治理則遵照道的原則; 任用那依循道的人才;
行動則合乎道的時間。

第十章

28. 載營魄抱一, 能無離乎? 專氣致柔, 能嬰兒乎? 滌除玄覽, 能無疵乎?
抱持道來安頓自己的魂魄, 能不兩者(道和魂)先已分離嗎? 抱守真
氣致使柔軟, 你可及得上嬰兒嗎? 洗淨心鏡, 能不心裏先有瑕疵嗎?

29. 愛民治國, 能無知乎? 天門開闔, 能無雌乎? 明白四達, 能無為乎?
愛護百姓治理國家, 能不自己運用智能嗎? 大自然陰柔產道闔門開
開關關, 能不自己視它做你的陰柔產道嗎? 明白道理通達四方, 能
不自己先學習知識嗎?

第十三章

39. 何謂寵辱若驚? 寵為下。得之若驚, 失之若驚。
什麼叫做榮寵和羞辱乃都令人惶恐的呢? 因為尊尚的榮寵總必成
為卑下的羞辱。所以, 得了榮寵乃惶恐, 這和失去榮寵是惶恐一
樣。

第十五章

48. 孰能濁以靜之徐清? 孰能安以久動之徐生? 保此道者, 不欲盈。夫唯不盈, 故能蔽不新成。
誰能夠用靜就令混濁得以漸漸清澈? 誰能夠用長久震動則使安靜
得以漸漸產生?(唯有道!) 知曉這道理的人, 不愛自滿。因為不自
滿, 故此才能夠隱藏自己, 決不會說親自成就了些什麼。

第十六章

51. 知常容。 容乃公; 公乃王; 王乃天; 天乃道; 道乃久。沒身不殆。
知曉常道, 便會容納一切。容納一切乃就大公無私; 大公無私乃就萬物所歸往; 萬物所歸往乃就遵循於大自然; 遵循於大自然乃就依循於道; 依循於道乃就恆久。這便終身不會危殆了。

第十七章

52. 太上, 下知有之。
最好的統治者, 是下面的百姓僅知他的存在(而不知他在統治)。

53. 信不足? 焉有不信焉!
不足信麼? 又豈會有不足信的哩!

第十九章

58. 此三者以為文不足, 故令有所屬: 見素抱樸, 少私寡欲。
上面這三個觀點由於論述的言辭未算足夠, 故此讓我再有所撰: 了解本性而持守真樸, 少點自我而捨棄私慾。

第二十章

62. 眾人皆有以, 而我獨頑似鄙。我獨異於人, 而貴食母。
眾人皆有個原因, 而我獨粗鈍兼鄙陋。我獨不同於人, 而祇崇尚生我育我的大自然。

第二十一章

64. 其精甚真, 其中有信。自古及今, 其名不去, 以閱眾甫。
它(德) 的真氣甚是純正不假, 它裏面有的是可驗證的誠信。從古至今, 這德從沒離開過, 靠它來賦與萬物的生長。

第二十二章

66. 曲則全, 枉則直。
曲從於道就可以保全性命, 彎曲就可以伸直。

第二十四章

73. 其在道也, 曰餘食贅行。物或惡之, 故有道者不處。
這在道裏面呢, 叫做殘羹穢臭與贅疣醜形。這都是人們常厭惡的, 故有道的人必不會處身其中。

第二十五章

76. 域中有四大, 而王居其一焉。人法地; 地法天; 天法道; 道法自然。
在人居處的地方裏面, 有四個大, 而天下所歸往者佔其中之一。人取法於地; 地取法於大自然; 大自然取法於道; 道取法於它自己的本然。

第二十六章

77. 重為輕根, 靜為躁君。是以聖人終日行不離輜重。雖有榮觀, 燕處超然。
重是輕的根基, 靜是躁的主宰。故此聖人外遊時, 笨重的行裝物資整天不會離身(寧願走慢些)。雖然享有榮譽, 抱的也衹會是閑居而超脫世俗的恬靜心態。

第二十七章

80. 是以聖人常善救人, 故無棄人; 常善救物, 故無棄物。
故此聖人常常依循道來幫助人, 本就不會嫌棄任何人; 也常常依循道來幫忙做事, 本就不會厭棄任何事物。

第二十九章

87. 故物或行或隨; 或歔或吹; 或強或羸; 或挫或隳。
畢竟在人裏面, 有些剛健, 有些溫順; 有些慣以鼻呼氣, 有些慣以口呼氣; 有些強壯, 有些羸弱; 有些挫服於道而自全, 有些不服於道而自毀。

88. 是以聖人去甚, 去奢, 去泰。
故此聖人丟掉溺好, 丟掉自誇, 丟掉驕縱。

第三十章

89. 以道佐人主者, 不以兵強天下。
用道來輔助君主的人, 不會以武力來鎮壓天下。

91. 物壯則老, 是謂不道。不道早已!
人若壯猛則必自衰弱, 這叫不依循道。不依循道, 早就完蛋啦!

第三十二章

95. 民莫之令而自均。
百姓無需命令, 也自會遵從上面的君主。

96. 始制有名。名亦既有, 夫亦將知止。知止可以不殆。
道生出了德。德既已有, 便須知道自己所應至和所應停的地方。知道自己所應至和所應停的地方, 就可以沒危殆了。

第三十六章

105. 國之利器不可以示人。
有利治理國家的工具(例如軍隊、律法等), 切不可以輕易展示百姓。

第三十八章

108. 上德不德, 是以有德; 下德不失德, 是以無德。
上等德行的人無需德行, 因此亦正顯示他本已具有德行; 下等德行的人不想失去德行, 因此反顯露他本來就是沒甚德行。

第三十九章

114. 故致數輿無輿。不欲琭琭如玉, 珞珞如石。
所以, 那些擁有數馬拉動車子的王侯公卿的高貴, 本就是建築在連車子也沒有的貧困平民的低賤之上。他們當不想自己耀目如珍貴的寶玉, 顯眼如頸上項鏈的寶石。

第四十章

115. 反者道之動。
使一切復返於道, 這就是道的力量和行動。

第四十一章

117. 大器晚成。
最大的具體事物(德), 是需要長時間來漸漸完成的。

第四十二章

121. 人之所教, 我亦教之。強梁者不得其死, 吾將以為教父。
人們所教化的, 我也用它來教化人。「剛強橫暴的人不得善終」, 我必用它作為教化的開始。

第四十五章

126. 大直若屈。
最大的正直, 乃是屈折(於道)。

127. 躁勝寒, 靜勝熱。
疾動或稍克服寒涼, 惟清靜卻終可克服苦熱。

第四十九章

134. 聖人無常心, 以百姓心為心。善者, 吾善之; 不善者, 吾亦善之。德善。
聖人沒有既定不變的私心, 祇以百姓的心作為自己的心。百姓喜好的, 我也喜好他們所喜好的; 百姓不喜好的, 我也喜好他們這個不喜好。這才得到與百姓完全一樣的喜(與不喜)。

135. 信者, 吾信之; 不信者, 吾亦信之。德信。
百姓信服的, 我也信服他們所信服的; 百姓不信服的, 我也信服他們這個不信服。這才得到與百姓完全一樣的信(與不信)。

第五十章

137. 出生入死, 生之徒, 十有三; 死之徒, 十有三; 人之生, 動之死地, 亦十有三。夫何故? 以其生生之厚!
從出生到死亡期間, 生的人, 有四肢九竅的身軀; 死的人, 也有四肢九竅的身軀; 人在生時, 每每往赴必死絕地來犯險, 亦同樣有著此四肢九竅的身軀。這是件什麼事情呢? 就是為了這身軀而令人太看重自己的財物和性命啊!

第五十三章

145. 朝甚除。
宮室建造太多。

第五十四章

147. 修之於身, 其德乃真; 修之於家, 其德乃餘; 修之於鄉, 其德乃長; 修之於國, 其德乃豐; 修之於天下, 其德乃普。
為了自身而修養道, 他的德乃就真樸; 為了家庭而修養道, 他的德乃就豐足; 為了家鄉而修養道, 他的德乃就更為增長; 為了國家而修養道, 他的德乃就更為豐厚; 為了天下而修養道, 他的德乃就更為全面而普及。

第五十五

150. 未知牝牡之合而全作, 精之至也。
(嬰兒)不曉得陰氣陽氣相調合, 卻能完好無損地成長, 這可說是真氣的極致了。

第五十七章

154. 以正治國, 以奇用兵, 以無事取天下。
治國依仗正道, 用兵認為不祥, 治天下憑藉不做大事。

155. 民多利器, 國家滋昏。
百姓得到更多有利自己的工具(例如貨幣、貿易等), 國家便益增混亂了。

第五十八章

158. 孰知其極? 其無正!
誰曉得這禍這福最終會是怎麼樣呢? 這實在沒有所謂美善的呀!

第五十九章

160. 治人事天莫若嗇。夫唯嗇, 是謂早服。早服謂之重積德。重積德則無不克。無不克則莫知其極。

在修養自己事奉大自然的事情上, 大家就比不上農夫了。祇有農夫, 才可稱做起初就已服從了大自然(德)。起初就已服從大自然, 乃可稱之為重視慢慢累積而得到收穫。能重視慢慢累積而得成果, 那就無所不能勝任了。無所不能勝任, 人們便不知道你能力的極限了。

161. 莫知其極, 可以有國。有國之母, 可以長久。

人們不知道你能力的極限, 你便可以治理國家了。用德來治理國家, 那就可以長久了。

第六十章

162. 治大國若烹小鮮。以道莅天下, 其鬼不神。非其鬼不神, 其神不傷人。非其神不傷人, 聖人亦不傷人!

治理大國如烹煮小魚(務必留神, 切勿傷害魚身的完好)。用道來治理天下的人, 他的敏慧不會是他的精神。並不是因為他的敏慧不是他的精神, 而是他的精神不會傷害人。並不是因為他的精神不傷害人, 而是遵道的聖人確實本來就是不會傷害人啊!

第六十一章

165. 故大國以下小國, 則取小國; 小國以下大國, 則取大國。故或下以取, 或下而取。

故此, 大國若以謙下來對待小國, 則取得小國的信服; 小國以謙下來接待大國, 則取得大國的信任。所以, 他們有些憑謙下以取得信服, 有些憑謙下而取得信任。

第六十二章

167. 道者萬物之奧。

道是萬物安棲的地方。

168. 人之不善, 何棄之有? 故立天子, 置三公, 雖有拱璧以先駟馬, 不如坐進此道。
對於不喜好道的人, 道又怎會丟棄他們呢? 故此, 確立天子設置三公, 雖則天子有拱璧之大的財寶, 三公有駟馬之車的尊崇, 倒不如自然而然地實踐此道。

第六十三章

170. 為無為; 事無事; 味無味。大小多少, 報怨以德。
幹那沒有私慾的行為; 做那沒有大功的事情; 嚐那沒有好壞的味道。無分大小多少, 我僅用大自然的規律(德)來回應仇怨。

第六十四章

173. 其安易持, 其未兆易謀。其脆易泮, 其微易散。為之於未有, 治之於未亂。合抱之木, 生於毫末; 九層之臺, 起於累土; 千里之行, 始於足下。
靜態的事情易於掌握, 未發生的事情易於謀策。脆弱的事情易於擊碎, 微小的事情易於破散。在事情未發生前要預先治理, 在事情未紛亂前要預先整治。給人砍伐的粗如合抱的巨樹, 生長自極細的幼苗; 甚費人力物力的九層巨大高臺, 開始於堆積第一筐的泥土; 令人疲累的千里外遊, 開始於你提起腳掌走的第一步。

175. 復衆人之所過。
讓人們復得所失掉的道。

第六十六章

179. 是以欲上民, 必以言下之。
故此, 若想居於百姓之上, 那就必須我先處於百姓之下。

180. 是以聖人處上而民不重, 處前而民不害。
故此聖人居於高位而百姓不覺得他是一重負擔, 居於領導而百姓也不覺得他會帶來傷害。

第六十七章

181. 天下皆謂我道大, 似不肖。夫唯大, 故似不肖。若肖, 久矣其細也夫！
世人都認為我說道大, 但它卻全不似大。正因為大, 故此它才全不似大呢。假若似大, 它老早就是細啦!

182. 我有三寶, 持而保之: 一曰慈, 二曰儉, 三曰不敢為天下先。
我有三寶, 常緊握而依仗著它: 一稱為篤愛於道, 二稱為節儉素樸, 三稱為不敢做天下的領導。

第七十章

190. 言有宗, 事有君。夫唯無知, 是以不我知。
言論要有個根本, 事物總有個主宰(德)。祇因人們不懂得這道理, 所以才不了解我。

191. 知我者希, 則我者貴。是以聖人被褐懷玉!
了解我的人極少, 效法我的更屬難能可貴。故此也證明了聖人身上穿的是卑賤的麻衣, 心內藏的卻是無價的寶玉呀!

第七十一章

192. 知不知, 上; 不知知, 病。
能知曉那些不懂道的, 此乃優尚; 沒能知曉那懂道的, 可就疲苦了。

193. 夫唯病病, 是以不病。聖人不病, 以其病病, 是以不病。
因為了解疲苦之所以成為疲苦, 所以才會不疲苦。聖人不疲苦, 因為他了解疲苦之所以成為疲苦, 所以就不疲苦了。

第七十二章

194. 民不畏威，則大威至。無狎其所居，無厭其所生。夫唯不厭，是以不厭。
當百姓再不懼怕君主的威嚇時，他們天大的怒威便即來臨了。不要遷移人們居住的地方，也不要傷害人們維生的生計。因為你不迫害百姓，故此百姓才不會傷害你。

第七十三章

196. 勇於敢則殺；勇於不敢則活。此兩者，或利或害。天之所惡，孰知其故？是以聖人猶難之！
勇於進取的那就喪命；勇於不進取的那就活命。這兩者，有利也有害。大自然之所厭惡，誰曉得箇中的原故呢？所以就聖人尚且覺得這是很困難的呀！

第七十四章

199. 常有司殺者殺。夫代司殺者殺，是謂代大匠斲。
然而，常道自有掌管殺戮的去殺。你替代掌管殺戮的去殺，這就叫做替代技藝高超的木匠來伐木了。

第七十五章

202. 夫唯無以生為者，是賢於貴生！
唯獨不貪求財物的君主，才肯定遠勝那些視財如命、徵收重稅的君主哩！

第七十八章

211. 正言若反。
合於正道的言論，乃是容納一切相反面而同返於道的言論。

第七十九章

213. 有德司契, 無德司徹。天道無親, 常與善人。

有德的人衹掌管田地約契, 無德的人掌管的是用稅制徹法來徵稅。
大自然之道可沒什麼親或不親的, 衹常常幫助那些喜好於道的人。

第八十章

214. 小國寡民。使有什伯之器而不用; 使民重死而不遠徙。雖有舟輿, 無所乘之; 雖有甲兵, 無所陳之。

理想的國家, 是小國少民。理想的治國之道, 是讓十倍百倍之多的
治國工具備而不用; 是讓百姓看重生死而不會移徙遠方。雖有渡船
馬車, 百姓卻不會乘坐它; 雖有軍隊, 國家也不會展示它。

第八十一章

218. 聖人不積。既以為人己愈有; 既以與人己愈多。

聖人不會為自己積聚財貨。既然已經把自己的施予他人, 那麼自己
就愈為富裕; 既然已經把自己的贈與他人, 那麼自己就愈為豐餘。

219. 天之道, 利而不害; 聖人之道, 為而不爭。

大自然之道, 乃利於萬物而不會傷害; 聖人之道, 是施與大眾而不
會相爭。

Tao begets all and nurtures all - *Tao Te Ching*

隸書 Clerical Script   122x35cm 2000AD
Source: *A Collection of Kwok Kin Poon's Calligraphy*

SECTION FIVE

Bibliography

The Universe is long-enduring and lasts for ages - *Tao Te Ching*

隸書 Clerical Script   67x35cm 2000AD
Source: *A Collection of Kwok Kin Poon's Calligraphy*

Bibliography

English

Legge, James, *Sacred Books of the East,* Volume 27, *The Li king,* edited by Max Mueller. Oxford: Clarendon Press , 1885.

Legge, James, *Sacred Books of the East, The Texts of Taoism*, edited by Max Mueller. Oxford: Clarendon Press :1891.

Poon, KS Vincent & Poon, Kwok Kin, *A Narrative on Calligraphy by Sun Guoting, Revised and Enhanced Edition* 英譯書譜增訂版. Toronto: The SenSeis, 2019.

Poon, KS Vincent & Poon, Kwok Kin, *English Translation of Classical Chinese Calligraphy Masterpieces* 英譯法書. Toronto: The Senseis, 2019.

Poon, Kwok Kin, *A Collection of Kwok Kin Poon's Calligraphy* 潘國鍵書法集. Toronto: The Senseis, 2019.

Chinese

王弼,《老子王弼注》, 華亭張氏本. 台北: 新興書局, 1964.

沈約, 《宋書》. 北京: 中華書局, 1974.

河上公,《老子河上公注》. 世德堂刊本, 出版地及年代缺.

高亨 ,《老子正詁》. 上海: 開明書店, 1949.

康有為,《孔子改制考》. 上海大同譯書局, 1897(?).

張默生,《老子章句新釋》. 上海:東方書社, 1946.

劉文典,《莊子補正》. 雲南: 雲南人民出版社, 1980.

潘國鍵,《 孫過庭書譜白話對譯 》. 多倫多: 尚尚齋, 2019 .

韓非,《韓非子》. 欽定四庫全書子部韓非子, 乾隆四十四年版.

Dictionary

段玉裁,《說文解字注》. 臺北: 藝文印書館, 1966.

《康熙字典》. 上海: 上海書店, 1985.

《漢語大詞典》. 上海: 上海辭書出版社, 2008.

《漢語大字典》. 成都: 四川長江出版集團, 2010.

Websites

中央研究院《搜詞尋字》. words.sinica.edu.tw/sou/sou.html.

中華民國教育部《重編國語辭典修訂本》. dict.revised.moe.edu.tw/cbdic/.

國家教育研究院《教育大辭書》. terms.naer.edu.tw/.

《漢典》. www.zdic.net.

Wear rags as coverings yet bear jades buried deep within - *Tao Te Ching*

隸書 Clerical Script 34x79cm 2019AD
Source: *A Collection of Kwok Kin Poon's Calligraphy*

SECTION FIVE

Tao Te Ching Scribed in Chinese Calligraphy

by KS Vincent Poon

歸其根歸根曰靜是謂復命復命曰常知常曰明不知常妄作凶知常容容乃公公乃王王乃天天乃道道乃久沒身不殆

太上下知有之其次親而譽之其次畏之其次侮之信不足焉有不信焉悠兮其貴言功成事遂百姓皆謂我自然

大道廢有仁義慧智出有大偽六親不和有孝慈國家昏亂有忠臣

絕聖棄智民利百倍絕仁棄義民復孝慈絕巧棄利盜賊無有此三者以為文不足故令有所屬見素抱樸少私寡欲

絕學無憂唯之與阿相去幾何善之與惡相去若何人之所畏不可不畏荒兮其未央哉眾人熙熙如享太牢如春登臺我獨泊兮其未兆如嬰兒之未孩儽儽兮若無所歸眾人皆有餘而我獨若遺我愚人之心也哉沌沌兮俗人昭昭我獨昏昏俗人察察我獨悶悶澹兮其若海飂兮若無止眾人皆有以而我獨頑似鄙我獨異於人而貴食母

孔德之容惟道是從道之為物惟恍惟惚惚兮恍兮其中有象恍兮惚兮其中有物窈兮冥兮其中有精其精甚真其中有信自古及今其名不去以閱眾甫吾何以知眾甫之狀哉以此

曲則全枉則直窪則盈敝則新少則得多則惑是以聖人抱一為天下式不自見故明不自是故彰不自伐故有功不自矜故長夫唯不爭故天下莫能與之爭古之所謂曲則全者豈虛言哉誠全而歸之

希言自然故飄風不終朝驟雨不終日

天地尚不能久而況於人乎故從事於道者同於道德者同於德失者同於失同於道者道亦樂得之同於德者德亦樂得之同於失者失亦樂得之信不足焉有不信焉

企者不立跨者不行自見者不明自是者不彰自伐者無功自矜者不長其在道也曰餘食贅行物或惡之故有道者不處

有物混成先天地生寂兮寥兮獨立不改周行而不殆可以為天下母吾不知其名字之曰道強為之名曰大大曰逝逝曰遠遠曰反故道大天大地大王亦大域中有四大而王居其一焉人法地地法天天法道道法自然

重為輕根靜為躁君是以聖人終日行不離輜重雖有榮觀燕處超然奈何萬乘之主而以身輕天下輕則失本躁則失君

善行無轍迹善言無瑕謫善數不用籌策善閉無關楗而不可開善結無繩約而不可解是以聖人常善救人故無棄人常善救物故無棄物是謂襲明故善人者不善人之師不善人者善人之資不貴其師不愛其資雖智大迷是謂要妙

知其雄守其雌為天下谿為天下谿常德不離復歸於嬰兒知其白守其黑為天下式為天下式常德不忒復歸於無極知其榮守其辱為天下谷為天下谷常德乃足復歸於樸樸散則為器聖人用之則為官長故大制不割

將欲取天下而為之吾見其不得已天下神器不可為也為者敗之執者失之故物或行或隨或歔或吹

260

道可道，非常道。名可名，非常名。無名天地之始；有名萬物之母。故常無欲，以觀其妙；常有欲，以觀其徼。此兩者，同出而異名，同謂之玄。玄之又玄，眾妙之門。

天下皆知美之為美，斯惡已。皆知善之為善，斯不善已。故有無相生，難易相成，長短相形，高下相傾，音聲相和，前後相隨。是以聖人處無為之事，行不言之教；萬物作焉而不辭，生而不有，為而不恃，功成而弗居。夫唯弗居，是以不去。

不尚賢，使民不爭；不貴難得之貨，使民不為盜；不見可欲，使民心不亂。是以聖人之治，虛其心，實其腹，弱其志，強其骨。常使民無知無欲。使夫智者不敢為也。為無為，則無不治。

道沖，而用之或不盈。淵兮，似萬物之宗。挫其銳，解其紛，和其光，同其塵。湛兮，似或存。吾不知誰之子，象帝之先。

天地不仁，以萬物為芻狗；聖人不仁，以百姓為芻狗。天地之間，其猶橐籥乎？虛而不屈，動而愈出。多言數窮，不如守中。

谷神不死，是謂玄牝。玄牝之門，是謂天地根。綿綿若存，用之不勤。

天長地久。天地所以能長且久者，以其不自生，故能長生。是以聖人後其身而身先；外其身而身存。非以其無私邪？故能成其私。

上善若水。水善利萬物而不爭，處眾人之所惡，故幾於道。居善地，心善淵，與善仁，言善信，正善治，事善能，動善時。夫唯不爭，故無尤。

持而盈之，不如其已；揣而銳之，不可長保。金玉滿堂，莫之能守；富貴而驕，自遺其咎。功成身退，天之道。

載營魄抱一，能無離乎？專氣致柔，能嬰兒乎？滌除玄覽，能無疵乎？愛民治國，能無知乎？天門開闔，能無雌乎？明白四達，能無為乎？生之畜之，生而不有，為而不恃，長而不宰，是謂玄德。

三十輻，共一轂，當其無，有車之用。埏埴以為器，當其無，有器之用。鑿戶牖以為室，當其無，有室之用。故有之以為利，無之以為用。

五色令人目盲；五音令人耳聾；五味令人口爽；馳騁畋獵，令人心發狂；難得之貨，令人行妨。是以聖人為腹不為目，故去彼取此。

寵辱若驚，貴大患若身。何謂寵辱若驚？寵為下，得之若驚，失之若驚，是謂寵辱若驚。何謂貴大患若身？吾所以有大患者，為吾有身，及吾無身，吾有何患？故貴以身為天下，若可寄天下；愛以身為天下，若可託天下。

視之不見，名曰夷；聽之不聞，名曰希；搏之不得，名曰微。此三者不可致詰，故混而為一。其上不皦，其下不昧，繩繩不可名，復歸於無物。是謂無狀之狀，無物之象，是謂惚恍。迎之不見其首，隨之不見其後。執古之道，以御今之有。能知古始，是謂道紀。

古之善為士者，微妙玄通，深不可識。夫唯不可識，故強為之容：豫兮若冬涉川；猶兮若畏四鄰；儼兮其若容；渙兮若冰之將釋；敦兮其若樸；曠兮其若谷；混兮其若濁；孰能濁以靜之徐清？孰能安以動之徐生？保此道者，不欲盈。夫唯不盈，故能蔽不新成。

致虛極，守靜篤。萬物並作，吾以觀復。夫物芸芸，各復歸其根。

人之所惡唯孤寡不穀而王公以為稱故物或損之而益或益之而損人之所教我亦教之強梁者不得其死吾將以為教父

天下之至柔馳騁天下之至堅無有入無間吾是以知無為之有益不言之教無為之益天下希及之

名與身孰親身與貨孰多得與亡孰病是故甚愛必大費多藏必厚亡知足不辱知止不殆可以長久

大成若缺其用不弊大盈若沖其用不窮大直若屈大巧若拙大辯若訥躁勝寒靜勝熱清靜為天下正

天下有道卻走馬以糞天下無道戎馬生於郊禍莫大於不知足咎莫大於欲得故知足之足常足矣

不出戶知天下不闚牖見天道其出彌遠其知彌少是以聖人不行而知不見而名不為而成

為學日益為道日損損之又損以至於無為無為而無不為取天下常以無事及其有事不足以取天下

聖人無常心以百姓心為心善者吾善之不善者吾亦善之德善信者吾信之不信者吾亦信之德信聖人在天下歙歙為天下渾其心百姓皆注其耳目聖人皆孩之

出生入死生之徒十有三死之徒十有三人之生動之死地亦十有三夫何故以其生生之厚蓋聞善攝生者陸行不遇兕虎入軍不被甲兵兕無所投其角虎無所措其爪兵無所容其刃夫何故以其無死地

道生之德畜之物形之勢成之是以萬物莫不尊道而貴德道之尊德之貴夫莫之命而常自然

故道生之德畜之長之育之亭之毒之養之覆之生而不有為而不恃長而不宰是謂玄德

天下有始以為天下母既得其母以知其子既知其子復守其母沒身不殆塞其兌閉其門終身不勤開其兌濟其事終身不救見小曰明守柔曰強用其光復歸其明無遺身殃是為習常

使我介然有知行於大道唯施是畏大道甚夷而民好徑朝甚除田甚蕪倉甚虛服文綵帶利劍厭飲食財貨有餘是謂盜夸非道也哉

善建者不拔善抱者不脫子孫以祭祀不輟修之於身其德乃真修之於家其德乃餘修之於鄉其德乃長修之於國其德乃豐修之於天下其德乃普故以身觀身以家觀家以鄉觀鄉以國觀國以天下觀天下吾何以知天下然哉以此

含德之厚比於赤子蜂蠆虺蛇不螫猛獸不據攫鳥不搏骨弱筋柔而握固未知牝牡之合而朘作精之至也終日號而不嗄和之至也知和曰常知常曰明益生曰祥心使氣曰強物壯則老謂之不道不道早已

知者不言言者不知塞其兌閉其門挫其銳解其分和其光同其塵是謂玄同故不可得而親不可得而疏不可得而利不可得而害不可得而貴不可得而賤故為天下貴

以正治國以奇用兵以無事取天下吾何以知其然哉以此天下多忌諱而民彌貧民多利器國家滋昏人多伎巧奇物滋起法令滋彰盜賊多有故聖人云我無為而民自化我好靜而民

或強或羸，或挫或隳。是以聖人去甚，去奢，去泰。

以道佐人主者，不以兵強天下。其事好還。師之所處，荊棘生焉。大軍之後，必有凶年。善有果而已，不敢以取強。果而勿矜，果而勿伐，果而勿驕，果而不得已，果而勿強。物壯則老，是謂不道，不道早已。

夫佳兵者，不祥之器，物或惡之，故有道者不處。君子居則貴左，用兵則貴右。兵者不祥之器，非君子之器，不得已而用之，恬淡為上。勝而不美，而美之者，是樂殺人。夫樂殺人者，則不可以得志於天下矣。吉事尚左，凶事尚右。偏將軍居左，上將軍居右。言以喪禮處之。殺人之眾，以哀悲泣之，戰勝以喪禮處之。

道常無名。樸雖小，天下莫能臣也。侯王若能守之，萬物將自賓。天地相合，以降甘露，民莫之令而自均。始制有名，名亦既有，夫亦將知止，知止可以不殆。譬道之在天下，猶川谷之於江海。

知人者智，自知者明。勝人者有力，自勝者強。知足者富，強行者有志。不失其所者久，死而不亡者壽。

大道氾兮，其可左右。萬物恃之而生而不辭，功成不名有。衣養萬物而不為主，常無欲，可名於小；萬物歸焉而不為主，可名為大。以其終不自為大，故能成其大。

執大象，天下往。往而不害，安平太。樂與餌，過客止。道之出口，淡乎其無味，視之不足見，聽之不足聞，用之不足既。

將欲歙之，必固張之；將欲弱之，必固強之；將欲廢之，必固興之；將欲奪之，必固與之。是謂微明。柔弱勝剛

(5 of 12)

強，魚不可脫於淵，國之利器不可以示人。

道常無為而無不為。侯王若能守之，萬物將自化。化而欲作，吾將鎮之以無名之樸。無名之樸，夫亦將無欲。不欲以靜，天下將自定。

上德不德，是以有德；下德不失德，是以無德。上德無為而無以為；下德為之而有以為。上仁為之而無以為；上義為之而有以為。上禮為之而莫之應，則攘臂而扔之。故失道而後德，失德而後仁，失仁而後義，失義而後禮。夫禮者，忠信之薄，而亂之首。前識者，道之華，而愚之始。是以大丈夫處其厚，不居其薄；處其實，不居其華。故去彼取此。

昔之得一者：天得一以清，地得一以寧，神得一以靈，谷得一以盈，萬物得一以生，侯王得一以為天下貞。其致之。天無以清將恐裂，地無以寧將恐發，神無以靈將恐歇，谷無以盈將恐竭，萬物無以生將恐滅，侯王無以貴高將恐蹶。故貴以賤為本，高以下為基。是以侯王自謂孤、寡、不穀。此非以賤為本邪？非乎？故致數輿無輿。不欲琭琭如玉，珞珞如石。

反者道之動，弱者道之用。天下萬物生於有，有生於無。

上士聞道，勤而行之；中士聞道，若存若亡；下士聞道，大笑之。不笑不足以為道。故建言有之：明道若昧，進道若退，夷道若纇，上德若谷，大白若辱，廣德若不足，建德若偷，質真若渝，大方無隅，大器晚成，大音希聲，大象無形，道隱無名。夫唯道，善貸且成。

道生一，一生二，二生三，三生萬物。萬物負陰而抱陽，沖氣以

(6 of 12)

夫唯無知是以不我知

知我者希則我貴是以聖人被褐懷玉

知不知上不知知病夫唯病病是以不病聖人不病以其病病是以不病

民不畏威則大威至無狎其所居無厭其所生夫唯不厭是以不厭是以聖人自知不自見自愛不自貴故去彼取此

勇於敢則殺勇於不敢則活此兩者或利或害天之所惡孰知其故是以聖人猶難之天之道不爭而善勝不言而善應不召而自來繟然而善謀天網恢恢疏而不失

民不畏死奈何以死懼之若使民常畏死而為奇者吾得執而殺之孰敢常有司殺者殺夫代司殺者殺是謂代大匠斲夫代大匠斲者希有不傷其手矣

民之饑以其上食稅之多是以饑民之難治以其上之有為是以難治民之輕死以其上求生之厚是以輕死夫唯無以生為者是賢於貴生

人之生也柔弱其死也堅強萬物草木之生也柔脆其死也枯槁故堅強者死之徒柔弱者生之徒是以兵強則不勝木強則兵強大處下柔弱處上

天之道其猶張弓與高者抑之下者舉之有餘者損之不足者補之天之道損有餘而補不足人之道則不然損不足以奉有餘孰能有餘以奉天下唯有道者是以聖人為而不恃功成而不處其不欲見賢

天下莫柔弱於水而攻堅強者莫之能勝以其無以易之弱之勝強柔之勝剛天下莫不知莫能行是以聖人云受國之垢是謂社稷主受國不祥是為天下王正言若反

和大怨必有餘怨安可以為善是以聖人執左契而不責於人有德司契無德司徹天道無親常與善人

小國寡民使有什伯之器而不用使民重死而不遠徙雖有舟輿無所乘之雖有甲兵無所陳之使民復結繩而用之甘其食美其服安其居樂其俗鄰國相望雞犬之聲相聞民至老死不相往來

信言不美美言不信善者不辯辯者不善知者不博博者不知

右王弼注本道德經

按老子道德經為先秦哲學偉大著作對後世中國思想文化影響極其深遠素為國人修身之所宗余習而書之於個人修養甚有裨益焉其中至理確非下士所能知也二〇一九年歲次己亥炎夏潘君尚於尚高齋

（右頁 9 of 12）

我好靜而民自正，我無事而民自富，我無欲而民自樸。

其政悶悶，其民淳淳；其政察察，其民缺缺。禍兮福之所倚，福兮禍之所伏。孰知其極？其無正。正復為奇，善復為妖。人之迷，其日固久。是以聖人方而不割，廉而不劌，直而不肆，光而不燿。

治人事天，莫若嗇。夫唯嗇，是謂早服；早服謂之重積德；重積德則無不克；無不克則莫知其極；莫知其極，可以有國；有國之母，可以長久；是謂深根固柢，長生久視之道。

治大國，若烹小鮮。以道蒞天下，其鬼不神；非其鬼不神，其神不傷人；非其神不傷人，聖人亦不傷人。夫兩不相傷，故德交歸焉。

大國者下流，天下之交，天下之牝。牝常以靜勝牡，以靜為下。故大國以下小國，則取小國；小國以下大國，則取大國。故或下以取，或下而取。大國不過欲兼畜人，小國不過欲入事人。夫兩者各得其所欲，大者宜為下。

道者萬物之奧。善人之寶，不善人之所保。美言可以市尊，美行可以加人。人之不善，何棄之有？故立天子，置三公，雖有拱璧以先駟馬，不如坐進此道。古之所以貴此道者何？不曰：求以得，有罪以免邪？故為天下貴。

為無為，事無事，味無味。大小多少，報怨以德。圖難於其易，為大於其細；天下難事，必作於易；天下大事，必作於細。是以聖人終不為大，故能成其大。夫輕諾必寡信，多易必多難。是以聖人猶難之，故終無難矣。

其安易持，其未兆易謀；其脆易泮，其微易散。為之於未有，治之

（左頁 10 of 12）

於未亂。合抱之木，生於毫末；九層之臺，起於累土；千里之行，始於足下。為者敗之，執者失之。是以聖人無為故無敗，無執故無失。民之從事，常於幾成而敗之。慎終如始，則無敗事。是以聖人欲不欲，不貴難得之貨；學不學，復眾人之所過，以輔萬物之自然，而不敢為。

古之善為道者，非以明民，將以愚之。民之難治，以其智多。故以智治國，國之賊；不以智治國，國之福。知此兩者亦稽式。常知稽式，是謂玄德。玄德深矣，遠矣，與物反矣，然後乃至大順。

江海所以能為百谷王者，以其善下之，故能為百谷王。是以欲上民，必以言下之；欲先民，必以身後之。是以聖人處上而民不重，處前而民不害。是以天下樂推而不厭。以其不爭，故天下莫能與之爭。

天下皆謂我道大，似不肖。夫唯大，故似不肖。若肖，久矣其細也夫！我有三寶，持而保之。一曰慈，二曰儉，三曰不敢為天下先。慈故能勇；儉故能廣；不敢為天下先，故能成器長。今舍慈且勇，舍儉且廣，舍後且先，死矣！夫慈，以戰則勝，以守則固。天將救之，以慈衛之。

善為士者，不武；善戰者，不怒；善勝敵者，不與；善用人者，為之下。是謂不爭之德，是謂用人之力，是謂配天古之極。

用兵有言：吾不敢為主而為客，不敢進寸而退尺。是謂行無行，攘無臂，扔無敵，執無兵。禍莫大於輕敵，輕敵幾喪吾寶。故抗兵相加，哀者勝矣。

吾言甚易知，甚易行；天下莫能知，莫能行。言有宗，事有君。